THE BUILDERS BEHIND THE CASTLES

THE BUILDERS BEHIND THE CASTLES

George Loorz & the F. C. Stolte Co.

by

TAYLOR COFFMAN

PUBLISHED BY THE

SAN LUIS OBISPO COUNTY HISTORICAL SOCIETY

SAN LUIS OBISPO, CALIFORNIA

1990

Cover and Titles Designed by Diana Bistagne
Typography by The Latest Word
Back cover photograph by Mike Littlejohn
Maps by Charles Collins and by Jan French
Pen-and-ink portraits by Charles Collins
Photograph of Julia Morgan from the Morgan North Estate
(courtesy of Sara Holmes Boutelle)
Photograph of William Randolph Hearst by James Manatt
(courtesy of the late J. C. "Pete" Sebastian)
All other illustrations from the Loorz family, the Loorz Papers, or photographs by the author
Manufactured in the State of California

Second Printing

Copies of this book may be ordered from the
San Luis Obispo County Historical Society
P.O. Box 1391, San Luis Obispo, CA 93406 (805) 543-0638

Copies may also be ordered from
E Z Nature Books
P.O. Box 4206, San Luis Obispo, CA 93403 (805) 528-5292

ISBN 0-945092-15-6

CONTENTS

PREFACE

APRIL 23, 1988, was a Saturday, an ordinary Saturday that found me working in my study. Early that afternoon the phone rang. The caller was Bill Loorz, the second of George Loorz's three sons. (I knew that George Loorz, during the 1930s, had been Julia Morgan's construction superintendent on the San Simeon job for William Randolph Hearst.) My ears perked up because I had long been wondering about the George Loorz Papers, which I knew were still being held by the Loorz family. And it was about those papers that Bill Loorz was calling. Mr. Loorz said that he and his brothers wanted to do right by their father's papers, that they felt the time to act had come, and that I might like to see some of the papers before any final decisions were made regarding their disposition. I naturally jumped at the chance. Two months later I was driving home from Los Angeles, with a few boxes of papers that Bill Loorz had entrusted to me for archival processing.

The project grew. By the end of 1988, I had been entrusted with nearly twenty boxes of George Loorz's papers—enough to keep me busy in my spare time for many months.

On June 26, 1989, Bill Loorz wrote me one of his typically encouraging notes. "I don't know exactly how these things work," he said, "but if you think there is enough in here of interest to Hearst-Morgan-San Simeon buffs, maybe we could underwrite your efforts to write a small book or pamphlet on the Loorz papers." I assured him that the papers contained more than enough information—largely untapped, unsuspected information—to warrant a book. I also assured him that a small book was the least we should consider, a pamphlet being too limited for the extensive, richly detailed Loorz Papers.

The idea of a small book also grew. Late in 1989, I completed several years of historical work for the Hearst Corporation and was free to pursue the Loorz project full time. Bill Loorz authorized me to proceed—to process an additional twenty boxes of his father's papers, to write a narrative based on the roughly forty boxes all told, and, as a culminating step, to direct the publication of a full-scale book befitting the subject. And so *The Builders Behind the Castles* was launched. I will be forever grateful to Bill Loorz and his brothers for having trusted me to carry out this challenging assignment.

A related assignment was to find a good home for the George Loorz Papers. That home proved to be the San Luis Obispo County Historical Museum, which is operated by the San Luis Obispo County Historical Society.

No one can act alone in writing a book like *The Builders Behind the Castles*. Bill Loorz, of course, was especially helpful from the very start. Later on I met Bill's older brother, Don, and his younger brother, Bob, both of whom likewise deserve my thanks; Don Loorz was most helpful, for instance, in discussing how his father and Fred Stolte became associated in 1928. Maurice McClure, a good friend of the Loorz family, deserves a special word of thanks. He was the one who mentioned me to Bill Loorz and urged him to sound me out. Few other "old timers" besides Maurice McClure are still with us from George Loorz's era. One of them, Conrad Gamboni, read the manuscript and made helpful suggestions. Another old timer, the late Carl Daniels, also read it.

Among my colleagues who read the manuscript were Shirley Shewmaker Wahl, who provided important information on Hearst's Wyntoon estate; Sara Holmes Boutelle, who interviewed George Loorz and Fred Stolte while writing her biography of Julia Morgan; Lynn Forney Stone, whose mother was Miss Morgan's longtime secretary; Dan Krieger and Mark P. Hall-Patton, who represented the San Luis Obispo County Historical Society; and of course John Porter, who has been my chief editor for several years.

This book is largely an edition of letters, and any such book requires a comment on editorial technique. George Loorz, the principal correspondent, typed nearly all his letters—and he usually typed them fast, with little if any fussing over misspellings and the like. I have preserved these quirks, these irregularities, within reason; I have "followed copy" more often than not. Some bracketed insertions have been necessary, and a very occasional "*sic*" crops up; however, I have tried to keep these devices to a tolerable minimum. Loorz was not alone in making slips in his writing. Julia Morgan certainly made some in hers. So did many of the others whose letters I have quoted. I hope the reader will enjoy seeing their words, their punctuation (or lack thereof), and their sometimes erratic phrasing, however flawed these elements may seem.

Saturday, May 26, 1990
Cambria, California

POSTSCRIPT: On July 22, 1990, Bill Loorz called me from Los Angeles. We both thought we had located all of George Loorz's surviving papers, but three more boxes had just surfaced—less than two weeks before *The Builders Behind the Castles* was slated to go to press. The three boxes were labeled "Burnett Road for 1932," "1933 Miscellaneous," and "F. C. S. 1936." Bill Loorz sent me the boxes the next day; I quickly confirmed that their historical value was comparable to that of the other boxes I had processed. The box from 1936, for example, threw much light on George Loorz's "outside work" for the F. C. Stolte Co. and on his dealings with Julia Morgan and William Randolph Hearst that same year. Would that I had had those papers at my disposal six months earlier! Yet just as sportsmen say that records are made to be broken, editors must concede that history is made to be rewritten—or at least amplified. The users of the George Loorz Papers will find endless grist for their mills in that regard. I wish them well in their efforts.

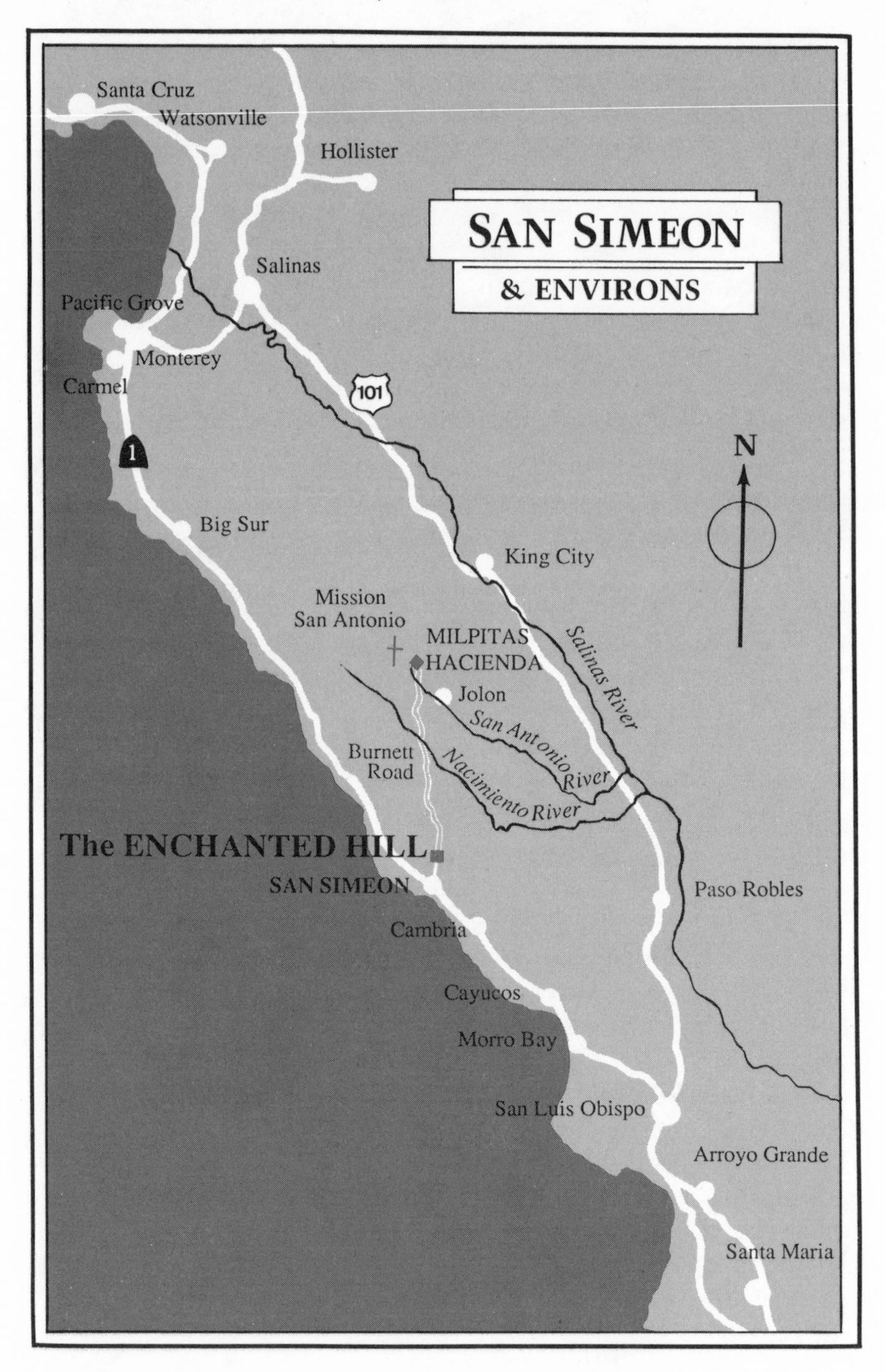
SAN SIMEON
& ENVIRONS
Santa Cruz
Watsonville
Hollister
Salinas
Pacific Grove
Monterey
Carmel
101
1
Big Sur
King City
N
Mission
San Antonio
MILPITAS
HACIENDA
Jolon
Salinas River
San Antonio River
Nacimiento River
Burnett
Road
The ENCHANTED HILL
SAN SIMEON
Paso Robles
Cambria
Cayucos
Morro Bay
San Luis Obispo
Arroyo Grande
Santa Maria

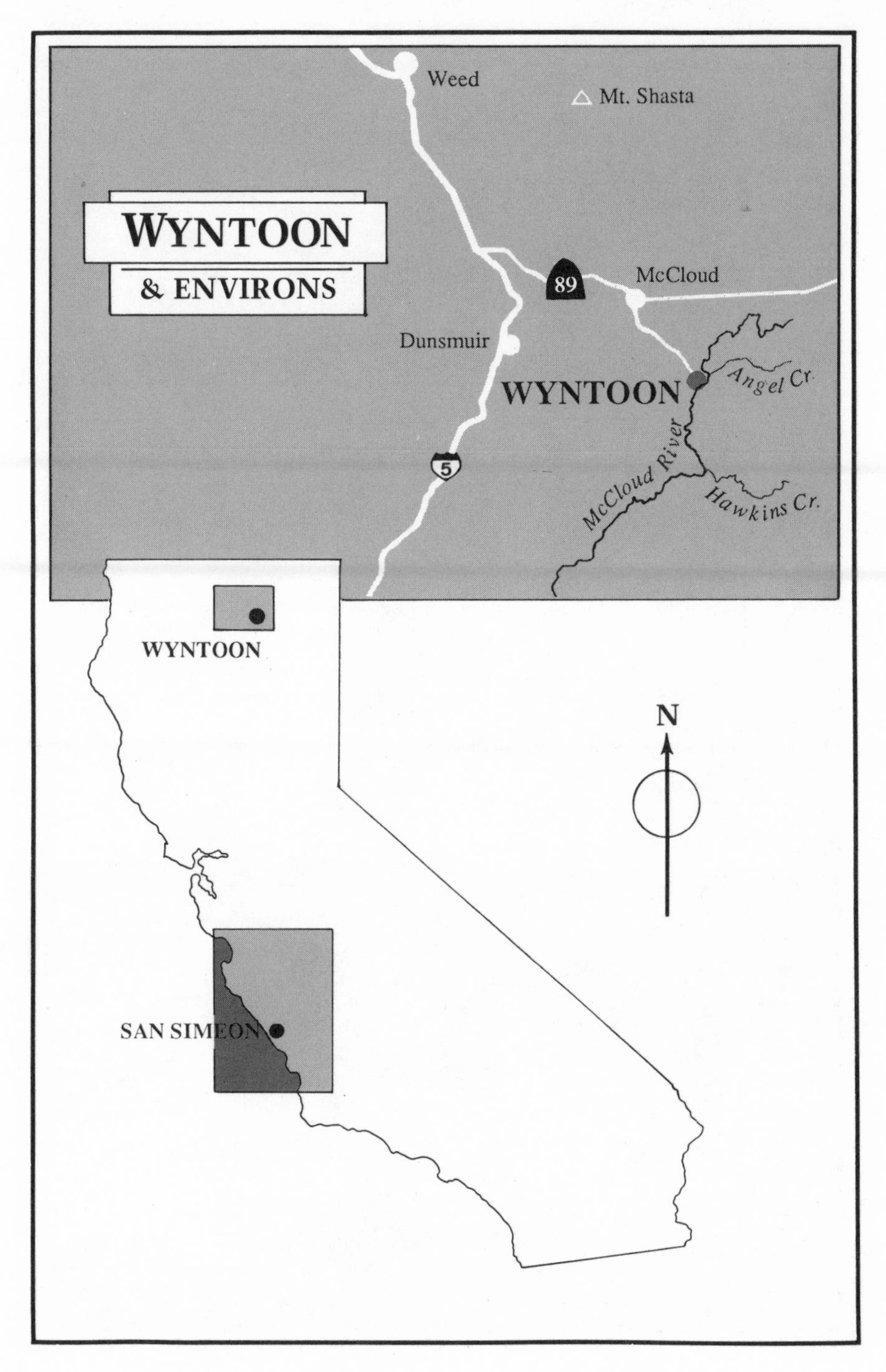
Weed
Mt. Shasta
WYNTOON
& ENVIRONS
89
McCloud
Dunsmuir
WYNTOON
Angel Cr.
McCloud River
5
Hawkins Cr.
WYNTOON
N
SAN SIMEON

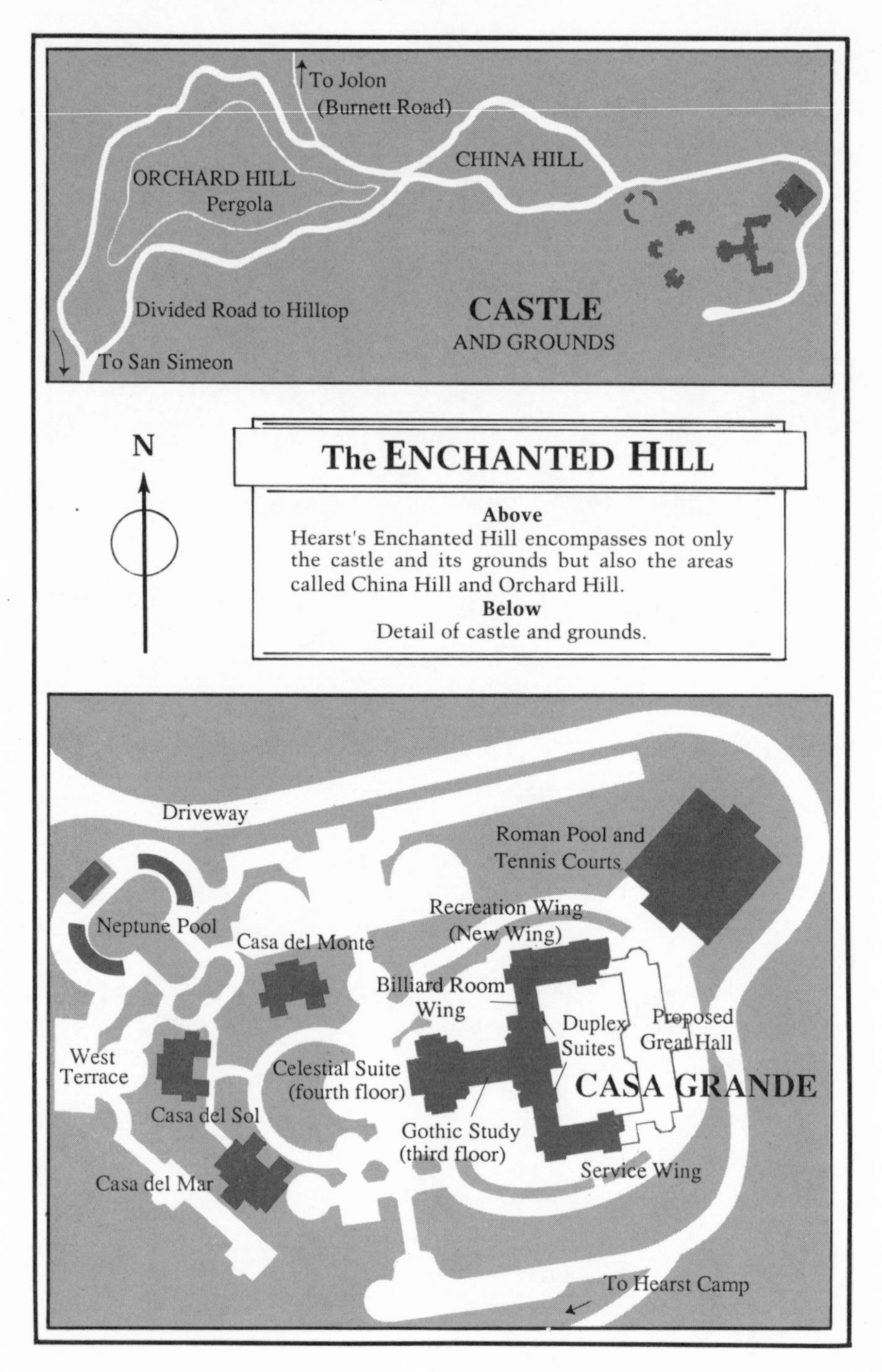
To Jolon
(Burnett Road)
ORCHARD HILL
Pergola
CHINA HILL
Divided Road to Hilltop
CASTLE
AND GROUNDS
To San Simeon
N
The ENCHANTED HILL
Above
Hearst's Enchanted Hill encompasses not only the castle and its grounds but also the areas called China Hill and Orchard Hill.
Below
Detail of castle and grounds.
Driveway
Roman Pool and
Tennis Courts
Neptune Pool
Casa del Monte
Recreation Wing
(New Wing)
Billiard Room
Wing
Duplex
Suites
Proposed
Great Hall
West
Terrace
Celestial Suite
(fourth floor)
CASA GRANDE
Casa del Sol
Gothic Study
(third floor)
Casa del Mar
Service Wing
To Hearst Camp

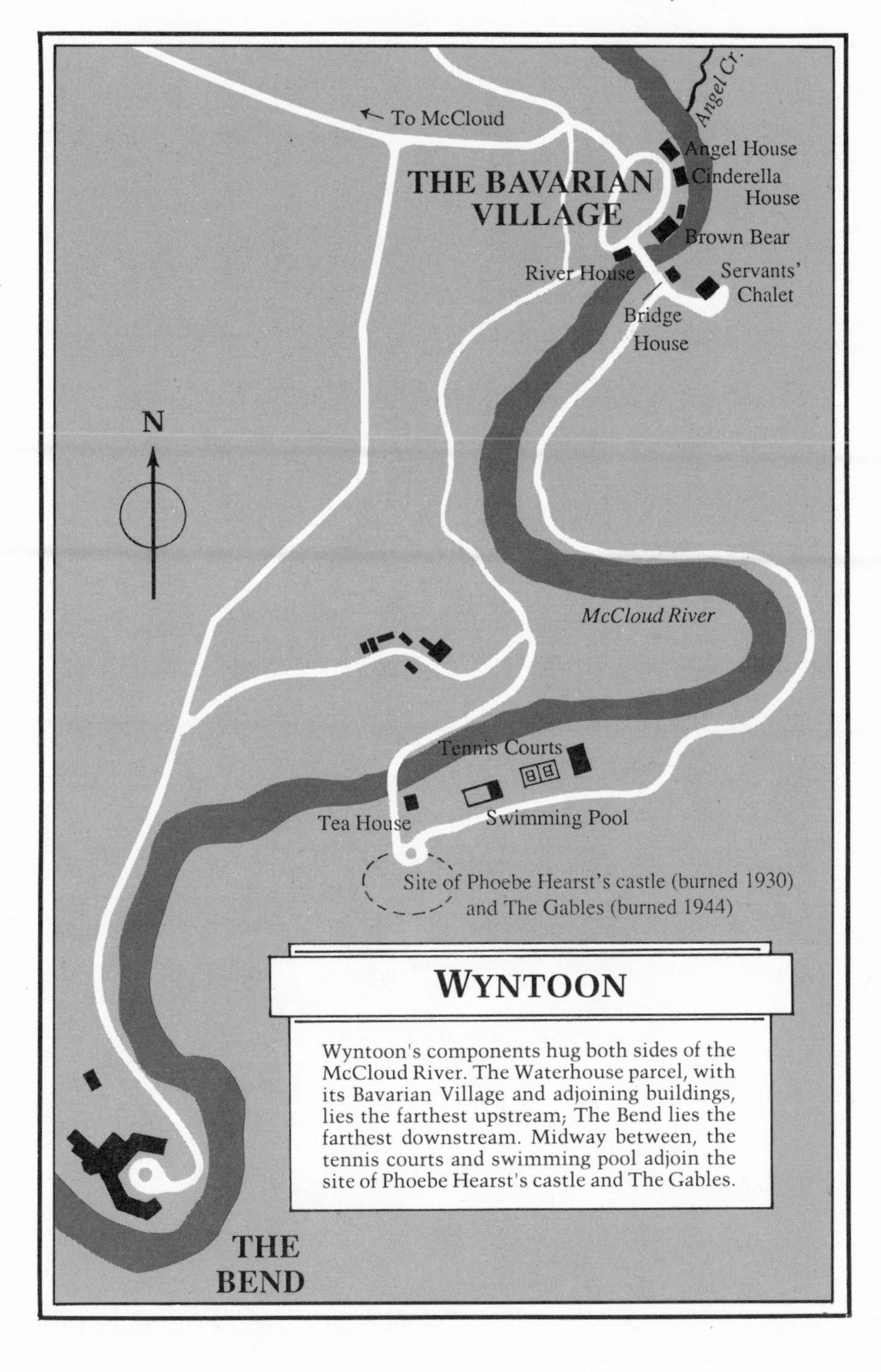

WYNTOON

Wyntoon's components hug both sides of the McCloud River. The Waterhouse parcel, with its Bavarian Village and adjoining buildings, lies the farthest upstream; The Bend lies the farthest downstream. Midway between, the tennis courts and swimming pool adjoin the site of Phoebe Hearst's castle and The Gables.

INTRODUCTION

IN FEBRUARY 1938, six years after he began working at San Simeon as construction superintendent, George Loorz received the following letter from William Randolph Hearst:

> I shall be very happy to have you refer anyone to me regarding the high quality of your construction work at San Simeon.
>
> I have had the most complete satisfaction with everything that you have supervised and executed.
>
> You have been most careful, not only about the quality of the construction, but about the cost.
>
> I cannot imagine it possible for anyone to be more competent and conscientious, and I am glad to testify to that effect.

Generosity was one of Hearst's winning traits, but he stopped short of lavishing undeserved praise. The only way George Loorz could have warranted those glowing words was to earn them.

Hearst's letter is one of thousands of documents that have come down to us as the George Loorz Papers, a choice collection on which *The Builders Behind the Castles* is principally based. Loorz was a packrat in the best sense, a man who saved his correspondence and other records in pasteboard letter boxes. As one of his sons later quipped, "The old man never needed a wastebasket." In reality, many documents that passed through Loorz's hands have long since vanished. But many others have survived.

California Polytechnic State University, San Luis Obispo, has the Julia Morgan Collection, and the San Luis Obispo County Historical Museum has the George Loorz Papers.

Together these closely related collections are unsurpassed in documenting the San Simeon of the 1920s and the 1930s. The Julia Morgan Collection runs thick through the 1920s but then thins to a trickle by the late 1930s. The Loorz Papers, on the other hand, run thick from 1932 through 1937—the six years George Loorz spent at San Simeon. They also continue into the 1940s.

The Loorz Papers document more than San Simeon alone. William Randolph Hearst had another country estate in California, a place called Wyntoon, hidden deep in the Cascade Range along the McCloud River, twenty miles south of Mount Shasta. And that is why the title *The Builders Behind the Castles* takes the plural form. For the Loorz Papers treat of Wyntoon as well as San Simeon; and because Wyntoon, unlike San Simeon, has been obscure for so long, the Papers are virtual Dead Sea Scrolls on that subject. Though San Simeon has been portrayed for years as *The Castle*—mostly to the exclusion of Wyntoon and the other residences Hearst had in this country—Wyntoon has features as striking, in many ways as castle-like, as those at San Simeon.

During his six years at San Simeon, Loorz lived just downhill from *that* castle, on the edge of San Simeon Bay. Greater San Simeon—the castle on the hilltop, the Hearst Ranch surrounding it, the little town alongside the bay—remained prominent in his correspondence throughout that period. During the first year, 1932, San Simeon was the leading subject of that correspondence. Wyntoon, a job superintended by Loorz's partner, Fred Stolte, attained equal stature in 1933. The two subjects, San Simeon and Wyntoon—the two "castles"—shared the spotlight from then on.

The Loorz Papers also contain a good deal of local history, most of it pertaining to San Luis Obispo County, some of it to Monterey County and other areas. Loorz and his many correspondents interwove those details between their discussions of San Simeon and Wyntoon, increasingly so as the six-year period unfolded.

George Loorz was a native of Lovelock, Nevada, where he was born on a small farm in 1898. He was a senior at Lovelock High School when this country entered the Great War in

1917. That spring he enlisted in the aviation branch of the army (he and other volunteers his age were granted their diplomas a month early). He served for two years, mostly in England and France. Right after the armistice in 1918, he severely injured his hand while defusing a grenade. He bore that injury permanently, though few would ever guess he was in any sense disabled. For Loorz was a big, robust man who was as strong and forcible as he was warm and gregarious. He was the perfect embodiment, in fact, of the "hail-fellow-well-met" personality. While in England he adopted a popular expression of the day, "Cheerio," which he used the rest of his life. "Cheerio" and George Loorz—the two seemed made for each other.

Loorz entered the University of California, Berkeley, in the fall of 1919. He completed a degree in mathematics in 1923 and another in civil engineering in 1924. He began working in construction around the San Francisco Bay Area; and in 1925 he married a fellow Nevadan, Grace Sullivan. Destiny soon crossed his path. Julia Morgan, one of San Francisco's best architects, was working on the Hills Brothers Building in that city; so was Loorz. Miss Morgan took an immediate liking to him. She regarded him, as his wife recalled years later, as something of a "prodigy" and as someone she could count on "anytime she needed anything." Loorz's trail through the mid-1920s remains faint nonetheless. He is known, however, to have worked for contractors like McClaren and later Dyer Brothers. He is also known to have worked on the Phoebe Apperson Hearst Memorial Gymnasium for Women, a building designed for the Berkeley campus by Julia Morgan and Bernard Maybeck.

In 1928 Loorz was construction superintendent under Julia Morgan on two jobs for William Randolph Hearst. One of the jobs was a swimming pool and tennis courts at Wyntoon—at the "old Wyntoon," where the late Phoebe Hearst had built a Germanic castle through Bernard Maybeck. (The "new Wyntoon" came along for the most part in the 1930s.) The other job was follow-up work in Santa Monica—at the great Beach House that Hearst was building for Marion Davies (and for himself as well). The Beach House job was evidently the one Loorz meant when he told a friend, "I worked for him [Hearst] under the roof where he lived for 8 months without meeting him." Despite Hearst's aloofness, Loorz got "many orders in writing thru another party from him" at the Beach House—a harbinger of things to come a few years later.

The year Loorz worked at Wyntoon and in Santa Monica, 1928, was the same year he became associated with Ferdinand C. Stolte, an Oakland contractor. Fred Stolte, as he was usually called, had been a builder since 1915, and a successful one at that in the days before the Great Crash of 1929. He and Loorz were a perfect example of that old saying "Opposites attract." Stolte was quiet and retiring; Loorz was garrulous and outgoing. The one thing Stolte had over Loorz was age (he was nine years older). Otherwise, Loorz was easily the more dynamic of the two. The F. C. Stolte Co. owed its name to Fred Stolte, but it increasingly owed its success to George Loorz. That became true as the two men endured the early years of the Depression and incorporated as equal partners in 1932; that remained true once the Depression began to ease in the mid-1930s and they hit their full stride. Above all, though, the two maintained a close friendship characterized by mutual respect and concern. Their partnership often seemed to have sprung from the pages of a storybook.

Another partnership—the term is figurative here—that at times seemed equally idyllic was that of William Randolph Hearst and Julia Morgan. "Fellow architects," they were once called, Morgan herself supposedly having chosen those words. In their best moments they indeed had an uncanny rapport; in still other moments they obviously strained each other's patience. In any event, they had been equally committed to their roles as patron and architect since the early 1900s (Morgan having worked for Hearst before San Simeon began in 1919), and they carried their commitment into the 1940s. The George Loorz Papers often reveal as much about Hearst and Morgan as the Julia Morgan Collection itself does; they just as often reveal considerably more through their realism, at times a gritty realism, that tends to be lacking in the Morgan Collection. Loorz, after all, could be a good deal less guarded in writing to a fellow supporting player than he could be in writing to Hearst or Morgan. The same was true, of course, for the supporting players when they wrote to Loorz. Occasionally, in writing to Loorz, Morgan herself dropped her guard long enough to qualify as one of those supporting players. Hearst, on the other hand, rarely if ever broke character. Whether he was writing to Julia Morgan, George Loorz, or anyone else, he would politely but unmistakably say what he thought. It was a great man's prerogative to do so.

Julia Morgan was the one who recruited George Loorz for San Simeon in the winter of 1932. Loorz's predecessor, Camille Rossi, had been there since 1922 and had been prolific as construction superintendent. During his ten years, Rossi had completed the three earliest houses, such as Casa del Mar; had begun the main building, Casa Grande, and had enlarged it greatly; had built two versions of an outdoor swimming pool (the eventual Neptune Pool); and had built the indoor Roman Pool, which he nearly finished before he left. He had also made great strides in the landscape architecture. And his work had gone past the hilltop in those big-budget days before the Depression took hold—had embraced several sites on the greater Hearst Ranch. But Camille Rossi, though an expert engineer, had finally run afoul of both Hearst and Morgan—he was exceedingly dictatorial, for one thing—and he was summarily dismissed once Morgan lined up Loorz.

Morgan was sure that Loorz, who was all of thirty-three in 1932, was equal to the challenge. He was; but things had changed since 1928, when she sent him to Wyntoon and Santa Monica. Loorz had Fred Stolte to consider now and the welfare of their contracting business in Oakland. In Loorz's absence the business might falter, might even go under with the Depression at its nadir. Furthermore, the proposal was that Loorz hire on independently, not on behalf of his company. Morgan and her office staff would keep acting as general contractor, just as they had from the outset in 1919; Loorz would strictly be her superintendent on the job, just as he had been for her on the other Hearst jobs in 1928. (In contrast, the F. C. Stolte Co. *was* brought in as general contractor for the work that began at Wyntoon in 1933—but only at Wyntoon, not at San Simeon.)

Despite certain drawbacks, Morgan's offer was too enticing to ignore. Loorz was promised $100 a week, a beachfront house in San Simeon, and a car for good measure. All he needed to do was to rent out his house in Berkeley, pack up his wife and two boys, and bid the Bay Area and the Depression adieu. Of course it wasn't quite that simple. He *had* to make sure Fred Stolte was ready to go it alone, even though he would be helping him out as much as possible, moonlighting from faraway San Simeon. Loorz's bids would still be needed for the company to secure its most important jobs.

Loorz made his arrangements; and with nothing more to count on at San Simeon than a single season's work, he went ahead and took what he rightly felt was a daring plunge.

NINETEEN THIRTY-TWO

1932

GEORGE LOORZ ARRIVED at San Simeon during the first week of February 1932. On February 6, he wrote to Julia Morgan in San Francisco. Thus began a stream of correspondence with her and others that would steadily flow through the six years lying ahead. Loorz had had a chance to look over the job before he wrote that first letter; he told Morgan, "I am very pleased with the definite and complete layout of the present construction program." He also said, "I can offer no alibis if I fail to make progress. Your assured cooperation in regards to the personel and the few kindly words that you must have used in conversing with others is already showing effects. I look forward to very sudden cooperation on the part of every craftsman in camp."

The camp Loorz mentioned was Hearst Camp, a kind of company town situated a short distance from the castle itself and occupied by laborers, artisans, and various other workers. Loorz had a gift for making friends quickly and keeping them. He spoke with nearly everyone in Hearst Camp during his first days on the job. Then he convened the foremen and addressed them:

> We are all working directly under the architect and thru her for Mr. Hearst. At present we are all in good standing in her office, and will remain so as long as we obtain results, satisfactorily and harmoniously. Her personal friendship, in your case and my case, is purely from a business point of view.
>
> I want your cooperation and thru you the cooperation of your men, in keeping our work and our camp, clean and tidy at all times. There are exceptions but most of us can improve. Anything that I

can do in the way of repairs and equipment in this respect, I will take up with those over me and do what I can. I'm an awful crank on good scaffolding, and safety precautions.

Loorz seldom came across that stiffly in his letters; but he obviously had to assert himself at the outset, especially in the wake of Camille Rossi's dismissal and the discord that was Rossi's legacy. (As the gatekeeper Ray Swartley later said, Loorz inspired "excellence where only mediocrity reigned before.") Most of the men Loorz addressed that day—men like the labor foreman, Frank Souza, and the carpenter foreman, Pete Petersen—soon became close friends.

Loorz and Julia Morgan had been good friends for the last six or seven years. Now that he was on the job, she had someone she could depend on implicitly, someone she knew would keep her closely apprised—above all, someone she knew would promote harmony in the ranks and keep the job running smoothly. San Simeon needed a strong dose of that in the winter of 1932. She also had in George Loorz someone who shared her penchant for work. Sundays, for instance, weren't necessarily days of rest, not when there was a job to be done.

It was on a Sunday, in fact, February 7, that Loorz next wrote to Julia Morgan, telling her about the mosaic decoration in progress at the indoor Roman Pool. The Roman Pool was one of many projects that had felt the pinch of the Depression during the last two years and that Morgan, and now Loorz as well, would push to completion for Hearst by the end of 1932. "Now Miss Morgan this has been a lengthy description and I ask you to pass frank judgment upon it," Loorz said of his report on the Roman Pool. "If it is of no use then I have wasted two hours and do not want to repeat it. Or if the idea is alright and my execution poor please say so, for it seems to me that this, more than anything else, is where I can best serve in connection with the several segregated crafts [like the mosaic sub-contract], those I mean that do not come directly under me."

Morgan's reply of February 9 assured Loorz that he was on the right track, that his comments were welcome. "I like people to express their own frank opinions and to make suggestions for betterments," she wrote. "It never hurts my feelings,—am glad people trust me enough to do so,—then it is up to me in the end to decide what solution is nearest best. There is no disloyalty if the opinion is contrary to mine, and no lack of appreciation on my part, if the opinion is not used. Let us all work on this basis."

The Roman Pool wasn't the only project the Depression had slowed at San Simeon. Several others had likewise felt the budgetary cutbacks Hearst periodically made as the national crisis worsened. But the carillon of bells he had ordered for the castle—for the twin towers of Casa Grande—had been withheld from installation for another reason. The towers already contained tanks of water (for a gravity-flow supply throughout Casa Grande); and Hearst feared that the heavy tanks, along with the weight of the carillon, would prove excessive—especially during an earthquake. He had even considered selling the carillon, but he had recently changed his mind; and on February 15 Morgan notified Loorz, "We have news today that the Carillon *is* to go in. The bells will be on this week's boat—the men [to install them] will appear any day." The "bell men" were from Tournai, Belgium, where the carillon had been cast. Two weeks later Loorz told Morgan he enjoyed the men's "Belgian humor." Yet he had to complain mildly that they monopolized his time and that he was "anxious to get this installation completed."

Ever the diplomat, Loorz paused long enough on March 9 to write to the deposed Camille Rossi in Needles, California:

> For the present at least things are going quite smoothly but the job and conditions are such that I'm certain I would not have as much patience as you had. Sorry we did not meet and talk before you left for I feel certain that you could and would give me a lot of downright good advice.
>
> I want to say without hesitancy that you left the job in first class condition structurally and it has been very easy for me [to] pick up and continue. I find the crew you had to be the best possible for this job and I have, to date, not hired a single new man, though I have and still am employing some 50 to 100 men continually in my business elsewhere. For this I am grateful and if you will accept, let me compliment you.

So much for diplomacy and kind words. In writing to Fred Stolte three days later, Loorz was more candid in describing the job that first winter:

The Big Boss here raised hell with everyone in General yesterday but left me out of it. Maybe it pays to be big. These people seldom say anything back so it is easy for him to let loose. It's all bluff for he never gets mad enough to lay them off. I don't blame him for they have worked for about two years and haven't completed a single extra bedroom for him. He has some 47 guests coming this week end and [his] need [of] another suite or two was the cause of the eruption. We managed to arrange one for occupancy although the decorating in them is about 5 months from being completed. It does seem impossible that it should take so long to decorate but with all of the feature painting and gold leaf work it is almost impossible to get men who can do the work.

Loorz's crew needed to finish eight bedrooms in all, plus an equal number of adjoining bathrooms, hallways, and, for the Celestial Suite, a sitting room as well. The Celestial Suite was perched in the towers, right above Hearst's own Gothic Suite. The other rooms were clustered at the back of Casa Grande, where they formed a honeycomb of passageways and staggered floor levels; these were the North Deck and South Deck bedrooms and, adjoining them, the two North Duplex suites and the corresponding South Duplexes.

Hearst's reduced budget was strained by these eight rooms alone, and had been for some time, to say nothing of the other projects he hoped to wrap up soon, like the Roman Pool. The landscape architecture was also making demands on the budget. Loorz, who was a skillful estimator, projected on March 18 a cost of $4,400 to bring in fifteen palm trees from San Luis Obispo. On top of that, he figured $700 for the replacement of four sickly palms in front of Casa Grande with some of the new ones from San Luis. In addition, he figured $800 more for the moving of five Italian cypresses to the Neptune Pool from the West Terrace, their places also to be taken by some of the San Luis palms. His total projected cost: $5,900. With the Depression holding fast, Hearst was counting pennies now as never before; many a proposed job at half that price or less had to be delayed or even abandoned during this period. But the moving of the palm trees from San Luis Obispo was important to him, and the $5,900 was one of the larger new expenditures he approved in 1932.

LOORZ'S WIFE, GRACE, and his two young sons, Don and Bill, joined Loorz at San Simeon shortly after he arrived. They moved into the stucco and tile-roofed house vacated by the Rossi family, overlooking San Simeon Bay; that idyllic setting remained their home, as things turned out, until the San Simeon job shut down in 1937 and they moved to Pacific Grove in 1938. Loorz described his good fortune in a letter to Fred Stolte on March 21:

> We certainly do like it there on the beach. Spent three hours frolicking up and down, jumping rope (seaweed) rolling old tires in the sand and gathering beachwood logs for the fireplace. You see we combined business with pleasure. . . .
>
> Everybody here has shown a great deal of interest and pleasure at our arrival. I have a cellar full of all kinds of vintage and cooling waters. One brought some nice fish caught yesterday and yet another promised some large Red Abalone for today. We visit all of them from laborer to Marble carver so we have laid the foundation for quite a pleasant sojourn.

Three hours was about as much as Loorz could devote to frolicking. Hearst had improvements in mind elsewhere on his ranch, not just on his Enchanted Hill with its gleaming white castle. The time had come, for instance, to improve the landing field. The field lay immediately west of today's private tree-lined drive that enters the Hearst Ranch from Highway 1. Among its other drawbacks, the field was too close to a row of utility poles. Both Hearst and some of his guests, and Julia Morgan as well, had landed on the field and knew its limitations; Morgan had done so as a passenger of Hearst's oldest son, George, who was a pilot and had his own plane. She told Loorz on March 30, "Mr. George Hearst's objection to the high tension poles is that it is necessary to begin to fall to the landing field only after passing them and that it shortens an already too short field by that amount. I've gritted my teeth several times thinking we would crash through the fence, so know it is fact." She asked Loorz to help Warren McClure, George Gillespie, and Arch Parks correct the problem. ("Mac" McClure, a draftsman, was Morgan's "representative" at San Simeon; George Gillespie was in charge of fence work on the ranch; Arch Parks was the ranch superintendent.)

Before long, though, the idea of merely moving the obstructing poles had blossomed into something larger, as Hearst's ideas so often had a way of doing. Hearst opted for an entirely new landing field, one having both north-south and east-west runways. The chosen site, roughly a mile east of the old field, is partly covered today by the Hearst Castle Visitor Center. Loorz later briefed Hearst on how the job was progressing:

> Mr. Parks has worked splendidly with me in clearing the new airport site. I am at present making a heavy railroad iron drag to smooth up the small irregularities of the surface. We will use horses to pull it as Mr. Parks says they need to be exercised. We hope to have the runway ready for Ray [Crawford] to make a few trial landings and take-offs when he comes tomorrow. He will then be more able to pass judgment. The cost so far has not been more than $200.

The cost soon exceeded $200, of course, especially when the lighting equipment was moved over from the old field and reinstalled; but Loorz watched the expenditures as closely as he could, a virtue never lost on Hearst.

Loorz also tried his hand at animal husbandry during his first months at San Simeon. Hearst's bull terrier, Buddy, needed a dog house; Marianne the elephant needed an elephant house. On a more urgent note, Hearst told Loorz and Carey Baldwin, the ranch zookeeper, to "do everything possible to protect the remaining giraffe"; that was on April 26. A giraffe had died the previous day, and another had died earlier that month—"a loss amounting to some $20,000," Loorz later told Julia Morgan, hence "the hasty order for quarters."

In April 1932 as well, Loorz notified Hearst's accountant in Los Angeles that he had received "written orders from Mr. Hearst to proceed immediately with a bridge across the creek in the ravine to the north where the Burnett road crosses." Hearst's orders to Loorz took the form of a hand-scrawled letter, in which he assured him, "Just a plank bridge will do for the present." And in his postscript he said, "We did more damage to the cars today than the bridge would cost." Here, again, was the germ of another expansive idea. For Hearst meant to do more than just build a bridge across his backyard creek; he meant to build a road across the rugged Santa Lucia Range that bordered the Enchanted Hill—a road that would ultimately link the San Simeon portion of his ranch with the uppermost portions more than twenty miles north, the portions surrounding the settlement of Jolon in Monterey County. There he and Julia Morgan had already built the Milpitas Hacienda, which Loorz would remodel a few years later. In 1932 the only ways of going from San Simeon to Jolon were inconvenient. One could drive through the Salinas Valley or fly to a landing field—a field as minimal as the one Hearst had decided to replace at San Simeon.

The Burnett Road, named for the creek that drained the coastal side of the Santa Lucias, was first and last an engineering job and thus right down Loorz's alley; as such, the job fell outside Julia Morgan's bounds, as diverse as her work for Hearst had been and always would be. Loorz told Hearst they should bring in a bonafide road contractor, someone with the right equipment and the men to operate it, rather than limp along with the equipment on hand and day labor out of Hearst Camp. That approach had already been tried under Camille Rossi in cutting the first few miles of road up Burnett Creek. To cross the Santa Lucias and, after that, to bridge the Nacimiento River en route to Jolon would require a new tack. Hearst agreed.

By June 4 Loorz could write to Fred Stolte, "We hear a lot about shortage of money here but they still spend thousands like water. I am letting a road contract to Tieslau Bros. [of Berkeley] for eight miles of pleasure road back thru the mountains here for some $30,000 so I guess all of the money is not buried as yet."

Stolte replied with "just a few lines" to let Loorz know he was "still doing business at the same peanut stand"—a stock phrase in many of his early letters.

"Seems strange to hear of someone who is spending real money," Stolte said. "A $30,000 pleasure road must be some job."

It was, and the eight miles Loorz mentioned were merely the first leg of the journey, a matter of extending the road as far as the main summit above Burnett Creek. To get from there to Jolon, through a torturous canyon leading down to the Nacimiento River, required two more years of work.

JULIA MORGAN WROTE to Loorz from her Merchants Exchange office in San Francisco on Friday, June 10: "Mr. Hearst will be up for next weekend [June 18-19]—and wants all rooms possible." She also told Loorz she planned to see him at San Simeon on the following Monday, June 13.

Loorz took detailed notes whenever he conferred with Miss Morgan on the jobsite. Within a few days of her latest visit he would type out his notes and send her a copy for her corrections and approval, much like a secretary submitting minutes of a meeting. These notes could be quite detailed, could run to as many as three or four pages with closely spaced entries—"Architect's Interviews," Loorz called them. His notes dated June 17, based on Morgan's visit of June 13, contained this entry: "As soon as plan of Great Hall arrives, stake it out for approval of Mr. Hearst."

(Hearst had proposed the Great Hall in April. The name was no exaggeration. Conceived as a link between Casa Grande's Recreation Wing and Service Wing, the Great Hall was to be part exhibit hall, part ballroom, part banqueting hall—the most spectacular room of its kind in this country, Hearst had told Morgan. His idea had its drawbacks, though, not the least of them budgetary. The Theater, which occupied the ground floor of the Recreation Wing, practically defied the abutting of a new structure. Hearst and Morgan could have juggled the aesthetics successfully enough, but to join the Theater and the Great Hall structurally, and spatially, was another matter. And then there were the oaks that grew smack dab in the path of the Great Hall—big oaks that could be moved only at much risk and expense. We may never know which of these obstacles was most responsible for ultimately thwarting Hearst's proposal; for the time being, his dream of a Great Hall remained alive.)

Morgan had told Loorz that Hearst would be at San Simeon over the weekend of June 18-19. On Thursday, June 16, however, Hearst wrote to Loorz from Los Angeles, saying he didn't think he could "get to the ranch before the last of the month."

Mid-July proved to be more like it. The distinction is important because on Friday, July 1, Hearst played the most fateful political card in his life—that of maneuvering the delegates he controlled at Chicago's deadlocked Democratic Convention in favor of Franklin Delano Roosevelt. And it was from Los Angeles that he played that card. His authorized biographer, Mrs. Fremont Older, placed him in Los Angeles for that historic gesture, the Julia Morgan Collection confirms his whereabouts, and the George Loorz Papers reinforce that fact still more. The popular account, however, has long been that Hearst was at San Simeon when he played his hand in Roosevelt's behalf.

On June 24, while Hearst was still in Los Angeles, Loorz wrote to E. E. Boss, the caretaker of Wyntoon, whom he had met there in 1928. Boss had written to Loorz earlier in June, telling him how tight the budget was at Wyntoon in 1932; the old bridge, for example, had "about seen its last" and no money seemed forthcoming from Hearst to repair it. Boss assumed Hearst was having difficulties "along with the rest of the world." Loorz told Boss, "Like yourself we are forced to run short handed this year." Boss had hoped a man he laid off at Wyntoon could hire on with Loorz at San Simeon. But Loorz told him, "Honestly I have so many applications daily that plead so for work that it certainly gives me an unhappy feeling to turn them down." Loorz could make no exception for Boss's man. What extreme, improbable contrasts—between Hearst's proposed Great Hall for San Simeon and the decrepit bridge at Wyntoon, between Hearst's maneuvering on the highest political level and Boss's agonizing over the humblest employee.

HEARST WAS BACK at San Simeon late in July. He and Loorz toured the hilltop, inspecting the progress to date; Loorz sent Julia Morgan a detailed summary. "In general regarding the construction in the Castle, " Loorz said, "he was well pleased with everything completed, and *very* well pleased with the nearness to completion of the Duplexes. His own statement was, after walking around, 'Well, things are beginning to finish up quickly, aren't they.'" Loorz also noted,

"He glanced into the South Deck Room as we walked by to the South Duplex and said, 'All ready to move into' and after a moment's hesitation, 'I like it better than the other one.'"

The two men also discussed the pergola—the columned arbor on Orchard Hill, just west of the castle. Hearst had decided to add to the existing row of columns and extend it around Orchard Hill. Nigel Keep, his longtime orchard man, was standing by all the while, eager to plant the grape vines the new columns would require, knowing it would be years before the vines matured. The placement of the columns, of course, had to be just so in the eyes of the perfectionist Hearst.

"Mr. Hearst has been down to the Pergola twice and is taking an active part in the location of the line to follow," Morgan learned from Loorz in mid-August. "We are now setting up a few poles to the finished height of the Pergola on the supposed course to see how it will look from the Castle above and from the road below."

As for further headway within the castle itself, Hearst's entertaining could cause delays. "It certainly handicaps us with the carpentry when we cannot hammer until noon," Loorz told Morgan in the same letter. "He has so many guests that any hammering in the forenoon bothers. I have plenty of work previously outlined that they can do but it does not permit real visible progress in any one room."

The pergola remained a priority as fall approached. Loorz brought Hearst up to date on September 19:

> We have the road machine working on the pergola extension. There are two fairly large pine trees which come directly in the proper location of the roadbed. The cost of moving and attempting to save these trees would be around $60 if they could simply be moved down the hill a short distance. Mr. Keep looked at them with me and said that . . . trees as old as they were would very likely die if moved. Said he could replace the trees with smaller ones for less than $50 each and thot it might not be advisable to attempt to move them. What would you advise?

"Move 'em," said Hearst.

In writing to Hearst in Los Angeles on October 10, Loorz related that "the pine trees on the Pergola road were moved quite successfully at a cost of about $55 each, net."

Hearst was actually in Cleveland, Ohio, at the time, not Los Angeles, recovering from throat surgery. 'Twas the season for the movers and shakers to pause a moment: Julia Morgan had recently undergone a mastoid operation at Stanford Memorial Hospital. On September 9 Loorz wrote to the electrician Louis Schallich, "Will welcome the lady back on the job. Don't seem to realize how important she is until she fails to show up." Morgan herself wrote to Loorz from the hospital a few days later: "Am having a longer stay than expected,—probably will not see the Hill for two weeks yet,—but maybe at the *end* of two weeks. . . . In their effort to save me, the office only brought up the questions on the West Terrace today—and do hope it has not delayed you." Apparently it had, though, for in writing to Fred Stolte on September 14 Loorz said, "Boy how I wish she was here. No one to select or approve anything, design or detail or whatnot. It keeps me humping to do some things way ahead hoping I can guess how she will want it."

Hearst was still in residence on September 14, hadn't left yet for Los Angeles or Cleveland; might not he have made the selections or given the approvals Loorz sought? The letter Loorz wrote Morgan the next day is illuminating:

> Several times he has mentioned or requested changes from things you have approved and when he mentions them to me I tell him what you had planned and explain the reason and nearly always he agrees with your ideas. When he requests these changes of anyone else I usually stall until I can talk with him about them or until I can write and consult you about them. The result is that, though he has never criticized or shown outward displeasure he knows that I consult you before proceeding with anything he requests in connection with architecture.
>
> In time I may lose his confidence because I do not do what he requests immediately and say "Yes" like a parrot. I do it for your sake and for the good of the job for he really asks for more things done than we could do with double the crew. If I kept jumping from job to job as fast as he requested, just to make an impression I would never get anything finished and he repeatedly remarks that he likes to get things finished.

Morgan was back on the job on October 4, Loorz sharing the good news with Stolte:

Miss Morgan is here today and though still unwell is very much on her toes and is a great help. Work is rushing at present in a vain effort to get the Roman Pool, showers, lounges etc ready by the 1st of December. We are concentrating on exterior terrace changes etc that should get underway immediately to be cleaned up when the rainy season starts. So you can bet your Uncle Dudley is a busy boy.

Wish I had time to tell you about my hike over thru the mountains to Jolon [on] the other ranch and my visit to the ruins of the old San Antonio Mission and the remnants of its old irrigation system. I enjoyed it immensely although the purpose of the trip was to locate the new [Burnett] road course.

The "exterior terrace changes" Loorz spoke of pertained to the West Terrace—more often called Lower C Terrace today—which Julia Morgan had mentioned in her letter from Stanford. Some of the palms in the recent shipment from San Luis Obispo were earmarked for the West Terrace, to replace its former row of Italian cypresses. But first the terrace was to be enlarged. Loorz told Hearst on October 10 that his crew was almost ready to pour the concrete. The job was going to be a big one and would require lots of gravel. The old gravel bed on the ranch had played out, and Loorz had found a new source at the mouth of Little Pico Creek, just below San Simeon Bay:

The road formerly used was washed out during the heavy rains last winter and the new bridge will cross it anyway so I asked the State Engineer on the new road if he would not make us a good road down. He gave it promptly and a very good one. I made arrangements with the Road Contractor to scrape up a lot of material with his tractor while there so we will have a supply out of reach of the tides for all of the present needs. With his machine right there it was more economical than using a team for a fairly long haul.

Loorz also told Hearst, "If I can continue on this wall [the West Terrace] with the majority of the present crew we should complete the concrete work within four weeks." He did so, through his labor foreman, Frank Souza, whose men used some thirty tons of reinforcing steel in the process.

At least one other big project was under way in these final months of 1932—the completion of the Billiard Room on the ground floor of Casa Grande. This passageway between the Morning Room and the Theater had promised for some time to become the Music Room. Now it was to be completed as the Billiard Room instead. The first step was to install the rare Spanish ceiling Hearst and Morgan had selected for it. Loorz had told Morgan on September 8 that W. R. Williams, the manager of the San Simeon warehouses, would locate the crates amid the rows and rows of Old World treasures he cared for. "He will open the beam one at least and determine the size so I can put the men on preparing the splices on the ends." In other words, the ceiling was slated for some skillful alteration before it could be installed.

COME NOVEMBER, HEARST returned to San Simeon after his stay in Cleveland. By November 22 Loorz could tell Julia Morgan, "Mr. Hearst looks much better than when he first came back. In fact, I have never seen him looking better. I have conversed with him at length but once and I found him to be in very splendid Humor."

That same day, Hearst sent a memorandum to Loorz and Warren "Mac" McClure, who had been on the job as the "representative" from Morgan's office since 1930. Among other points he addressed, Hearst told Loorz and McClure:

> I do not know about the elephant pond. That is beyond me. I should think an elephant hose would be pretty good. If we have a puddle of some kind I do not see that it need be ornamental. . . .
>
> Any additions to the Roman pool building are a matter of the distant future. The next building to be built will be the proposed great hall.

Dream on, Mr. Hearst. He closed that memorandum of November 22 on a more pragmatic note:

> I realize we have bills to pay and that is the reason I want to reach the irreducible minimum point as soon as possible and pay the bills.
>
> We will, of course, keep some men at work during the winter. The unfinished duplexes should be finished, and so should the so-called music room [the Billiard Room]."

Julia Morgan was technically the architect, Mac McClure her representative, and George Loorz the construction superintendent; but each of them had to be ready, at a moment's notice, to assume duties above and beyond the usual. It fell to

Loorz as the season drew to a close, as Hearst Camp battened down its hatches for a winter recess, to do some financial tallying. He wrote to Hearst's accountant in Los Angeles on December 12, "One has to be somewhat of a contortionist to keep a completed, balanced record of accounts that are so mixed up as many of these have been but we have a real system and record that is of great value to me as regards to costs and exact information." Make no mistake about it, Loorz would far rather have been pouring concrete (a particular passion of his) than tapping on his adding machine.

Would Loorz be back for another season at San Simeon? Having just turned thirty-four he was hardly ready to retire. And the business he had left behind in Oakland in Fred Stolte's hands was scarcely setting the world ablaze. Fortunately, Julia Morgan had reassuring words for him on December 14:

> Your vacation plans I am sure will be acceptable, and I will write Mr. Hearst today explaining them, so that you can bring up the details with him as may seem necessary, and you come back when your vacation is over whether any number of men are put on immediately after the holidays or not—as it gives a chance to catch up on detail, as well as to be on hand in emergency.

Loorz stayed on till December 21. The next day he and his family drove to San Francisco, where they picked up his younger brother, Claude; then they set out for Lovelock, Nevada, the Loorz family home, which George hadn't visited since 1928. Before leaving San Simeon he wrote to Fred Stolte: "Of course things look dull for you there next year, just as it has to us each year for the past four at this time of the year. Cheer up it cannot last this way forever." Then he told his partner about his trip to Nevada and about how Hearst had said he could be gone more than two weeks if he wished. "It certainly has been a pleasure to work with him," Loorz said.

NINETEEN THIRTY-THREE

1933

THE SAN SIMEON of 1932 recalled *The Great Gatsby*—as though in a time warp, to be sure. So did the San Simeon of 1933—but it also foreshadowed *The Grapes of Wrath*. The contrast between those two years was pronounced, especially through the first part of 1933. True, the Depression had nipped at Hearst's heels during 1932; yet he still achieved some spectacular results at San Simeon that year. By the time George Loorz got back from Nevada, the Depression was more than just nipping at Hearst; it was threatening to swallow him whole. As long as it was merely threatening, though, the job could move ahead, albeit cautiously.

On February 13, Loorz wrote to the electrician Louis Schallich, who was holed up in the Crest Hotel, San Francisco: "Well we are starting up tomorrow with a small crew of about six or seven men. The intention is to finish the two Duplexes and the Billiard Room." Schallich's services would not be needed just yet; Loorz told him to "keep a stiff upper lip." Then he wrote to King Walters in Los Angeles, who operated a Caterpillar on the Burnett Road in 1932. "There will certainly be no work on the road before April 1st or 15th," he told Walters. "At that time we will likely start up but will use but one cat."

And then a shock wave rolled through the local area. "The Cambria Bank closed its doors yesterday with a little over $100 of my cash and some $1200 to $1500 of Mr. Hearst's in my name depending upon how many checks issued have gone thru," Loorz told Fred Stolte on February 17. "It certainly did hit the natives here for most of them had a lot of confidence in it and had most of their savings in the bank."

The news was brighter a week later—and more customary. "We expect Mr. Hearst with a party of 50 here for the coming week," Loorz told Stolte on February 25. "He will see lots of things that he wants and we no doubt will have to step on things a bit, even if we are right up to the budget at present." Hearst's visit revolved around the wedding of his third son, John, on March 4. "Talk about an array of new cars, musicians, floral pieces etc.," Loorz told some Berkeley friends that day. "I wonder if it really is *wonderful* to be rich." Stolte, meanwhile, didn't have to wonder for a minute. He told Loorz that same March 4, "Well, we apparently are in the midst of a real tough time and we thought two or three years ago was bad." Stolte explained, "The jobs that we have had are showing a fair profit—about 10% but there is no volume to speak of."

Loorz wrongly assumed that Hearst would want him to "step on things a bit." Hearst returned to Los Angeles soon after his son's wedding, and he called Loorz on March 8, telling him to "cut down to the absolute minimum." The job limped along for two more weeks, until Hearst came back on March 24; he lost no time in telling Loorz that times were bad. Loorz spelled things out for Stolte in writing to him on the 25th:

> Well the hatchet has fallen at last. Mr. Hearst notified me yesterday that I should arrange to complete the rooms I am working in at present as soon as possible and shut the camp down for a couple of months at least. He says times are a little too tough for him to keep on spending as we have been. . . .
>
> Will let you know as soon as I know definitely what is going to happen. As long as things are as tough as they are there [in the Bay Area] I might even try to work for Mr. Hearst in some other capacity.

Stolte replied in a humorous vein, saying, "[Hearst] can *probably get along* on the building that is finished." But then he said, "Personally I feel that he has been quite a sport to continue up to the present." Loorz and the few others who were still on the payroll undoubtedly felt the same.

Things changed by the minute with William Randolph

Hearst—they always had; they always would. He soon decided to forge ahead at San Simeon, Depression or no; and by March 31 Loorz had better news for his partner in Oakland:

For the present at least I am definitely located here. I will spend but $4000 or $5000 per month. That means just 10 men with the expensive materials they use. I am to complete two more rooms which will take at least three months, with all of the modeling, casting and figure decorating. I refuse to worry about time beyond that limit, it may never get here. I am assured that I will not be cut below $75 per [day], which is quite fair with 10 men.

Loorz also referred to the Victory Highway Garage in Lovelock, Nevada, a building he had figured for the F. C. Stolte Co. in his spare time. (The bid was unsuccessful, but Loorz was hoping to retain the client's "good will in the home town.")

Then he mentioned that he had begun figuring a job for Hearst at Wyntoon, San Simeon's counterpart along the McCloud River in northern California:

I am going over an alteration job at McCloud that we will get if it goes ahead. I'd guess about $20,000. I want to make certain the money will be available. I am now six weeks behind in paying the men and I don't like to mention how many thousands for materials. If it does go ahead Fred I thot you could meet Miss Morgan up there and arrange to handle the work. It will be a rush job and you would have to be there quite a bit yourself, leaving some old reliable like Mr. Carlson, or someone equally loyal and pleasant, and real active [in charge in Oakland]. I will let you know when and if it turns up.

Stolte assured Loorz that he would be pleased to work with Miss Morgan at Wyntoon, that he would "make a special effort to make the job easy for her," and that he would hope for the best on Hearst's coming through for all concerned.

"Business here is just the same," he added, "a few new beer buffets have come to stay, however I can't figure that people are going to buy much beer at 15¢ per glass."

The prospect of work at Wyntoon is barely detectable through the rest of April 1933; however, we can be sure from what soon materialized on that job that Hearst was giving it plenty of thought. In the meantime, the Billiard Room and the South Duplexes saw continued work at San Simeon; these rooms fairly dominated Loorz's periodic consultations with

Julia Morgan, according to the "Architect's Interviews" he compiled. Loorz also typed out notes and questions in advance for Morgan. For her visit of April 10, for example, he submitted this question: "Just how much do you wish the decorators to do in livening up the antique ceiling of the Billiard Room?" Her answer in part, as Loorz recorded it, was to "do more antiqueing on woodwork of panels and beam soffits before going ahead with any more decorating on the new section of the ceiling." She had more to say about the same matter on April 27: "Continue cracks in ceiling beam sides thru patches at ends so as to match in character the original beam sides." No detail was too trifling for these people to consider.

In mid-April, Loorz wrote to Camille Solon in Mill Valley. Solon had been the chief designer of the mosaic tile work in the Roman Pool, which was now completed, and he was eager to see the building; Loorz knew, though, that Solon was none too keen on bumping into Hearst:

> He is here at present and may be for a long time but you know he is not around until afternoon and you could have most of your *snooping* completed by the time he gets around. . . .
>
> The pool is still clear but not quite as nice as last week. We have to date added thirteen tons of salt and have five more to add later. At first the salt made it a bit dirty but it is now clearing up again. Who said we couldn't have ocean water without waiting years for the proposed pipe lines from San Simeon?

The water in the Roman Pool may have been clearing, but the eighteen tons of salt soon played havoc with the plumbing system, which had to be revamped entirely. Tons of salt were also added to the outdoor pool in 1933. Hearst was about to remodel that pool, now that the indoor Roman Pool was completed. (He had avoided working on both pools concurrently so that he and his guests could always swim in one or the other.) As Loorz said in some notes he made on the outdoor pool later that year, "Pool pipes were not originally intended for salt water and will corrode. As pool will be changed this may not matter."

The sub-contractor in charge of plumbing at San Simeon was James Rankin of Oakland, an old and very close friend of

Loorz's and a fellow member of the Exchange Club in that city; Loorz wrote to him on April 18:

> Well no doubt Alex [Rankin, James Rankin's son] is keeping you posted on the job. Some crew with about nine men total. I thot you would be down roughing in [the plumbing] for the bedrooms upstairs over the Billiard Room by this time. I asked the lady [Miss Morgan] about it last week. . . . She said, "Oh that won't be ready for a long time and I'm not quite sure the arrangement Mr. Hearst wants." She added that she would take it up with him on her next visit. I again reminded her about it in my written notes and she answered that she'd see him soon. If you chance to be talking to her just cry a little bit about hard times and she'll let you come on down for a little vacation.

Hard times at San Simeon—the image is almost too improbable. Yet compared with the high-flying 1920s, when Hearst's monthly budget often ran in the tens of thousands, these *were* hard times.

THE HARD TIMES ASIDE, Hearst had recently approved the resumption of work on the Burnett Road. A new arrangement was in the offing for the 1933 season. The work would be done directly under George Loorz, rather than by contract with Tieslau Brothers, although Henry Tieslau would be part of the new crew. So would King Walters and one or two others from the previous year. Loorz wrote to Walters in Los Angeles on April 26:

> This is the brief fact. If you can move just 3/4 as much dirt per hour as you moved last year the net cost to me will still be cheaper than Henry's net cost last year. Counting what Henry made you only have to move 1/2 as much dirt per hour to make the same net cost to me.
>
> At the same time you personally will make more than you did. You will have a lot nicer job, fewer worries and have a hell of a lot more time to visit with me and hoist a few beers occasionally.

But the hard times were far from over, of course, in April 1933, this second month of the new Roosevelt Administration. A colleague in San Francisco told Loorz on May 5, "You are quite right in saying that the contracting business is in the doldrums." The man also told him, "It goes without saying that jobs are being taken at ridiculous prices and in the main by contractors who just have to take them in order to keep the creditors away." Hard times had set in closer to home, too. May 6 found Loorz answering a letter from Ernest Baumgartner of nearby Cayucos:

> I regret to state that it is positively impossible for me to employ any more workmen at this time. When and if things open up a little later on it may be possible to give you some kind of work.
>
> I was talking over the contents of your letter with some of the boys [in Hearst Camp] and they were very anxious to help you over the tough spot you seem to be in.
>
> I enclose herewith $15 in cash with which we hope you will be able to have your lights hooked up and purchase fuel. We are having a small supply of staple foods set up and are sending them to you by courtesy of Ed Harkins of the Valley & Coast Transit Co.
>
> We will still have on hand a balance in the fund with which we will send another grocery order at a later date. If you are in greater need of something we have not considered kindly let me know at once.

The Loorz Papers contain receipts from Sebastian Bros., the cracker-barrel store still operating in San Simeon today, for the first shipment to the Baumgartners: a pound of salt for 7¢; ten pounds of flour for 29¢, and ten pounds of sugar for 44¢; twenty-five pounds of potatoes for 39¢; three boxes of Post Toasties for 23¢; six pounds of bacon for $1.14; and so on. The grand total came to $6.82, roughly a day's wages for a man lucky enough to be on Loorz's current payroll. The money and groceries arrived in Cayucos the next day, May 7, and both of the Baumgartners wrote notes of thanks to Loorz and "the boys." Mrs. Baumgartner said, "The $15 looked as big to us as $500." She also said that she and her husband had been "without the greatest necessity for 4 days—bread!" Their words were heartfelt, and no doubt tearful.

Julia Morgan was at San Simeon the same day Loorz wrote to Mr. Baumgartner, May 6. She left Loorz with a "Probable Summer Program," which included "Fall and Winter possibilities," that must have made his head spin. The program called for the completion not only of the Billiard Room and the Lower South Duplex but also of Heart's private Gothic

Study. In addition, Loorz was to "have all materials on hand to begin [remodeling the] outside pool with fairly large crew on about September 1st and perhaps continue work thru winter to have [it] ready for first warm weather of spring following." And he was to "build necessary concrete walls of new extended East Terrace [behind Casa Grande], fill and move oaks from proposed site of Great Hall, to have site ready for actual work on Hall next year." The hard times seemed to be softening for Hearst.

Loorz, with his wife and sons along for the ride, had recently driven Hearst's new Cadillac convertible into San Luis Obispo to be worked on. He related the story to his parents on May 8, telling them how he and his family froze going home since the top was down and evidently couldn't be put up:

> However, the history of that car is interesting since it was a personal gift to Mr. Hearst from Arthur Brisbane a few months back. They went back thru the woods here with one of Mr. Hearst's old cars and it got hot and wouldn't pull. After many trials Mr. Hearst said angrily to my chauffeur, "Tell Mr. Loorz to buy some new Fords and Chevrolets that can climb these rough roads without stalling." Brisbane was present and the next day when he went thru L.A. he bought this Cadillac and had it driven here to Mr. Hearst.

Loorz got busy with his latest assignment. "Personally would prefer to buy good condition second hand car," he noted on a list he submitted Hearst. "One very fine looking 1929 Buick can be had for $300 cash in San Luis. It is a large seven passenger car and they are willing that we put it to [the] test over the picnic roads."

"*Get it,*" Hearst scrawled in the margin.

LOORZ WROTE TO Fred Stolte the same day he wrote to his parents, May 8; the prospect of work at Wyntoon had blossomed abundantly that spring:

> Mr. Hearst is here most of the time and keeps everyone on their toes all the time. Time does not drag on one's hands. They have continued to hash over developments at Wyntoon until they now have sketches, plans and exteriors of quite a large New Castle. He says it is nearly finished and that they can plan on starting the

engineering drawings within the week and hopes to get started up there in about a month.

It now looks more like $300,000 than the $20,000 I talked about before. I don't know whether that will eliminate us or not. They may want to do it like here [acting as their own contractor] but I don't think so. At best I don't believe he would spend more than $30,000 this summer up there. That would be one unit, the dining room living room & kitchen only. However, as always, no telling how many times it will change before going ahead if at all.

I understand that his business has picked up quite a little and that may cause his income to increase until he can actually go ahead up there.

On May 10 Loorz told Charlie Badley, one of his fraternity brothers from Berkeley's Phi Kappa Tau chapter, "If [Hearst] starts the big job up there after these small alterations and we are lucky enough to land it, it will be good for a long time to come, perhaps as long as weather permits, for the next three years." Loorz wrote Harry Thompson on May 20 also; Thompson had just been chosen to be foreman on the "small alterations" the F. C. Stolte Co. was about to begin at Wyntoon:

Harry this little job is not much in itself but I have a lot of hopes for better things. As it now stands they have not told me that we will get the big job that they have recently designed for up there. However, Mr. Hearst seems anxious to get started upon it and has even made motions toward raising the funds. I feel certain that some work will begin on it before the summer is out.

You can help a lot by getting this [small] job done in a hurry. That is what Mr. Hearst wants. He wants to go up there with a party as soon as possible and at present there are not enough accommodations for his guests. Do your best to satisfy.

The people in charge up there, Mr. & Mrs. Boss, are not particular friends of Miss Morgan, or Mr. [James] LeFeaver [Morgan's office manager] but I believe she is some distant relative of Mr. Hearst's, and I hope you will endeavor to make them your friends. . . .

You know Mac McClure the architect who was here. He is in S. F. now completing the drawings as Mr. Hearst had him sketch them here. He will be up there on the big job and might be sent up on this small one. In any case do whatever he asks and promptly. I believe Mr. Hearst likes him better than anyone in Miss Morgan's office and he knows Mr. Hearst's likes and dislikes best.

Loorz closed by wishing Harry Thompson the best of luck; as things turned out at Wyntoon, Thompson needed it.

From San Francisco on May 12, Mac McClure contributed the first of his many letters to the George Loorz Papers. His clear, graceful script is always a thing of beauty; and the insightful, often animated details he conveyed are usually to be savored to the last word:

> We are still "Wyntooning" on a big scale. I have been busy getting the plans into shape and tomorrow there will be a gathering at the site of Miss Morgan, Steilberg, Huber, Rankin, various sub contractors and me. I am going up with Rankin. J. M. goes on the train tonite. . . .
>
> LeF[eaver] told me that it was impossible for the "office" to stand the expense of the various Castle projects' plans without some payment and that he would have to collect for the Arizona [Grand Canyon] house—etc. Also one reason for my leaving [San Simeon] was to prevent Mr. H. making further changes. However I'll wager that Mr. H. will continue making plans and changes either with or without me! I can't see what "expense" is entailed except my salary.

That must have been quite a meeting of the minds at Wyntoon—the architect Julia Morgan, the architect-engineer Walter Steilberg, the engineer Walter Leroy Huber, the plumber James Rankin, and the draftsman Warren McClure (for "Mac" was not an architect, despite Loorz's having called him that in his letter to Harry Thompson). Whether it was the "small job" or the "big job"—or both jobs—that occasioned that meeting can best be answered by the Loorz Papers. We can turn, for instance, to the letter Mac McClure sent George Loorz on May 22, 1933:

> There is quite a lot of new sash and frames, a Colonial entrance door, 4 wood mantles, stair rail, and a lot of pilasters and panel mold to dress up the interiors. Miss M. seems to be a trifle afraid it may cost too much and is putting brakes on a little. Mr. H. asked her if it would cost under 5 or 6000. There are 4 new baths as well as a lot of fireplaces etc. Perhaps it can be done.

The building Mac described was River House; that, along with some nearby but unnamed buildings, represented the "small job." River House stood on what was called the Waterhouse property (named for Clarence P. Waterhouse, whose heirs had sold the parcel to Hearst in 1931). The Waterhouse property was on the McCloud River, just upstream from the site of Phoebe Hearst's original Wyntoon Castle—most of which had burned down in 1930. (The tennis courts and swimming pool Loorz had worked on in 1928 adjoined the remains of Phoebe Hearst's castle.) References to the "big job," meanwhile, can be detected between the lines further on in that same letter Mac McClure wrote to Loorz on May 22:

> I called on J. M. at her house [in San Francisco] Saturday and heard a lengthy and confused account of [her recent] San Simeon trip. Apparently W. R. H. is undecided and vague about building here and apparently left her discouraged. However [Walter] Steilberg and [John] Wagonet [Wagenet] are to make the drawings and I am to stay here at Wyntoon probably until the job is finished. That is O. K. with me as it is at least a "change" here if not very lively. At least I will have my Sundays—perhaps.

Loorz, the tireless correspondent, answered Mac promptly:

> I believe Mr. Hearst misses you and the Wyntoon sketches for he comes in my office a lot now and of course we have such a little to talk about except figures and facts which soon gets tiresome. . . .
>
> Yes Mr. Hearst did send Miss Morgan away feeling rather discouraged about the [big job at] Wyntoon last week but I believe most of his anger was because she told him how tough the excavation etc were [going to be] if they built the building where it was originally located. She suggested moving it forward and he seemed peeved about it. After he thot you had worked it out to the best advantage for excavation to have her tell him how much it really amounted to hurt just a little.

The Wyntoon sketches Mac had done for Hearst at San Simeon were for the big job, not for the small one; the latter, in fact, would soon be finished under Harry Thompson, the foreman for the F. C. Stolte Co. And it was the big job that Loorz, and Stolte too, anxiously awaited word on, the two men having prepared a "preliminary estimate" of the "Bedroom Wing"; Loorz sent their estimate to Julia Morgan on May 31. That one wing alone—conceived as a concrete structure four stories high—would need 125 tons of reinforcing steel and would take twenty-two weeks to excavate and pour. The estimate also addressed the 190 windows and the 200 doors the plans called for. But the estimate made no allowance for "plastering as concrete is to be allowed to set for some time before plastering (none this year)." Nor did it allow for "painting, plumbing, electrical, heating, mantels, fixtures, decorating and furniture." The "tentative" costs were left untallied, but we can readily add them up ourselves: $64,405, most of which applied purely to rough structural work. The big job was going to be very big indeed.

(The projected cost of $64,405 was as competitive as Loorz and Stolte could make it. To put that figure in perspective: the two men had recently been awarded the Walter E. Buck house for $80,000, on which their profit would be minimal. The Buck house was a mansion in the exclusive Bay Area community of Woodside, and the F. C. Stolte Co.'s rock-bottom figure covered everything from excavation to interior finish.)

Just what *was* this big job at Wyntoon, this job for whose bedroom wing the concrete work alone would cost that much? The Loorz Papers fail to say—probably because Hearst eventually had to abandon the big job in favor of more affordable work. And so he, and Loorz and the others in turn, began focusing their attention elsewhere in the continuing saga of Wyntoon. But just for the record: the big job would have entailed the use of tons of stonework from a Spanish monastery, the monastery of Santa Maria de Ovila, which Hearst had bought in 1931 through the Madrid antiquarian Arthur Byne and which now lay dismantled in a San Francisco warehouse. Julia Morgan and Walter Steilberg had also taken part in that complicated transaction, hence the latter's mention in the Loorz Papers of 1933. (Another Bay Area architect, the great Bernard Maybeck, had preceded Mac McClure in making sketches for the big job.) No other architectural fantasy of Hearst's—not the Enchanted Hill at San Simeon; not the Beach House in Santa Monica; not St. Donat's Castle in Wales,which he bought in 1925; not the house he envisioned for his Grand Canyon property, which he had owned since 1913—could quite equal what he had in mind for his Spanish monastery at Wyntoon. Yet why all the concrete work that Loorz and Stolte had figured for the proposed bedroom wing and that they would have figured for other portions of the big job had it gone ahead? Because the ancient stonework of Santa Maria de Ovila was to be appliquéd, in effect, to the modern concrete shell. The same thing had been done at San Simeon with old ceilings, mantelpieces, and other building fragments

Hearst had bought through the art market. For Wyntoon, though, the application of crate upon crate of medieval stonework to the "large New Castle," as Loorz had called it in writing to Fred Stolte on May 8, would have been unprecedented in its scale.

COME THE SUMMER of 1933, San Simeon had its share of activity, even as the small job at Wyntoon gave way to a kind of medium job (though it was never called that). At San Simeon, Loorz's tiny hilltop crew was still pushing the Billiard Room and the Lower South Duplex to completion; in addition, Julia Morgan had brought in a man named Martin Charles to solve a complex puzzle, the layout of a Spanish ceiling for Hearst's Gothic Study. (Hearst had bought the ceiling in 1930, through the same Arthur Byne who had procured the monastery of Santa Maria de Ovila for him in 1931.) Loorz's crew on the Burnett Road, meanwhile, was inching past the Santa Lucia crest on its way to Jolon. Loorz mentioned the road to Mac McClure on June 19; he gave us an invaluable glimpse of social history while he was at it:

> Spent a most uncomfortable Saturday afternoon accompanying the party on a picnic to the end of the new road and thence over a very rough trail on horse-back to the Nacimiento River. They complained so much about the rough road (quite unfinished) and the hazardous, steep, rough, narrow trail, that I felt sick when we reached the other side. Did Marion [Davies] kid W. R. about his fine trail. You might know that she was persuaded to take the trip after long and lengthy teasing and coaxing by Mr. Hearst.
>
> Anyway I suggested to Mr. Hearst that they take the Davis Trail back and that I would go back over the trail and have the cars at Davis [Flat] when they got there. He accepted promptly. I know he felt, several times, like telling me a few things about my trail but was very gracious about it and just laughed. He certainly does have to control his temper to put up with some of the things he must have known to be very sarcastic, this referring to many remarks made by the guests about the beauty etc. Was I glad to get back. The worst part for me was that I was in the same car with Eddie Kane and did he rave and criticize the possibilities of any fun on a picnic way back there. The reason being that he always gets very car sick going back, so does Marion and a few of the others.

That was probably one Saturday night when Loorz didn't hoist a beer with King Walters and the rest of the Burnett Road crew.

Hearst and his party left for Wyntoon on June 26. The next day, Loorz wrote to Martin Charles, the man that Julia Morgan had brought down to work on the Gothic Study; Charles had recently returned to San Francisco:

> Martin, will you pardon me for my frankness, but I must tell you a part of a discussion with Mr. Hearst last evening shortly before he left. It was up in the Gothic with him, me in a nice soft chair.
>
> Anyway, I told him he could tell Miss Morgan that I had plenty of work outlined ahead, so if she didn't feel very well it would not be necessary for her to hurry down here. I said, following the above, "Thanks to Mr. Charles the Study had been worked out very efficiently and carefully, so that barring changes, I had it all quite clearly outlined." He said, "Is that so—I'm glad to hear it—Miss Morgan thot and talked very highly of him." He asked, "Is he here?" and I told him you had left last week end. He said, "What was the matter, didn't he like the place? Maybe he would have enjoyed it better if we arranged for him to move into the house and be with the guests. We'd be glad to have him. Maybe he can come back and work with you on getting the Billiard Room finished, we must have that."

Hearst evidently meant exactly what he said about Martin Charles. But Charles wanted no part of the offer. Charles told Loorz he didn't want to return to San Simeon. "How is that for rank ingratitude?" he wrote. "Mr. Hearst's suggestion about herding me with the guests does not help matters in the least, as you can imagine. I prefer being with you and remaining a member of the humble, but honest, construction camp." Just what Charles was upset about is hard to say; the Loorz Papers leave that question unanswered.

WITH HEARST HAVING LEFT for Wyntoon on June 26, the question was who would be the first to tell Loorz about the great man's arrival. The distinction fell to George Wright, an engineer, a wit, and an expert in reinforced concrete (albeit a "Stanford man," as Loorz jokingly warned Julia Moran):

> We landed in the midst of a whirlwind of excitement that was blown up by the preparations for the arrival of W. R. and his party.

Getting everything in ship shape in the allotted time looked like an impossible task but it was done. W. R. was apparently pleased. Poor Miss Morgan was just about a wreck by last night [June 27]. Truck load after truck load of furniture arrived and every piece had to be placed just so. An ash tray on the wrong table worries her. She deserves the vacation she thinks her trip to San Simeon will be.

Fred Stolte, the superintendent on the job, gave Loorz a similar account on June 30. "And I surely take off my hat to Miss Morgan," he added. "She was the first one on [the] job and the last one leaving." Harry Thompson, the foreman, also told Loorz on June 30, "They have been running Mr. McClure ragged with changes and additions. We are now to build another house about 30 x 60. The Castle [the monastery] seems to be a minor consideration at present."

Not until July 7 did Mac McClure have a chance to write to Loorz—to unburden his soul, as he put it:

The past month has been the most hectic I have ever endured. As you know we have had J. M. for long visits, one for eight days and one for four, and she just left last night again after a two day stay.

The pressure of work and responsibility is very great. The worst was the three days preceding W. R.'s arrival—house unfinished—3 van loads of furniture all at once—most of it dis-assembled and crated and green hands to do the work. By working at top speed all day long we just barely got things in order for the Chief. I would have had it done sooner but J. M. threw a few monkey wrenches the last day—paint colors must be changed—furniture moved and removed etc. When I finally took Miss M. to town [McCloud] at 10:30 p.m. she very nearly collapsed—never saw her so bad. W. R. arrived and liked what we had done but the next day sent me a very sharp note about broken and marred furniture, and all instances which he mentioned were made before unpacking here—it was unjust and beyond my control entirely but I had to take it. W. R. since has been O. K. but yesterday when J. M. was here he flew into a terrible rage because the laborers cut some underbrush to put in some high stakes for [the] new castle. Again I took the rap although Geo. Wright and Ed Hussey [of Morgan's office] did the dirty work while I was busy elsewhere. However I think things are quiet again and part of W. R.'s bad mood was due to [the] fact that J. M. was trying to sell more castle designs over his own plans.

At any rate we are still alive but things are not as pleasant as could be wished. The program of building is most undecided—W. R. changes his mind from day to day and I would not be surprised if he did very little to main building. Please keep this under your hat.

He is talking about building more cottages and altering present buildings at Waterhouse immediately which I think will go ahead.

Apparently Mr. H. likes it here very much but expects the smooth machinery at San Simeon to be duplicated here at once.

Here is a little item which you are to keep to yourself or I am to be shot at sunrise.

Two weeks ago when Miss M. was here she told me she was going for a short walk by the flume and not to bother about her. 3 hours later she returned covered with mud, blood, and bruises to such a degree that I had to take her to the hospital. She had fallen off the flume down the wet and rocky bank about 20'—cutting her head open and severely bruising herself. Fortunately and miraculously she was not badly hurt and was out again in two days. Can you beat it?

Loorz heard from the "Wyntoonites" throughout July 1933. Harry Thompson wrote, "I'm glad Miss Morgan is pleased with the work we have done. I couldn't possibly do any more with what I've had to work with and she makes so many changes that it slows up progress." That was on July 9. On July 14, George Wright said, "We have one large labor crew that does nothing else but go around and pull up stakes as fast as they are placed." He also told of Fred Stolte and Miss Morgan's having just returned to the job. "They both seem to think that this time some definite decision will be made regarding the Castle. At any rate W. R. intends to go ahead with a cottage to be erected at the site of the Waterhouse barn. And we have a short road to build. That's better than nothing." Harry Thompson wrote again on the 17th, saying, "We will have one more new cottage to build at least that is the plan at present." Mac McClure wrote on the 28th, "We are to have two houses built and furnished by October 1st, as well as general revamping of existing buildings. . . . The amount of work to be done is so great that if we get one half accomplished we will fulfill my expectations." He also said, "W. R. left [for San Simeon] in a good humor. I made him a new castle sketch (on a new site) which he liked or at least it aroused his interest again, however I do not expect any castle this year, if ever." James Rankin also wrote on the 28th, relating that

Harry Thompson had nearly cracked under the pressure but had managed to pull through. "Perhaps the fact that he was finally able to make a good catch of fish and treat us all to a nice fish dinner helped him over the hump," said Rankin, "for in fact I guess it helped us all." Miss Morgan herself, in an undated letter from San Francisco, said, "It certainly is beautiful up there, & I am so glad Mr. Hearst could be there & catch all our errors as well as *vacationate*." What a saint she must have been to choose those words over a hundred other possibilities.

Loorz answered Mac's letter on August 4:

> As you know the party are here with us again and all hands are at the wheel. Though very pleasant and full of Pep, Mr. Hearst seems more interested in things up there than here at present. When everything is going O. K. and he doesn't get excited about things it certainly means he isn't particularly interested, doesn't it?
>
> He would like to start work on the outside pool, start a new reservoir etc but told me yesterday, "I want so many things but haven't got the money." Poor fellow, let's take up a collection.

He also answered James Rankin, the prince of plumbers, on August 4, greeting him as "Dear Jimmie":

> W. R. seems more interested in the work up there than down here but that makes it easier for us to keep pegging at the same things we are on and get them completed. We are not making a big showing but we are still spending money.
>
> I thot you would be down to put in those two fixtures in the Tennis Court Dressing Rooms but now I don't know when we will do much more plumbing. We are concentrating on the Billiard Room and Gothic Study in which there will be no toilets, thank God.

Loorz wrote to Fred Stolte the next day and told him, as he had Mac McClure, that Hearst wanted to build a new reservoir and that it would cost "about $30,000." And when he told Stolte, as he also had McClure, that Hearst had said, "I want so many things and I haven't got the money," he added that Hearst had laughed in making the statement. "He has been in splendid humor all week and I've enjoyed chatting with him," Loorz told Stolte. "Hope we can keep him that way and send him back up there feeling the same way."

Stolte replied with two letters on August 7, upon returning

to Oakland from Wyntoon. In his first one he said, "The program is changed somewhat—and several 8 or 9 room cottages are to be built." In his second one he said, "I am very glad to hear that Mr. Hearst is in a good humor. For a while, I thought things looked rather bad, he was real peeved, about the castle site." Stolte described himself as having stayed in the background while Hearst was at Wyntoon, as having let Julia Morgan do the talking. Like the Loorz of 1928, Stolte had yet to meet Hearst.

Stolte's letters moved Loorz to confide in him on August 8:

> Between you and me Fred I don't think he felt he could afford to start such a large building at this time and had to find some fault with the whole scheme. I have felt that way about it even before we started up there. About the time each new set of plans was about ready to start work he would make major changes.
>
> Anyway Miss Morgan is quite satisfied in spite of everything so that is what really counts. As I told you in my last letter I never mention Wyntoon to him for a definite reason. When it becomes that last resort I will tell him.

What Loorz meant by those final words was that his and Stolte's partnership was unbeknownst to Hearst. Loorz was employed independently at San Simeon, not on behalf of the F. C. Stolte Co., and he was afraid one of those "conflicts of interest" that are all the rage nowadays would spoil his rapport with Hearst. His fears proved unfounded. Before long he and Stolte learned that their company had been chosen to return to Wyntoon in 1934, apparently with Hearst's full knowledge and approval. The prospect of the big job, however, remained as much in limbo as ever.

Loorz paused long enough to portray the idealized San Simeon for his parents. "Mr. Hearst, the twins (about 18) [Randolph and David Hearst] and many guests are here but will leave for L. A. about Sunday," he told them on August 10. "Miss Davies will start another picture and is diligently training in tap dancing etc. It is not all easy to keep trim for pictures. I think Mr. Hearst personally sees to it that she does keep practicing. The boys are very nice and sociable and full of fun." And on August 15 he told them, "All of Mr. Hearst's guests and the boys left last night for L. A. Mr. Hearst will leave by aeroplane this morning. Then it will be a little lonesome for a few days for me. Most of the crew like it better while he is away for they can swim in his pools, ride some of his horses and things like that. I like it better while he is here for everybody seems to take his business more seriously."

In the meantime, of course, there was work to be done at San Simeon and especially at Wyntoon. The first clear indication of the "Bavarian Village" that was soon to emerge on the Waterhouse parcel at Wyntoon lies in Harry Thompson's letter of August 18: "We have three houses to enclose before winter and they are going to be some shacks." Thompson's reference to what became Brown Bear, Cinderella House, and Angel House is revealing; but it was Mac McClure who consistently provided the insider's view; he prefaced his letter of August 27 by saying, "I suppose you are tired of hearing about the troubles at McCloud":

> When W. R. left here he left a pretty definite program with approved designs of proposed houses for us to follow. However since then they have been regularly and completely changed as often as J. M. visited San Simeon. After Miss Morgan's last visit here (a 4 day visit) we were told to proceed without drawings or other data other than some charcoal smudges and other indefinite data.
>
> I might also say that I received daily letters last week requesting so much data and drawings on the other houses that I had no time whatever to do necessary drafting for job progress.
>
> At any rate last Friday morning she called me up and was much incensed because we had not done more "as we had *all* the necessary information."...
>
> To cap our program, I received a wire from [the] office this morning saying, "Stop all work on houses until Thursday, when I will be there with new ideas" from J. M. at San Simeon last night. This probably means she will be here over the holiday week end—which I have planned to take off. Such is life.

Loorz assured Mac he was always happy to hear from him, even if his letters sounded "a little discouraging":

> I'll only add that I think Mr. Hearst is personally more responsible for the changes than she is. He just simply keeps her busy all day changing while she is here. She brings down rather completed drawings for his approval. However, it may be that she has already instigated changes which he is not in sympathy with in the face of the fact that you and he had done them up there.

We are plodding along slowly but surely here. She hasn't been down a lot and [*sic*] two times on Sunday and I was away all day. Last Sunday however, I came up about 7 in the evening and stayed with her until after 11 that night. She was to stay in S[an]. L[uis]. that night so had lots of time. But she was already too tired from her afternoon with W. R. and his drastic changes of Wyntoon that I got little or no information from her. However, she was in a good humor and I enjoyed the hours with her anyway.

On September 13, Loorz alerted Fred Stolte that Hearst and Morgan were planning to fly up to Wyntoon in a day or two. Loorz told Stolte, "I think he is just a little hostile toward Miss Morgan for changes she is making to plans that he and Mac produced. When that is going on I find it much better to keep away." Poor Stolte. He had written to Loorz, "I told Miss Morgan that I would be pleased to go up before and during Mr. Hearst's visit there, (seeing that she has placed this confidence in me)." But as he had confided, "I get the JITTERS When I think of having to go over the job with Mr. Hearst." Loorz tried to calm him by saying, "I know you will enjoy it a lot after the first few times. He is just as shy and bashful as you are and it takes a long time for him to become familiar and sociable. I've always found that it is best to beat [it] as quickly as our business is completed for it is embarrassing when we suddenly run out of something to say." And to think Loorz was nine years Stolte's junior!

WHILE FRED STOLTE was taking deep breaths, George Wright, the engineer and wit, was driving to Wyntoon from San Simeon, where he had seen Loorz. The various buildings at Wyntoon would require a revamped power supply; Wright was helping to plan a new system of poles and wires. His account of his trip north to pursue that work left Loorz in stitches:

I thought I should let you know that I am here [at Wyntoon], lest you start worrying that either the car or myself had gone to pieces on the way.

I had my first flat tire this side of Morgan Hill; a rim slipped over the wheel flange, started running at a wild angle in San Jose; I refused to buy a new tube in San Francisco, put on a dainty patch the size of a bed spread.

After cleaning off some of the grime I headed for the Merchants Exchange [Miss Morgan's office]. My face looked like a boiled lobster from wind burn (the top had blown in two at Cambria) but I put my pride in my pocket and marched up to the office. The door was locked, the place deserted. I phoned [James] LeFeaver [the office manager], who told me that he knew nothing about any map, knew nothing about the power line, did not know that I was going up. Wasn't that just swell! I phoned Miss Morgan, who was glad I called, who arranged to meet me at her office at noon. She showed me the map, explained what they had in mind. She said that the poles hadn't yet been purchased and that she would remember the information regarding cedar poles. For Mac's peace of mind you might assure him that I put up a good sales talk for cedar.

There was more to Wright's adventures—"at Pinole a valve stem sheared off," "at Arbuckle the head gasket went out," and so on. Back on the job site itself, he had to contend with Hearst's frowning on the removal of any underbrush in the way of the new power lines. Wright figured an act of nature might make the work easier. He concluded his long letter to Loorz by saying, "Can you arrange with God to have Him start a fire up here with a bolt of lightning?"

Loorz knew what Wright was getting at. "I believe the little shrubbery cut this spring caused more discomfort than anything since the Johnstown Flood," he answered on September 16, referring to Wyntoon.

Along with working on new power lines and framing three new houses, the Wyntoon crew had also begun remodeling The Gables, which adjoined the swimming pool and tennis courts Loorz had worked on in 1928. The Gables was downstream and across the McCloud River from the Waterhouse parcel, with its remodeled River House and the new houses that would become Brown Bear, Cinderella House, and Angel House—the components of the architectural group called the Bavarian Village. The Gables also adjoined the remains of the original Wyntoon Castle, which Bernard Maybeck had designed for Phoebe Apperson Hearst at the turn of the century. The late Mrs. Hearst's castle had been almost completely destroyed by fire in 1930. A wing had survived, though, and it was to that structure that Hearst had affixed The Gables soon thereafter. (The insurance settlement after the fire of 1930 had funded the building of The Gables, as Mac McClure recalled years later.) For Hearst, a building two or three years old, like The Gables at Wyntoon, was a building already in need of a facelift. McClure, Thompson, and the rest of the Wyntoon crew had their work cut out for them as the summer of 1933 ended. The medium job, as it were, was getting bigger all the time, even with winter just around the corner.

Back at San Simeon, the Billiard Room and the Gothic Study remained at the forefront, as before, and so did the Burnett Road. Loorz briefed Hearst on the latter job on September 22, writing to him at the Beach House in Santa Monica:

> The road is going nicely again. We are able to progress several hundred feet per day which is somewhat of a relief after the gorge. Fighting that hard rock certainly caused breakage and delay on our tractors but all are repaired [and] in excellent shape and should cause no further trouble. Unless I am too optimistic, I believe we will be able to get thru nicely without putting on the extra machine and crew from the other side.

Loorz's optimism about the Burnett job proved sound. By October 2 he could tell Hearst, who was still in Santa Monica, "We are up to the point where it is necessary to select the bridge site over the Nacimiento River."

Julia Morgan paid a visit to San Simeon in the meantime. Concerning the Billiard Room she told Loorz on September 25 that it was "O.K. to send for Joe Giaritta [Giarritta] for setting [the Persian] tile arches." She also instructed him to "complete steps, buttresses and mantel hearth border as outlined to Mr. Cardini." (L. Cardini was a San Francisco marble sculptor who had done extensive work at San Simeon since the 1920s.) For the Gothic Study, she told Loorz that Cardini was to "make and antique stone inner jambs and lintel for mantel." There were sixteen other matters for Loorz to oversee, according to his "minutes" of that meeting.

Loorz wrote to Fred Stolte right after Julia Morgan's visit on the 25th:

> Miss Morgan reports everything going along nicely up there now [at Wyntoon], with reference to the construction crew at least. She is certainly not happy with the way the Chief and Mac are changing and adding. She went to L. A. yesterday to see him and was going to

tell him that the present budget would not enclose those buildings this winter. Let's hope he is in a position to get more [money]. I am cutting down here as much as possible to leave more for up there. They want so many things though that it is hard to cut down.

The latest reports from the south have it that they are rushing through the [Marion Davies] picture and will come here, in force, in about two or three weeks. Whether they will go north at that time will be doubtful but no one knows.

Hearst and Mac had made their most recent changes and additions (on paper) while Hearst was at Santa Monica, Mac having gone down to work with him there. Mac was back at Wyntoon by October 5, the day he next wrote to Loorz:

Haven't heard much from J. M. since returning. A letter received yesterday however says we aren't making enough speed getting frames up. Have you seen the designs? The roof framing is, for the most part, very complicated. I have no fear that the houses will be covered before the snow comes, but the Gables remodeling is another big item which is on our hands. The patio, as you probably know, is to be roofed and the downstairs almost entirely revamped. If this is to be done this Fall we will have a full program. If you have any idea how long we will be operating here let me know. Miss Morgan indicated they might try to keep going most of the Winter—Hope not!

The next day was Friday, October 6, and that evening saw some of the camaraderie for which the Loorz household in San Simeon was justly renowned. Loorz told the electrician Louis Schallich about the gathering in a letter of the 7th:

Joe Giaritta [*sic*] and his brother left this morning after a few days setting the tile panels in the Billiard Room. Last night they and Cardini were down for a feed and later Arch Parks and his wife dropped in. We had some of the same old thing, you know, wine and song. Anyway a goodly time was enjoyed by all. Wish you had been with us. Joe brought down a gallon and so did Cardini so they furnished their own stuff so to speak.

We can only hope Loorz went easy on the rotgut, for he had to confer with Miss Morgan on Saturday. Her instructions to him about the Billiard Room tended more toward the fine points, now that the Giarritta brothers had set the Persian tiles and the other finishing touches were soon to be applied.

"Place selected furniture as directed as soon as room is completed," Loorz noted in his minutes. And, "Place one pool table in center and permit Mr. Hearst to approve before having the other two placed." (The room was eventually furnished with two such tables, not three.)

FROM SAN SIMEON, the globetrotting Julia Morgan made straight for Wyntoon. Loorz wrote to Mac McClure on the following Monday, October 9, "No doubt Miss Morgan is there with you this morning. Hope things are going to her satisfaction." He also told McClure, "I left her Saturday night at 10:30 (the rest of the afternoon off) after a rather busy day of furnishing the Billiard Room though it is still full of scaffolding, stone masons, plasterers, decorators etc." Morgan, who was sixty-one in 1933, was seemingly as tireless as ever; but she had yet to recover fully from the mastoid operation she had had the previous year, as Loorz related in that same letter to McClure:

> She was quite strong, that is she lifted heavy chairs etc but Oh the equilibrium. I think she staggered more than ever. While we [were] going thru one of the tapestry boxes in the Vault she just simply fell into it. She said, "I certainly have a jag on tonight." Again she was sketching something learning on her elbow on a table and went flop down with her face on that. Each time I merely put my arms around her [and] pick her up bodily and set her in the nearest handy spot and go right on with the business. It is really pathetic.

He also addressed the questions Mac had raised in his letter on the 5th:

> As for Wyntoon, I know they will work there as long as weather permits. I am cutting down here as much and as fast as possible to allow more funds for up there. Like yourself she is worried about the Gables alteration starting so late but she says Mr. Hearst wants that to be far enough ahead so they can finish it promptly for an early spring trip up there. She doesn't think he will go up there this fall. He has had a cold and has not felt any too well. I had a long phone conversation with him on Saturday. He heartily approved the idea of cutting down here to help out Wyntoon, but not to stop Gothic Study, Billiard Room. He still wants to start the outside pool in

November. If you are far enough ahead or shut down because of weather I think he will insist on it.

Before Mac got a chance to write back (Loorz told him on October 17, "You owe me a letter"), George Wright checked in on the 14th, writing from the Hotel McCloud, where most of the crew lived during that first season at Wyntoon:

> I think Miss Morgan has been irritated no end by trivial things that have not suited her fancy. At San Simeon, though you *may* have foremen who carry out instructions to the letter, the chief reason for the smoothness with which the job operates is your ability to handle Miss Morgan. If you were running this job it would be duck soup. Since his superior happens to lack the knack, Harry's job is difficult. Am I plain enough?

Harry Thompson checked in with Loorz a few days later, likewise by writing from the Hotel McCloud. "Have four good sized jobs under way have roof on one expect to have two more covered in next week and the fourth in about three weeks if the weather holds out." Three of those jobs were the eventual Brown Bear, Cinderella House, and Angel House—the components of the Bavarian Village on the Waterhouse parcel.

Mac finally got around to writing to Loorz again on October 22:

> Our job here has grown to cover a lot of operations. Three new houses [the Bavarian Village] of no mean size and the Gables remodeling which in itself is a "job." Needless to say I have had my hands full and can't give anything the complete attention it merits. The drawings necessary alone would be more than I could turn out if it weren't for the other interruptions and demands on me. However I am doing this [work]; I hope to get the buildings up and covered and let future details be worked out as they may. In any case the probable finish will be different than planned now any way.
>
> Of course we hear much talk about "Getting the feeling" and a lot of time and money consuming antics are indulged in as usual.

Despite those and other drawbacks, the season had not been without its merits, Mac assured Loorz. "I think my efforts and hard work have been appreciated and I believe J. M. has a higher regard for me than she once had."

Loorz, in turn, assured Mac, "I am confident that Miss Morgan has a lot of faith in you and feels that she could not have put a better man on the job. She remarked several times how well you got along up there and how much help you had been."

Yet another Wyntoonite wrote to Loorz from the Hotel McCloud—and did he write! Hayes Perkins, a veteran of Hearst Camp who joined the pilgrimage to Wyntoon in 1933, hammered out three tightly spaced pages of local history and descriptive prose on November 1:

> McCloud is a one-man town, or rather, a company town, for the Shevlin-Hixon Lumber Co. owns everything here but the dairy, and all the land and timber for a long radius about the place. . . .
>
> Mr. Hearst's present place is about seven miles distant from the town. Most of us stay at the hotel, where charges for rooms are from $9 to $10 per month. The rooms are very good, steam heat, a good lobby, well conducted and as good as anyone could ask for the money. We commute daily to our work, about a half hour in truck or car. . . .
>
> There is no comparison between this place and that at San Simeon. This site is in a deep valley taken up by dense forest. The largest forest trees grow about the houses, and the McCloud River, a flush stream that varies little during the entire year is immediately behind every house. It is very rapid, so there is no possibility of boating whatever. There is a good sized lawn, perhaps an acre and a half, well cleared and sown to grass at the upper place called locally the Waterhouse, and a smaller area a half mile below at the old [Phoebe Hearst] castle site, now called the Gables. Of course everything is more or less upside down now on account of the construction, but when it is finished, can be easily put into condition again. . . . Personally, I like the Waterhouse site the best. Mr. Hearst seemed to prefer it when here last summer, and stayed at that place all the time. When completed, it will be truly a sylvan retreat, more secluded than is San Simeon and embowered in virgin forest unspoiled.

Perkins concluded his letter many paragraphs later by saying, "This is about all I know, Mr. Loorz."

Loorz heard from Mac McClure a month later; Mac was still at Wyntoon on December 1:

> The buildings are all covered and a fair amount of exterior work done on them. More than I expected has been accomplished.

However it is expected that the Gables and one house here [on the Waterhouse parcel] will be finished before W. R. comes up next Summer. This leaves a lot to be done next Spring—as no interior work is done on either the Gables or these houses.

Then on December 17 Loorz heard from the Chief himself, William Randolph Hearst, who was in residence at San Simeon and who summarized his plans for that estate in 1934:

After the holidays I would like to hurry up the [Gothic] study and get the decorators into it as soon as possible.

I would then like to start on the three bedrooms over the billiard room.

I would also like to alter the ladies' dressing room as planned. And I think while doing this we could tile and finish properly the kitchen and pantry.

Perhaps we can also do the stairs after a model I have given Miss Morgan.

We might put in the north wing elevator and do the bowling alley.

Outside on the grounds I would like to do the outdoor pool beginning February first. I think we can finish the west terrace at the same time.

I would like to complete the pergola and the road wall also in time for Autumn planting.

We should enlarge the smaller reservoir to enable us to double our water supply.

Of course we will finish and straighten the road to Jolon when the fine weather comes.

And I think we should make a shorter road from the castle to the creek.

Dream on, Mr. Hearst—dream on.

NINETEEN THIRTY-FOUR

1934

HEARST REMAINED AT San Simeon through Christmas and New Year's, with a large party. Loorz wrote to Mac McClure in Los Angeles on January 5, 1934, telling him, "The party is to leave about January 15th. Mr. Hearst said they intended to be away a couple of months returning about April for a short stay and away again." As for the resumption of work at San Simeon, or at Wyntoon, Loorz made it clear he was getting mixed signals from Hearst:

> Yesterday forenoon he seemed to want to get started with a small crew soon. Later in the day while talking to Miss Morgan and I, he said he was in no hurry and we could remain shut down until March or April. No less than two weeks ago he sat down and wrote me a long letter on Sunday [December 17] which laid out a large program for this year with the hopes that we go right on and get some of it done right away. So there you have it. He even told Miss Morgan yesterday that she needn't rush Wyntoon Gables and houses for he was comfortably located here and could remain here this summer and she could get it ready for the following summer [1935], up there. Now if you know any more about it after all this you are a magician. In spite of all this he looks very well and seems very happy. Except of course that the north wind is causing the East Room Fireplace to smoke too much.

Mac knew that Loorz planned to take his vacation as soon as Hearst left in mid-January. "Hope you and the family have a good time and a chance to forget W. R. H.—J. M. and all the rest of the outfit," went his reply of January 8.

Hearst delayed a week in leaving, but the Loorzes took off just the same for a much-needed eight days at Gilman Hot

Springs, east of Riverside. Upon returning, Loorz found two baseballs awaiting him on his desk. Hearst's secretary, Joseph Willicombe, knew Babe Ruth and had asked him to autograph the balls for Loorz's young sons, Don and Bill. Loorz resumed his unending correspondence by thanking Colonel Willicombe, as he was called (the U. S. Army Reserve having given him that title honorarily in 1927). "You certainly must have a drag with the Babe," Loorz said. Then he told Willicombe about his recent trip to Gilman Hot Springs. "It may not be a *Carlsbad* but it affords a real place for rest and health improving for those of moderate incomes." He also mentioned having seen the Marion Davies movie *Going Hollywood,* which the Loorzes thought would be a big success. "Miss Davies certainly did herself justice," he said.

But Loorz had more pressing correspondence to get out that January 30. "As per previous conversations we are starting up construction work with a small crew," began a detailed letter he sent to Hearst in Santa Monica:

> A few men will work on the [Gothic] Study and a few will start about Monday on the outdoor pool. Perhaps not more than ten men for a few weeks on this work. No doubt I will hear from Miss Morgan with more definite instructions in a day or so.
>
> There is a lot of miscellaneous odd jobs that have been requested from time to time and which could use quite a crew if we attempted them all very soon.

The jobs Loorz mentioned ranged from fence work at the Hearst Ranch poultry plant to the installation of a new elevator in Casa Grande—and from the building of additional tennis courts to the transplanting of an Italian cypress tree from Paso Robles.

Hearst replied immediately. "I think you will have to enlarge your crew," he told Loorz, "because all the things which you mention in your letter should be done and should be done more or less promptly." He was especially concerned about the Italian cypress:

> Please take great care in moving the cypress tree from Paso Robles. Please take a very liberal amount of dirt with the tree,—more than you think necessary for safety,—more than enough to leave what you consider a sufficient margin of safety and then some more.

We must surely preserve this tree. I do not know where we could get another one of that size. . . .

In fact to get all these things washed up, I would be willing to defer starting work on the [outdoor] pool until the first of March, if necessary; although I would like to begin on the first of February and get all the noisy work of taking out the concrete finished by the middle of March.

Loorz soon had firm orders to begin working on the Neptune Pool and certain other jobs. His conference with Julia Morgan on Saturday, February 3, yielded this note: "Start work with the approved crew on Monday Feb. 5th. Approx. six laborers. [Frank] Frandolich on swimming pool, Alex Rankin to start removing pipes with labor helper. [Pete] Peterson & one carpenter on Billiard Room doors and forms for present. [Frank] Gyorgy to polish Dining Room tables and stain doors only for present. Plasterer, bricklayer, helper and Glazier to complete present hilltop construction crew. Labor total to be approximately $3000 Mo." Concerning the pool, Loorz also noted that the crew was to "move all of group statue[s] to safe location from pool and fence [them in]." His notes contained these references as well: "Move temple marble, columns and stone, to safe location, perhaps on south side of pool. Layout carefully keeping all pieces in position as at present"; "Can start removing concrete with compressors as soon as antiques are safely out of the way"; "Frandolich can chip out the marble ladders to make certain they are not damaged."

Loorz provided Hearst with a detailed progress report on February 13:

The cypress tree is safely loaded and enroute this morning. We have a nice tight ball of earth and should have no trouble. Will see that proper guys are placed as you suggest. . . .

The outdoor pool is being wrecked but as you know that concrete is hard and requires considerable handling to get it out to the dump.

We are busy moving the doors to the [Gothic] Study from the Gothic Hall. We will proceed promptly with this so the hall should be completely finished before the middle of March. This is not a large job but requires everything from brick & concrete work to marble & decorating. . . .

It is a real pleasure to have a crew again and see things real active. Few of the men had a days work since they left the hill. Some of them had been away five months.

In mid-February Hearst flew up to San Simeon briefly for what Loorz called "a little family reunion," the group revolving around Hearst, Marion Davies, and Hearst's two oldest sons, George and Bill. Hearst wrote to Loorz from his hilltop office on the 14th:

Regarding the work inside the hacienda [the castle], there are two things I wish we could do and have them over with.

First, and most important, is the fireplace in the East Room. I would like to have this fixed right even if we have to take down all that end of the building. But I do not think we will have to do that.

The fireplace in the East Room, or Morning Room, had smoked badly for years; Hearst suggested some possible remedies. Then he elaborated upon the second problem:

The other thing is the stopping of noises in the tower—in fact in both towers. The north tower, however, is much the worse. If I believed in ghosts I would think it was haunted.

Whenever there is any kind of a wind, even a stiff breeze, the moans and groans in the tower are pitiful to hear.

I do not know what the trouble is, although it may be the weather vanes, which are probably old and rusty and creak when the wind moves them.

If it is not that it must be something connected with the bells. . . .

It is a bad trouble, however, and makes sleep almost impossible.

There is a slight moaning in the south tower, but it is only slight in comparison and only noticeable when the wind is particularly strong.

It may be due to some similar cause, but it expresses itself in a much less aggravated and aggravating manner.

If we can get these two things fixed up—the fireplace and the ghosts —the house will be much more habitable.

Loorz replied to Hearst's secretary, Joseph Willicombe, on February 22. "We have enjoyed reading his *Ghost Letter* several times and use it as an excuse to write the enclosed letter":

Being favored with a strong appropriate Southerly, I sent out a scout to locate the position of the enemy, the Ghosts of La Cuesta Encantada.

Within a short time the scout returned, reporting that he had located the stronghold of the enemy. He volunteered to go out single-handed and route [*sic*] the ghosts with a hammer and two plugs. This being done promptly all is again quiet on the Gothic Front.

There were two small stubs of pipe projecting about 6 inches thru the roofs of the stair towers, these are the elevator tower and the one on the south. The wind blowing over the tops of these small open pipes made very prominent rumbling noises, much as I imagine Ghosts make. For certain, they would be most disturbing to slumber. In fact, they were so perceptible that they were clearly audible and even disturbing to the noisy workmen in the Gothic Hall.

Loorz assumed a more serious note in explaining that the stormy weather had prevented his working on the East Room fireplace; he also summarized his progress on the odd jobs he and Hearst had discussed. He saved the most serious note for last. Hearst's bull terrier, Buddy, whose recent disappearance had prompted Hearst to offer a fifty-dollar reward, had possibly died on the slope below Hearst Camp; one of the men had spotted some buzzards circling there. Buddy was very dear to Hearst, having been his "only house pet" since 1918.

Hearst enjoyed Loorz's account of the ghosts as much as Loorz had Hearst's; Hearst wrote to Loorz from Los Angeles on February 25:

I am very glad the expeditionary forces have completely routed the enemy.

Do you not think decorations of some kind are in order.

Your description of all that is going on at the Hill, not only in the way of work but of weather, makes me feel that it is just as well that we are away during this period.

As for his beloved Buddy, Hearst proved to be straightforward on the question of death, a subject absurdly rumored to frighten him: "I suppose of course Buddy is dead. But if he is, I would like to be sure of it." We may never know what became of Buddy since the Loorz Papers contain nothing further on the matter.

THE WINTER OF 1933-34 was getting to be a wet one, as Loorz told his parents on February 27:

> Well I hope old Jupiter Pluvius has been as good to you with his rain as he has with us. We really don't want any more for a while. It could wait three or four weeks before we could benefit by more. Everything is knee deep in mud. The fields are so soft that even my caterpillar is stuck out of sight. . . .
>
> Except for rain we would be doing quite a little work. I have quite a few men and things sound good around here again. I like to see things move. That is why I get pretty disgusted during the winter months when we are shut down.

In writing to Fred Stolte the next day, though, Loorz disclosed another reason for the slowed pace:

> I have quite a little work going on so life is interesting again. All sorts of equipment from caterpillars to shovels operating but not too many men, in fact, I would like a lot more. However, I am purposely holding down for a good and sufficient reason. You know why, that is so there will be more to clean up Wyntoon debts.
>
> Talking to Miss Morgan, day before yesterday, she said that they would be able to clean Wyntoon up entirely on the next payment. That sounds too good to be true, does it not? However, we cannot kick on that job. It has even helped a little on the others. . . .
>
> I wish things would hurry up and start on the up and up. I'm getting tired of this confinement. Though I do love to work with Miss Morgan and Mr. Hearst. Both have been wonderful to me. He writes very amusing letters while away and jokes with me while here.

The subject of Wyntoon had come up often in recent weeks. Loorz told Charlie Badley, "For this year they merely plan on completing some of the work started this [last] year. The big proposed castle will not be started." Harry Thompson inquired about the new year's prospects, and so did George Wright. Loorz told Thompson, "Miss Morgan does not plan on starting up at Wyntoon until some time in April at the earliest. . . . Right now, Mr. Hearst does not appear to be in a hurry for anything up there but will no doubt change before summer"; he gave Wright a similar answer.

James Rankin, on the other hand, wondered how soon he

would be needed at San Simeon, where work had begun on the Neptune Pool; Loorz answered him on March 8:

> The excavation is, as you know, very slow on the pool with the wrecking of that concrete and rock cut, with a short crew and all hand work. So I cannot predict how soon we will have space for you to begin laying pipe. I don't think it will be for about six or eight weeks anyway. In the meantime they may want to start the bathroom over the billiard room. I hope so. . . .
>
> All is well on the Hilltop. Peace and quiet reigns. Miss Morgan has been awfully nice for many months, not a single real complaint. Maybe that is why production has slowed up? Don't you say yes.

By March 21 Loorz, having talked to Morgan the day before, could tell Fred Stolte, "It looks like we can get started [at Wyntoon] before very long." He also told him about the Burnett Road job at San Simeon. "This last week end I drove around to Jolon to start the road crew on that side," Loorz said. "I will work from both ends to get the road open. In about 20 minutes the Caterpillar went out of sight and the driver and I shovelled as fast as we could for four hours to get it out. Some Sunday!"

But hold the show. On March 25 Joseph Willicombe gave Loorz a message Hearst dictated the night before:

> Please tell Miss Morgan and Mr. Loorz that I do not want anything else undertaken up here until that fireplace in the East Room is fixed. I have been talking about that for a long time and I do not get anywhere. It is a miserable thing. It smokes all over the house, and when they do not want it to smoke they open the doors and create drafts all through the house. So I wish Miss Morgan or Mr. Loorz would kindly just fix that fireplace whether there is anybody here or not.

Needless to say the show went on, smoke or no smoke. Loorz's notes from his meeting with Morgan on March 27 contain these entries under "Gothic Study":

1. Leave mantles as is at present while Architect looks for appropriate stone mantles. Mr. Hearst not satisfied with present wood lintel mantles.
2. Proceed with plastering and completing West end wall then follow with girders to be ready for decorators.

3. Mr. Solon to be sent down next week or about to put sketches on East end girder of main room.
4. Crew can be increased to hasten speed in this room.
5. Arch[itect] to get out detail of bookcase, order grilles from [Ed] Trinkkeller, and sample carving for lower doors from [Jules] Suppo.

Those same notes of March 27 contain five entries under "Outside Pool"—that is, the Neptune Pool, which saw increasing activity with the onset of spring. "I certainly have a crew of men and I'm right busy and on my toes," Loorz told George Wright on April 9. "It looks like a madhouse around that outside pool. I'm spending the money this month that was expected to be spent at Wyntoon. You birds certainly rob this establishment when you work up there."

Loorz resorted to capitals in compiling his notes from his meeting with Julia Morgan on April 19: "LATE ORDERS BY PHONE FROM MR. HEARST TO MISS MORGAN: PROCEED TO COMPLETE ALL ROOMS OF RECREATION WING TEMPORARILY FOR USE FOR LARGE PARTY FOR WEEK END OF April 29th." Now *that* was a tall order. But not until May 3, when he wrote to Fred Stolte, did Loorz come up for air long enough to explain the meaning of those words:

Well we are settled down again to a more even program. Perhaps you have heard of the grand rush for his Birthday Party.

One week before his party they called me at 8 P. M. while I was having dinner with the folks at the [Cambria Pines] Lodge. The order was to try to get all of the rooms in the Recreation Wing completed temporarily for occupancy in time for the party.

You remember that dead concrete wing over the Theater with nothing in the openings but tar paper storm covers. Besides that the floors were full of antique stone for later use in the openings of this wing etc. One of the rooms was my paint shop with filled shelves.

Anyway within six days we turned the place over to him furnished with all rooms, closets, bathrooms, including showers, ready for use. That is 11 rooms complete with baths & closets and 2 tower rooms quite comfortable for use but no bathrooms. Rankin did wonderful to get as much [done] as he did. Note that the form wires were still in place and had to be cut thruout. The ceilings were painted, the concrete exposed walls were painted and the floors, rough concrete tinted. Hand rails galore up and down steps. In fact, they turned out to be very comfortable and the only difference between temporary and permanent was plasterboard instead of plaster & rough floors.

Loorz concluded by saying, "Mr. Hearst is still in splendid condition and seems very happy. Told me yesterday that he would be in Europe for three months and outlined what he wanted complete when he returned . . . oh boy. . . you should read the list."

LOORZ HADN'T HEARD from Mac McClure in quite a while; Mac finally wrote on May 10, saying he would be returning to Wyntoon that night for the new season. Loorz hastened to reply on the 11th:

> Glad you will be back at McCloud. Hope you will be there when Mr. Hearst arrives. He expects to make an inspection trip of one day on Monday [May 14]. As you well know, that is not a promise. . . .
>
> W. R. and Marion flew down to see the preview of Operator 13 last nite. I understand that he is in the plane homeward bound right now (4:30 P. M.). From a hint from Mr. Willicombe the picture was not received well and W. R. is returning with spirits at low ebb. Suggested that it was not the proper time to touch him for an increase in funds.
>
> They plan on leaving about Tuesday or Wednesday for their extended sojourn. The Dame Rumor has it that the party of companions is increasing to be nearly a gang.
>
> Of course, the bunch up there [at Wyntoon] heard the Rumor that he bought the Wheeler place. If he paid the figure that I saw in the correspondence, I commend Wheeler on his excellent salesmanship—W-O-W. Now he will move the proposed site of the Dream Castle.

The Wheeler place was downstream along the McCloud River, below The Gables and the Waterhouse parcel—downstream where the McCloud turned prominently, hence The Bend by name. The attorney Charles S. Wheeler had owned the property since the late 1800s, not only The Bend itself but also, until recent years, the property Hearst now called The Gables—the site of Phoebe Hearst's original Wyntoon castle. Mrs. Hearst had leased that property from Wheeler and had retained Bernard Maybeck as her architect; Wheeler himself had built his own country house at The Bend through the equally renowned Willis Polk. And now The Bend was Hearst's, The Bend and all the land Wheeler had kept after Hearst bought the land his mother had only leased. Indeed, Hearst had now consolidated his holdings along the McCloud River—from above the Waterhouse parcel, past the site of his mother's castle, where The Gables now stood, and on below Wheeler's last stronghold at The Bend. If Wheeler was gloating over the sale, as Loorz suggested, Hearst no doubt was gloating even more over the new prospects of remodeling and development that lay before him.

At San Simeon, meanwhile, Hearst was still "preparing to leave for a three months tour of Europe," Loorz told King Walters on May 12. "He has had us on our toes expecting a trip thru to Jolon but the time is getting so close for his departure that I'm inclined to doubt it. The boys will be disappointed as they have rushed to get the road cleared and fairly smooth for this picnic." In all likelihood that was one picnic Hearst and his party cancelled; their last day at San Simeon, until the fall of 1934, was Sunday, May 13.

Hearst's protracted absence meant Loorz and his men could do their work with gusto—no worries, for instance, of a noisy jackhammer disturbing anyone's late-morning slumbers. The Neptune Pool and the Gothic Study were the two main jobs on the hilltop itself; the Burnett Road was the main one elsewhere on the ranch; of course a miscellany of other jobs, small and large, also came under Loorz's superintendence. Despite the increased tempo, Loorz kept up with his correspondence, as always. On May 23 he answered a letter from Phil Smith, with whom he had served in France during World War I and from whom he hadn't heard in years. "I'll only add that, my business in Oakland, contracting, is continuing on fairly well," Loorz wrote, "and I could and should go back to it right away. However, this is a very interesting place. I answer to no one but Mr. Hearst personally and his Architect. Both have trusted and shown appreciation of [my] efforts in every way so that I would hate to leave them. They have been wonderful to me and pure business is too often cool." Many of Loorz's letters contain such references—to his feeling of isolation at San Simeon, to his homesickness for Berkeley and the Bay Area, to his concern for the welfare of the F. C. Stolte Co. in his absence. But they also refer to the challenging nature of his work, to his deep sense of loyalty to Hearst and Morgan—and, on occasion, to the handsome salary he enjoyed in the midst of the Depression.

In writing to Mac McClure on May 11, Loorz had asked Mac to keep him posted on Wyntoon—that way Loorz could "look intelligent" when Hearst or Morgan mentioned the subject. Mac, though, was apparently too busy for the moment to correspond; but George Wright came through for Loorz on June 2:

> The two new carpenters that arrived today brought the total pay roll up to twenty-three. When Rankin and [George] Addison get here with their crews, we will very nearly be back to last year's strength. There is certainly enough work to be done to keep all hands busy.
>
> As a fire retardent we started whitewashing the Brown Bear [house] today. Can't you imagine the mess? I suggested that we rename it the Polar Bear.
>
> The power line voltage and layout is still undecided. As you suggested, I have refrained from arguing about the merits of the various systems. The various possible plans have been submitted for their consideration, and we are just sitting back and waiting to put in whatever they decide upon. . . .
>
> I wish you were here to go fishing with Harry and me tomorrow.

By keeping in close touch with Julia Morgan, and by being a partner in the company that had the general contract at Wyntoon, Loorz undoubtedly knew more about that job than he had let on to Mac McClure. On June 4, for instance, he wrote to Fred Stolte in that regard:

> Went over Wyntoon work with Miss Morgan and things seem to be satisfactory but she was not real enthusiastic. It was proper for me not to ask any questions as she felt so good about everything here [at San Simeon] that I certainly wasn't going to spoil it. . . .
>
> How are the accounts receivable coming with the Wyntoon work? Remember that when we took the thing at 3% it was definitely with the idea of cash monthly payments. Now we won't be mean or anything but in a nice way I will mention it sometime if they are falling behind.

Three days later he again wrote to Stolte about Wyntoon. "No Fred," he said, "I don't think Miss Morgan is displeased with our work. I think she would have grumbled about it a bit if she felt that way. What I think is, that she resents the many many changes that she has to make that Mr. Hearst and Mac made without consulting her. Also she resents the excessive cost of the finish etc when he is not providing funds accordingly. I did not mean to worry you."

THAT SUMMER THE LOORZES sent their two boys, Don and Bill, to stay for several weeks with Loorz's parents in Lovelock, Nevada. Loorz wrote to his sons, who were six and eight, right after they arrived in Lovelock in early June. "I know you will have a good time with Grandma & Grandpa and I hope you will be nice to them," he said. "Can't you gather the eggs for her and bring in the wood and help her? Can you try to eat properly and use your best manners all the time? If you can I am sure that Grandma and Grandpa will be proud of you and Daddy and Mamma will be so pleased." A week later Loorz wrote to his boys again and also to his parents in the same letter. "We wanted so to get into San Luis on Saturday to see the Fiesta Parade with Don Poncho [Estrada] leading it but we could not, I had to pour concrete. . . . Well Dad I hope those boys don't get into everything like we used to. All I say is to watch your tools and nails. They sure can use a lot of them when they start manufacturing anything."

The concrete Loorz poured on Saturday, June 9, may well have been at the Neptune Pool, whose new walls he had begun pouring on June 6. Loorz's notes from his meeting with Julia Morgan on June 14 began with these instructions: "Make certain to strip forms carefully & completely." More of his notes pertained to the Gothic Study and the work of Camille Solon and other artisans in that room. "Mr. Solon's figures too 'wispy' and grouping should be more in panels than to appear continuous up and down girder," went his final entry, the reference being to Solon's paintings on the main arches in the Study. "Instruction given direct to Mr. Solon with other suggestions. (Note: Mr. Solon came down from scaffold next morning after working an hour, quite a nervous wreck bound for S. F. and a few days rest. After 15 minutes of my most sympathetic conversation, he laughed, threw his shoulders back and climbed back up the scaffold. I hope it was a cure.)"

Loorz wrote to Stolte the day after Julia Morgan's visit of June 14:

> Miss Morgan was here yesterday and told me about progress and changes at Wyntoon. She still grieves over the many changes and says that with them all they have not improved the houses. So it is not our work that makes Wyntoon a bit of a "Black Eye" or tooth ache for her.
>
> I am going out the [Burnett] road this morning to make my weekly visit and I'm taking the Mrs. with me. She has a cart load of books to read while I am arguing with the foreman. She apparently knows just what to expect. It is seldom that she gets to go with me on this job. Taking advantage of the kiddies being away. . . .
>
> . . . I have a lot of detailing and designing to do on this job all the time. I have just designed a 100 ft. bridge and will have time [over the July 4 holiday] to detail all joints.

Loorz's bridge was a wood-trusswork span over the Nacimiento River—a crucial link in connecting San Simeon with Jolon at long last.

Stolte wrote to Loorz on June 16, in reply to Loorz's letter of the 7th; he touched on the fortunes of the F. C. Stolte Co., and not just with respect to Wyntoon. "I am becoming a little more optimistic as to the future. Conditions seem to be better or we have found a way to live in the worst possible situation—1933—and get by." He mentioned having landed another General Petroleum gas station job—a Stolte standby in those days—this time in Stockton. The company had also landed a private job in San Francisco (Miss E. Schilling) for which Julia Morgan was the architect; Loorz and Stolte's connection with Miss Morgan was beginning to pay off apart from the Hearst work. Stolte further mentioned that the company had made a profit of roughly $4,000 thus far in 1934, a marked improvement over its performance in 1932 and 1933. As for Wyntoon, where Stolte was still construction superintendent, he had this to say about James LeFeaver, Morgan's office manager and one of her engineers: "Mr. LeFeaver seems to have *loosened up* toward me just a little and chats a little more. I have attempted to consult him in most of engineering items."

LeFeaver could seem formidable to those who didn't know him well, much as Hearst's secretary, Joseph Willicombe, could to the uninitiated. Loorz assured Stolte, "He [LeFeaver] is really a fine fellow when you know him. He is slow to make friends but when he does I think he will stand by them."

Loorz wrote to Julia Morgan on July 6; she was wondering how his appointment with Dr. Marshall in San Luis Obispo had gone:

> While examining me he noticed that my back was very sunburned and asked me how come. I told him I had worked the whole of Sunday in our back yard with my back exposed. The day being slightly overcast and the sun not very hot I had not expected to burn much and was still at that moment not particularly painful. He leaned back smiling quietly at me and said. "It takes a college education to make a man do *smart tricks* like that, you are going to blister plenty."...
>
> How truthfully he spoke, Miss Morgan, you can never imagine. However, I have spent most every hour from Tuesday morning until right now and for at least another day, confined to a small over-heated room. Over heated because it has been unbearable to put any clothing on the above mentioned back. I could not describe the immensity of the blisters without exaggerating so I won't try. . . .
>
> So you can see that I had to abandon some carefully made plans of things I had hoped to accomplish in the office while the boys were away on vacation. It is very difficult to do any office work when the crew is working. I wanted to list my steel and material for the [Neptune Pool] Pavillion and order [those items]. I wanted to sketch up those partitions for the bear pits which I hope we'll be able to get before Mr. Hearst returns. . . .
>
> You wouldn't think at my age and experience, it would be possible *TO BE QUITE SO DUMB AND YET SO HAPPY*, in reference to much of the above letter.

Loorz had more to say about his sunburned back in writing to Fred Stolte on July 10—and about the reason for his "own darn foolishness" in the first place:

> The wife and I are very busy all evenings, mornings, Saturday afternoons and Sundays trying to get a small swimming pool ready

for the boys when they return. We hope to surprise them and hope they will like it and continue to. They certainly like the water. Don knows how to swim and stays under the water most of the time.

We dug the pool by means of horse and slip scraper and car and slip and by main strength with shovel. There is a lot of clay so I worked the clay up and plastered the pool to exact shape. Now I am running a skin coat of plaster over it hoping that it will hang together while I'm working. When I get the water in I'm sure it will be O.K. It is 30 feet long, 16 feet wide, sloping from 2-6 to 4-0 in depth. So far it has cost me about $35 for the cement, drain pipe and valve and a little help on labor. When a bum comes and wants something to eat we give him a few hours digging at 35 or 50 cents per hour.

Loorz urged Stolte to bring his family down for a week's vacation at San Simeon. "Better come and help us initiate the pool," he said, meaning his homemade, backyard pool—not the spectacular Neptune Pool, which was likewise approaching completion on Hearst's Enchanted Hill.

On July 14 Loorz wrote again to his sons and parents in Lovelock, making sure of course not to mention the pool:

Since I've been able to get out with a shirt on my back Mamma and I have been working in the back yard a lot. Our flowers look fine. The tomato vine you two planted has lots of tomatoes on it. The squash is now bearing heavily. The squash grow quickly and we will have a lot more than we can use. The corn is also doing nicely. . . .

The strike is certainly affecting us here. We will be unable to get supplies and I may have to shut down if it holds out very long. Thank goodness we have the ocean handy with plenty of fish and some vegetables in the back yard.

The strike Loorz mentioned had erupted on the San Francisco waterfront as "Bloody Thursday" on July 5 and was about to culminate in the historic general strike of July 16-19. In the midst of his European sojourn, William Randolph Hearst pulled strings long enough and powerful enough to help choke that strike from six thousand miles away.

THE GENERAL STRIKE was in its second day when Loorz wrote to Mac McClure at Wyntoon:

The marble men are very busy with a large crew in the [Neptune] Pool. Frandolich is setting up those marble columns for the Colonnades or Pavilions at either end of the pool. We are making good headway but as you know it is very expensive work and I've had to keep quite a crew busy. We are making good headway in the [Gothic] Study but that too is so detailed with carved stone and carved wood and expensive ornamental and figure decorating that it is necessarily slow.

Certainly Mac I will let you know as soon as I hear about when the party will be back. I just heard that the Twins [Randolph and David Hearst] have been given permission to go up there but are not to come to the hill here. So if you have not heard the rumor you have it. I don't even know that they want to go there but Mr. Willicombe himself said they had that permission.

Camille Solon of Mill Valley, the decorator of the Gothic Study and the beneficiary of Loorz's pep talk in mid-June, had evidently taken a temporary leave after all. Loorz consoled Solon on July 30, saying he hoped his letter would not remind him of "the Discomforts of the Hilltop":

We have made you the *cutest* scaffold that you can move around like a wheelbarrow, all over the Study Floor. However, greater complications turned up. After taking down your scaffolding and erecting the portable [one] the floor was still so jammed that you couldn't have moved ten feet. Consequently I have three men lowering plaster materials, work benches etc. We really need these articles but will have to take them up as we actually use them or you couldn't get anywhere. So Camille, in case there is still some few obstructions will you please bear with me as I'm really doing my best.

Both Loorz and Julia Morgan were concerned that the Gothic Study be finished before Hearst returned from Europe; Solon was worth coddling if need be. Loorz closed by telling Solon how refreshing his backyard pool was in the recent hot weather. "You'll certainly have to join us some evening after work." The ploy was successful. As Loorz told Miss Morgan on August 2, "I expect Mr. Solon to be on deck for Monday quite fresh and ready to cooperate. I had a card from him which stated that 'He was happily recuperating from his *Grouch*.'"

Julia Morgan herself could show a tempermental streak on occasion. Dell Clausen, a plasterer working at San Simeon, could vouch for that, as Loorz told Stolte on August 3:

> The type that can please Miss Morgan are few and far between Fred. It took Dell several months to really win her over although she knew from the beginning that he was exceptionally good. In fact, she has since gone back and is using his own textures that he started with and has almost entirely abandoned the textures she used to use. . . .
>
> According to Miss Morgan things are going quite O. K. up there [at Wyntoon]. She is just now beginning to feel that you really are getting somewhere and is really satisfied with the altered buildings. Says they look real fine. Keep up the good work.

Loorz also said, "From now on I'm going to keep an eye open for prospects of the Hearst type when they visit up here," meaning Hearst's guests. "The trouble is that most of them are from Los Angeles. Maybe we can open up an office down there someday." Always thinking, always looking ahead—that was George Loorz at his most typical.

The Burnett Road had recently been completed, a job Loorz was proud of. Stolte was planning a trip to San Simeon; Loorz encouraged him to try the new route:

> I just wanted to tell you that it would be a lot closer for you to come down by way of our new road thru to Jolon. It is rough and very dusty and will be until the first rain when we can grade it properly. However, it is an interesting ride and I would drive thru to Jolon and meet you with my keys. It saves 80 miles but not a lot of time as it is a slow road. You turn right just as you approach the bridge going into King City and drive 20 miles over perfect highway to Jolon. If you would phone me the night you leave Oakland and tell me about when you will reach Jolon, I'll be there. At the same time I'd take you thru the big place there at Milpitas.

(That trip would be impossible today unless one had unlimited access to the Hearst Ranch and the adjoining lands of Fort Hunter Liggett. Hearst sold his Milpitas property, surrounding Jolon and Mission San Antonio, to the government in 1940; the "big place there" was the Milpitas Hacienda, which became the headquarters at Hunter Liggett once the government took over.) Loorz closed that letter of August 11 by telling Stolte, "I am certainly booming now with over a hundred men and all small jobs necessitating changing every few hours."

The Gothic Study and the Neptune Pool continued to dominate the work at San Simeon. Jules Suppo, who had done fine woodwork for the project since the early 1920s, had been retained to inlay the bookcases for the Gothic Study; Suppo worked out of his studio on Polk Street in San Francisco. "Everything seems to fit nicely," Loorz told him encouragingly on August 14—everything, that is, that Suppo had completed thus far and forwarded to the job. By September 5, with Hearst's return drawing closer, Loorz adopted a more urgent tone: "We are anxious to get the inlay work as soon as possible. We have all of the cases nearly roughed in and can complete them as quickly as we recieve your work." The Neptune Pool, meanwhile, was far enough along for Loorz's notes from his August 16 meeting with Julia Morgan to contain this entry: "Try to get temple started to indicate proper balance from approach on roads up hill." The temple was a Roman ruin that Hearst had bought in 1922 and that had lain in wait on the hilltop ever since; its ultimate role as the centerpiece of the remodeled and enlarged Neptune Pool was soon to be realized.

MAC McCLURE WAS OVERDUE in writing his memorable letters to Loorz; on September 6 he came through with a good one, datelined "McCloud":

It has been an eventful summer on the whole. The houses have moved along steadily toward completion (externally) and now the place has quite a finished appearance, with much of the half timber and plaster on and the grounds and pathways neat and shining. I think Miss M. is more or less satisfied and I hope W. R. is likewise but who can say?

We have an artist lady here painting shutters and decorations. She came about a month ago with a carload of baggage and a large parrot in a cage. I met her at Mt. Shasta and hauled as much as possible in the coupe and Geo W[right] went over later for the rest and "Nicky," the parrot.

Nicky is the apple of her eye and although she has been told to keep him out of the McCloud Hotel she hates to leave him out on the job and occasionally spirits him into the hotel via the back stairs. It is more fun than trouble, however, and is O.K. by me.

I think the shutter decorations will prove expensive however and doubt if $50 each will cover them—(there are only about 60 of them).

Very little changes have been made by Miss M. She has a few suggestions, chiefly about the garden, but spends much of her time, when here, working on the cataloging of the San Simeon "treasures."...

The new plasterer "got the feeling," at least partly and our plaster is no longer "nervous" but is "happy" or at least so we are told....

The days are getting much cooler here—or the nights I should say. I hope W. R. does not wait too long or he will freeze in his unheated houses—Waterhouse & Wheelers.

Loorz answered Mac on September 11, beginning with, "Boy I was pleased to get your letter":

Yes I know that Miss Morgan is quite pleased with Wyntoon. She admits that it turned out much better than she anticipated and much better than originally planned.

I know the artist lady Miss [Doris] Day. At the beginning of the decorating in the Study Miss M. talked to me about the advisability of having her come and work with Solon. I only shrugged my shoulders and she knew how I felt about it. She brought her out here and she went over everything and raved about most everything. It was the proper thing to do for she is now working isn't she.

Anyway it was decided to bring a young decorator Ted Linforth, a son of one of Miss M.'s clients and very personal friend. Young and inexperienced but very talented and a smart boy. But—it is too long a story to go into detail—try as the boy might he could not please the master and he was reduced to slinging paint with [Frank] Gyorgy and Mr. Solon has done the big job almost single handed. The space is covered with typical Solon sketches and dull tones. According to Miss M. he must go over all of it again and really do the job. That is put more color in the costumes and improve figures above the sketchy layout. You know as well as I do that they are just as Solon planned them and the best he can do and perhaps alright to some. For myself I think she is right but I told her she could never get it out of Solon. We have one real good one rich in color and not too bright but that was done by Ted. That was his Waterloo for too many admired it and Mr. Solon heard. Besides that Ted made the mistake of talking to Miss M. when she came down. It is Solon's drawing and story but Ted's hand and coloring.

Just as we are about to complete the Study we are obliged to make such changes as tear out two cast Stone Doorways, replacing one with an Antique and the other with a carved stone imitation. We must tear down an end wall to build supports for a heavy Antique Stone Panel etc. Boy you know the story too well. We have gone all too nicely until now. If we get the room completed by the return of Mr. Hearst I miss my guess. By the way talking to Mr. Willicombe over the phone yesterday he said he expected him back in about two weeks. That meant N. Y. of course.

Loorz wrote to Louis Schallich the next day, September 12, about the Neptune Pool:

The marble men are thru in the large pool and soon will be in the upper. Dell [Clausen] is plastering the walls above the marble and Mac [Max Mindner?] is setting the main Venus statue. We hope to put water in the pool sometime next week. I don't know how we can do it without Jimmie [Rankin] so I suppose he will be down to show us how. I hear that he raved when he got to Wyntoon because of the amount of work they had done without him. Says it is all wrong. Poor Jimmie and he is so nice to kid and dig into.

San Simeon experienced a late-summer, tropical rain on September 19; Loorz described the event to George Wright, who was still at Wyntoon:

We had a great electric storm Wednesday and lightning struck all over the place. Burned the upper log barn in the animal field. Started fires near Chileno Camp and several around Pine Mt. Actually struck and shattered a pine tree on China hill, you know the one just across the road from the approach to the Castle. Many eye witnesses swear they saw a bolt strike the North tower and sparks fly in all directions. It sounded like it in the office where I was hiding as it was pouring down at the same time. . . .

It is still very foggy actually dripping but not quite enough to be called a rain. We needed it as we will soon need a lot of water for the pool. The pool is already for water except for the placing of the heavy statues where Miss M. wants them. The light 7 ton bases of brick are now on rollers so that we can put them about promptly. Sounds bad but really she has ordered them moved but once so far and they are awaiting a second inspection.

From Fred Stolte at Wyntoon came surprising news on September 24: E. E. Boss and his wife had been relieved of their duties as caretakers. But it was even more surprising

George Loorz

The Enchanted Hill

San Simeon

Loorz residence, San Simeon

Julia Morgan

William Randolph Hearst

The Roman Pool building and the back of Casa Grande

The Roman Pool

Site of the proposed Great Hall, Casa Grande

Fred Stolte

F. C. STOLTE CO.
GENERAL CONTRACTORS
TELEPHONE ANDOVER 2311
3498 LAGUNA AVE
OAKLAND CALIFORNIA

6-30-33

Dear George:-

Well, I guess you know that Mr. Hearst and party arrived at Mc Cloud, Tuesday 10 P.M.

Everything seemed to finish up in good shape- However, I had <u>many</u> misgivings, a day or two before.

And I surely take off my hat to Miss Morgan. She was the first one on job and the last one leaving.

I have spent the last week here and, also, the family have been here with me. The Mrs. has had a very bad cold, and I thought she would shake it here.

OAKLAND LAKE MERRITT

Fred Stolte to George Loorz, June 30, 1933

The Gables, Wyntoon

Brown Bear, Wyntoon, October 1933

Two Bay Area houses built by the F.C. Stolte Co., early 1930s. Above: A. J. Sweetland house, Piedmont; below: Walter E. Buck house, Woodside

Two views of the pergola, Orchard Hill

William Randolph Hearst and George Loorz, Burnett Road, 1933

Davis Flat, Burnett Road

George Loorz and Ray Van Gorden, Nacimiento River bridge

Nacimiento River bridge, 1934

View downstream from the Nacimiento River bridge

Digger pines, Burnett Road

The Gothic Study

that Stolte and Jim LeFeaver of Miss Morgan's office had gone fishing together! "He, Bob Lang, Harry & myself went down the river yesterday (Sunday). Caught a nice mess." Stolte added, "The job seems to be progressing satisfactorily. Landscaping & roads are complete and plaster & outside trim is progressing nicely and almost finished."

A week later George Wright answered Loorz's "newsy letter" of September 19; he referred, as Stolte had, to the Bosses' dismissal and then gave other details of life at Wyntoon:

> The hotel is bulging with a construction crew that is about the same strength as that on the job last year. The so-called permanent guests may resent the intrusion of such a large foreign element, but that is there [*sic*] hard luck. When I first came up here and found out how little work was definitely planned, I didn't think that the architectural office would be able to keep up with decisions fast enough to keep as large a crew going as we have had here for some time.
>
> At the first of the season it seemed as if there would be little need for laborers outside of a few to keep the carpenters supplied. But there has been many a time when Harry would [have] liked to have supplemented the crew of fourteen that have been steadily employed ever since the job has been well under way. . . .
>
> Two of the buildings [on the Waterhouse parcel] are completely plastered, the third nearly so. Tile is going on the roofs, and of course exterior carpenter work is done. Within a short time all scaffolds will be down. Mrs. Day is just about finished painting pictures on the Brown Bear. So you can send the chief up here to give the place the once over when ever you are through with him down there.
>
> We, who have seen both [decorators], feel very thankful for Miss Morgan's choice of Mrs. Day for the decorator rather than another we could name.

As for E. E. Boss and his wife, they had somehow run afoul of Julia Morgan. "It doesn't pay to cross Miss Morgan," Loorz told Louis Schallich on October 1. Loorz also told Schallich, "Now we are expecting the party home any day and all work on the pool has stopped. We are to concentrate on the study only and greatly reduce my crew as soon as possible."

The shadow of Hearst was falling upon the land, the presence of the great man could almost be felt. Loorz relayed the latest news to Stolte on October 6:

Mr. Willicombe phoned me that it looked like Mr. Hearst would leave N. Y. on Tuesday and be in L. A. on Thursday. That means we can expect him here or in Wyntoon any time. *RUMOR* has it that he intends to fly to Wyntoon before coming here. He has written Miss Morgan that he has a lot of new ideas to try out at Wyntoon, so make up your mind that you'll make lots of changes. Ho Ho. I'm glad he didn't say he'd try that here.

Mr. Hearst sent a special maid to accompany 11 small blooded dogs of various types back from N. Y. and Europe. I have to rush up kennels with large runs within a very few days to accommodate them. I started yesterday to move the garages to make room. One section is moved and the kennels are started this morning. Can you beat it?

Stolte, it turns out, had been doing his homework. "In reading several of Mr. Hearst's European articles," he replied on the 8th, "I felt that we may expect some new or rather very old ideas—incorporated—in the plans for Wyntoon. Did you read the last article on Germany and the walled towns?" Stolte also told Loorz he had signed up two more General Petroleum stations, one in Santa Cruz and the other in San Francisco, and that he had "started the Berkeley job for Miss Morgan"— a remodeling, apparently, of her Seldon Williams house on Claremont Avenue.

Loorz's pulse surely quickened when he read the first line of Joseph Willicombe's letter, dated October 12 in Los Angeles: "Confirming telephone message I have following memoranda from Chief regarding your report of September 14th on construction at San Simeon":

Referring to paragraph six of BURNETT ROAD item, in which you discussed running new and better road from hilltop to first bridge at bottom of canyon, Chief said he would like to discuss this with you. Therefore advise delay until he returns. . . .

Referring to your suggestion in paragraph three of PIPE LINE BEARTRAP SPRING TO BURNETT item in which you state that you could construct the reservoir at the Beartrap Flat, etcetera, Chief says:

"This would make grand fishing hole. We can make it extra large."

You stated regarding the STUDY that Solon hopes to have very presentable job by October 4th. Chief says in that connection that he will be home about October 20th.

As telephoned, Chief hopes that the Breakfast Room [East Room] fireplace "works well." When you talk with him on the telephone I suggest that you discuss this also.

Chief says finally:

"A lot more has been done than I had hoped. I will be coming home to a different ranch. Please thank Mr. Loorz."

He also is glad that you are enlarging the kennels.

Chief indicated in his letter that he may go to Wyntoon about November first, from which you may infer that he is likely to be at the ranch between the date of his arrival, October 20th, and the end of the month.

Hooray! The Chief was in a chipper mood!

JULIA MORGAN WAS AT San Simeon on October 20 for Hearst's arrival. But Hearst didn't show up until Tuesday the 23rd, as Loorz explained to Stolte that evening:

Well it is now 7 P. M. and the chief just arrived a few minutes ago. We have been expecting the plane to land all day and Miss Morgan has been waiting for him since Saturday. She is very tired but really had not much to do to make ready this trip. She has walked around looking over things in general and going over winter programs etc with me.

We had company for dinner tonight but she felt a bit weak and really wanted me to stick around to help in case of necessity. . . . If she is with him for many hours I'll certainly enjoy the wait till she leaves. I have enjoyed her visit a lot. It is about the first time she has remained over night since I've been down here. That is excepting the rush when we fitted up for the xmas party.

She feels that things are in good shape at Wyntoon and thinks the new manager or caretaker will be O. K. About all she has to worry about, I think is that as always at this time of year she finds herself deeply indebted to everyone. I hope this time that she will be able to get a bit more from the chief. It would make things much easier for all concerned. . . .

The wind is blowing and it is quite cold. It means all fireplaces must be booming and that always means trouble for sooner or later one will flare up and smoke. If I can only keep those I've constructed behaving properly.

Well all I hope is that we can get Mr. Hearst to loosen up a bit with funds for Miss Morgan and permit at least a small crew on

Wyntoon over the winter months. She cannot do it at the present rates.

I'm beginning to realize how impossible it will be for me to get away from here. She would be disappointed and that would take all her other work away from us. Boy we would certainly miss her work, wouldn't we?

Loorz touched on the same point the next day in writing to his old friend Jack Hall: "I don't see how I can possibly plan on getting away from here as I'm afraid Miss Morgan would be too disappointed. That would mean a lot to us just now as we have the big job up north and several smaller alterations from her in the bay district. She has been awfully good to me Jack. I owe her a lot."

On November 1, Loorz heard from Frank Hellenthal, his counterpart at the Beach House in Santa Monica. Hellenthal sought the name of the man who had made the "silvered wire screens" for the bookcases in that building. Loorz's answer was enough to make an archivist's mouth water. "Frank," he said on November 2, "I have some old Beach House records in the attic of my Berkeley home, now rented. This man's name will be in those records. My tenant might gladly send the files to me." The Beach House records are probably long gone; the Loorzes sold their house in Berkeley in 1936.

Hearst's anticipated visit to Wyntoon around the first of the month prompted Loorz to write to Fred Stolte on November 3:

Well I guess your rush is over for this year. Hope you made personal contact with Mr. Hearst and that you enjoyed it. He has been very pleasant to me and I look forward to an enjoyable winter working with him here on the hilltop. This in spite of the fact that we get some very unreasonable calls when we least expect them.

The day before he left, Willicombe called me at about 9 P. M. and said that Mr. Hearst had just told him to consult me about getting the zoo off the hilltop as soon as possible. Willicombe said, "If you meet a few tigers and bears and lions etc on your way up the hill in the morning you will know what it is all about, just get busy and house them someway."

Stolte wrote back that, yes, the rush at Wyntoon was over "for a while":

Despite the rainy weather, I believe Mr. Hearst enjoyed the visit; he surely didn't mind walking around in it.

I met him the second day for a few seconds only—I thought that Miss Morgan could answer any embarrassing questions.

The first eve, on their arrival, I fell into the job of showing them around the houses. So if he should ask you who the guy with the spotlight was—why you are prepared.

Hearst's trip to Wyntoon bore the usual fruit, as Loorz explained to Stolte on November 15:

Mr. Hearst is very active, comes out everyday and talks over this and that with the vim and vigor that he had 7 years ago when I first knew him. You know he has Mac back making alterations and interiors of the Wyntoon houses. Oh boy, if he doesn't change his mind again Harry will have a headache when he hears about some of the changes. The nice tile roof just completed may have to be altered quite a little. Ho Ho, Let's hope he lives a long time doing just the same things that he has in the past.

It is good to have Mac back. Between the two of us we manage to entertain Mr. Hearst several hours each afternoon. Mac of course is with him most of the time. He has been very pleasant and very interesting so it really makes things on the hill worth while.

Loorz and Stolte's recent correspondence had also touched on the possibility of their working in the Los Angeles area. Loorz addressed the question further in writing to his partner on November 17:

I had thot about the job moving the [Marion Davies] cottage and theater from the Metro Goldwyn Mayer Studio [in Culver City] to Warner Bros. [in Burbank]. However, Fred, Frank Hellenthal has been doing all of Miss Morgan's work in Los Angeles for the past ten years and more. After I left Santa Monica he got in on the Hearst work and has done every bit of it since. Mr. Hearst knows him personally and likes him very much. He just finished the theater, in fact, Mr. Hearst never even went to look at it, so naturally he is already doing the moving job. I thot it best not to say anything about it. Besides all this LeFeaver and Hellenthal are graduates of the same University and are very friendly. In fact, Frank is a very fine fellow.

However, Fred, Mr. Hearst has been very friendly and frank with me and I will spring the question of work in L. A. one of these days. I don't want to scare him so I'll work up to it gradually. He's getting familiar enough so that he kids me now, tells jokes and laughs lustily.

Harry Thompson, the foreman on the Wyntoon job, wrote to Loorz that same day, November 17. Thompson said, "It is also a big help to hear that you feel both Miss Morgan and Mr. Hearst feel satisfied with our carrying out of their work." Loorz assured Thompson there was nothing to worry about. "Mac and Mr. Hearst are spending hours per day making nice pictures for you up there," he said. "It looks like you'll be there a long time if it all goes ahead as he plans it and then is changed a couple of times. He selects the fanciest trim he can find in all available books and Mac draws them up."

After she and Hearst made their quick visit to Wyntoon early in November, Julia Morgan sailed for Europe, leaving James LeFeaver in charge. The Neptune Pool still required some finishing touches, which Loorz took up with LeFeaver on November 27:

> Well I talked to Mr. Hearst after talking with you yesterday and he says we can do as we please. I started off with a laugh, saying that I wanted to ask him a question and thot I knew his answer but would ask anyway. He laughed heartily and said, "Alright, what can I do for you?"
>
> I put my question this way, "We can pour the second pavilion by xmas by concentrating definitely upon it but not if rain delays us anything like on the present one." He said, "It is almost certain to rain and it really doesn't matter, you do just what you think best."
>
> With the weather even threatening right now and with your permission I will begin reducing the crew after we pour next week. It is certainly not worth the chance to risk leaving the plaster forms over the winter. There is also the possibility of saving many or most of the coffers when we strip them from the present pavilion. This will save a good deal of labor and material in castings.

LOORZ FOUND TIME for a family outing on November 25; he told his brother, Claude, about it on the 28th. "Last Sunday I took the whole gang duck hunting on Morrow Bay," he wrote. "We rowed out on the bay at daylight and rowed and rowed until noon. We had very little shooting but lots of excitement especially when Bill fell overboard in shallow water." Loorz went on to say, "It seems funny but little boys really do more thinking than we give them credit for. They still get into lots of mischief but are not bad":

> Day before yesterday they came in very late for supper and we didn't know where they were. Here they come and Oh Boy you should have seen them, smell WOW. After dark they were near the corrals looking for mushrooms. They walked into what they thot was plowed ground and it was wet manure freshly scraped from a very sloppy cattle corral. Well Bill went in first and got absolutely stuck. Don said, "I couldn't come home and leave him there so I had to wade in and get him." He managed to get Bill out and then got stuck himself. While walking home a friend stopped and asked them if they wanted to ride in his car. They declined stating the facts and of course they were not begged to enter. Fortunately I built a shower in the garage and we herded them in there for a general cleaning.

The Loorz boys enjoyed an idyllic childhood in San Simeon. They rode their plowhorse, Pat, launched their driftwood raft on the nearby lagoon, swam in their backyard pool, romped through the poison oak in the ravines, climbed about the ruins of the old whaling station on San Simeon Point—and slipped in more cowpies than they cared to recall. Don was in the third grade that fall of 1934 at the one-room Pacific School, across the street from the Loorzes' house; Bill was in the first grade. Mrs. Loorz, meanwhile, was pregnant with her third son, Bob, born the following March.

One of the Loorzes' close friends, Arch Parks, had left his job as Hearst Ranch superintendent earlier that year in favor of ranching in Gilroy. He had nothing but praise for Loorz in writing to him on December 1. "And George I want to tell you," he said in part, "that after you got on that job, it was a different out fit all to gether, both on the hill, and down at the ranch." And then an unexpected, revealing barb concerning Loorz's predecessor: "Rossi was a queer make up. Seemed to glory in human misery."

Loorz wrote to James Rankin in Oakland on December 11, concerning the Neptune Pool:

> Jimmie, I know you are anxious to come down and play with those pipes and fittings on that gorgeous pool. Well I'll try to have my forms stripped and cleaned up by next Wednesday so that you can be here at that time and start filling the pool. Don't start telling

me that you need more time than that for it will be impossible to give it to you before that. My concrete will then still be too green to do it wisely but I'll take that chance. Now Jimmie, put your hands together, throw your shoulders back, get that ghastly twinkle in your eye and *quietly* have the water in the pool and partly filtered by *Xmas*.

The next day, Loorz wrote to James LeFeaver in San Francisco, likewise concerning the Neptune Pool. "It looks now that it would be unwise for us to shut down next Saturday," he said. "Mr. Hearst wants water in the pool for xmas and we should completely strip and cleanup around the pool so they could really use and get the benefit of that portion that is completed." Loorz went on to say, "Perhaps it is not too soon to discuss our winter program"—whereupon he hammered out two paragraphs of details. And then he said, "My idea is, if we can continue to show Mr. Hearst some progress around the pool he may not request that we start any new rooms in the Castle. This is what Miss Morgan hoped. Of course she outlined some rooms but hopes we will not have to do more than [the] small vault towers off the Study."

LeFeaver visited San Simeon on December 17, much as Julia Morgan would have if she had not been in Europe. Loorz wrote to Stolte about his meeting with LeFeaver:

Things turned out just as I wished and I will continue thru the winter with a very small crew to complete the things that Mr. Hearst wants right away.

We did a little talking about Wyntoon but only in general and about the plans and changes. Mac is going up to his office now to do some detailing on the Gables so that we can get some millwork ready for a rush start.

Loorz wrote again to Jack Hall in Berkeley on December 20. He admitted having supported Upton Sinclair for governor instead of Frank Merriam in the November election— "A choice of accepting the lesser of two evils," as he put it. (That was one bit of news he undoubtedly declined to share with Hearst.) "I'll be laying nearly all of the crew off tomorrow and it will be quiet around here," Loorz told his friend. "I will have plenty to do personally but there won't be a lot of planning and worrying about it. There'll be no rush except getting xmas trees put up and placing packages and sending. It becomes quite a mad-house."

A madhouse indeed. In the midst of the activity, Hearst decided that December 23 would be a fine day for a trip to Jolon over the new Burnett Road. Colonel Willicombe told Loorz on the 22nd:

> Chief was very much surprised when I told him the road to Jolon was not an all-year road, that it was not passable in winter.
>
> He asked that you proceed to make it an all-year road, building bridges where necessary and fixing the surface so that cars can pass over it at all times of the year.
>
> Chief says there is rock enough along the route to take care of the surfacing, and he surely wants it navigable for twelve months.
>
> Best wishes to you and yours for the holidays.
>
> P-S The trip to Jolon Sunday has therefore been abandoned.

Was there to be no rest, for either the wicked or the saintly? Willicombe wrote to Loorz again, this time on Christmas Day: "Discussing the all-year road again today Chief says where the road goes through that canyon there is enough rock, if you widen the road a little, to pave all the road. You might have this in mind when you talk about it."

But Loorz had other things in mind when he wrote to Hearst the next day. "Words cannot express my appreciation of the finest gift I have ever received. The *one* thing I really wanted was a good wrist watch. . . . I accept it as an expression of your personal regard rather than because I happen to be one of your many fortunate employees. I only hope that my activity in your interests have merited such a fine gift."

Loorz also owed Jim LeFeaver a word of thanks—"for the many boxes of candied fruit." He used the occasion to bring LeFeaver up to date:

> As you know things are real quiet on the hill, that is in the construction department. Even if we had men it would be too wet to do anything. In the household, however, tonight and tomorrow bid fair to be the first and largest day in the year. They have one of their largest crowds here with every room filled. Oh boy, the headaches there will be around here on Tuesday & Wednesday.
>
> Mr. Hearst writes notes and calls me on the phone almost daily to request some little things immediately and ask for some larger

things to be done as soon as he leaves. In a way it seems that it is a waste of time to be here when the crew is gone but it just works out that you'll have to keep a man here when Mr. Hearst is here. They want such things as heaters, phones, felt strips, doorclosers, rattles stopped etc. I manage to take care of a few of these each day. The pool looks wonderful & a *few* have used it.

Loorz's letter closed out the year; he dated it, "December last, 1934."

NINETEEN THIRTY-FIVE

1935

IN WRITING TO Jim LeFeaver on the last day of 1934, Loorz predicted a lively New Year's celebration for San Simeon. Early in January 1935 he wrote to Mac McClure, recounting for him that the preceding Christmas celebration had been just as lively:

> For the Party, you will know that all got gloriously drunk and were dumb with headaches and hangovers the next day. The 10 trees were an ugly display of wealth and superfluous tensil & ornaments. Really very beautiful except that you could see no tree. As promised, Mr. Williams [the warehouse manager] did not complete decorations until 8 A. M. xmas morning. As he planned, he was present to receive his envelopes from Mr. Hearst & Miss Davies on that tired xmas day. I don't mean to be unkind Mac, just talking our usual line.

He also said that Julia Morgan had sent each of his sons a postcard from the Canary Islands. "She made a few wisecracks in her own inimitable manner and they were interesting."

Loorz wrote to Fred Stolte on January 5:

> You knew that Mac went East for the holidays, did you not? Well he is to go back up to the [Morgan] office to start detailing [for Wyntoon] as soon as he returns. As soon as they get out any details we should get the mill started running the stuff. Mr. Hearst wanted the Gables and one of the houses by July if possible but of course he does not insist when they tell him they will need additional funds. Let's wait till Mac gets back and then I'll inquire again. I could have Mr. Hearst write LeFeaver asking him to get going but I rather

hesitate to do that. I feel certain that he would if I suggested it. He has told Mac but Mr. LeFeaver doesn't take orders thru Mac very seriously.

Mac was back on the job in San Francisco on January 7. "The office work is much the same as ever," he told Loorz the next day. "LeFeaver is leaving a lot to my own discretion and direction. Miss Morgan wrote a letter to the office family—apparently all is O. K."

The winter of 1934-35 was a rainy one—Loorz told Frank Souza in mid-January that the hilltop had had nearly thirty inches already—and the rains would last well into the spring that season. Loorz gave Jim LeFeaver a briefing on January 11:

> Mr. Hearst says it will not be necessary to hurry back on construction as long as it is raining and as wet as it is at present. That means that it might be better not to figure on starting on the colonnade work around the first of February.
>
> John [Vanderloo] is back with his one moulder and helper. Pete [Petersen] is doing some necessary repair work and between rains is working with one more carpenter and helper trying to get the third log barn constructed [for the zoo animals].
>
> Val Georges is back working on the fire screens as we planned. Mr. Hearst likes his screen very much and cancelled his order for some of them from Los Angeles.
>
> How soon will we receive those shades for the standards in the Study? Those with the old parchment shades.
>
> Mr. Hearst keeps wanting more and more lights and I think Miss Morgan keeps wanting dim. Oh boy when she sees all the lights he now has in the Study.

On January 15, Loorz wrote to Olin Weatherford, a key man in the F. C. Stolte Co. who superintended many of the "General Pete" gas station jobs:

> Well it looks like Fred manages to keep a few of you fellows busy anyway. Hope it continues that way. I'd really like to get back into the old office for a change, especially during the winter here when I have few men. I have plenty to do but I don't seem to be able to get the pep to do it for it lacks interest. We like it when we really produce something, patching leaks, handling cook house and ordering chauffeurs & mechanics around is a job but there is little real production to it. . . .

Maybe Olin, if we get this alteration job in San Luis, you will be able to come down on it.

The job Loorz meant was the W. T. Reid Company's Ford showroom and service station, on the southeast corner of Monterey and Santa Rosa streets in San Luis Obispo. Soon after Loorz went to San Simeon in 1932, he had begun to figure several jobs for the F. C. Stolte Co. in the Bay Area and elsewhere in his spare time; however, the Reid job was the first one in San Luis Obispo County that he figured and, as such, was the harbinger of many more to come. (Mac McClure, in fact, contributed some helpful sketches on the Reid job.) Loorz was familiar with local conditions through his three years at San Simeon. He saw the county and its adjoining areas as a virgin middle ground between San Francisco and Los Angeles—as a territory whose jobs were often too small for the metropolitan contractors and, just as often, too big for the contractors based in San Luis, Santa Maria, Salinas, and the other towns. Besides, the worst of the Depression was over, and Loorz was itching to get back into the contracting game. But for the time being the Hearst job at San Simeon remained his prime responsibility, despite Hearst's erratic budget and the persistent rain.

LOORZ HAD AMPLE TIME for his correspondence that month. He wrote to George Wright the same day he did to Olin Weatherford, January 15:

Right now things are quiet as you know but with his Highness here and calling every day or so and wanting to discuss work for the coming summer it is necessary that I be here. So when he leaves they tell me to get and take a couple of weeks right away before work starts up again in Spring. What a hot time to take a vacation, especially with my family expecting the stork about the first of April. Maybe now would be the time to go to the big city and step out a bit.

I enjoyed having Mac here for the few weeks. He certainly has a sense of humor and we collaborated at length on every detail. My spare time did not hang heavily. Right now I miss him. . . .

. . . It has stopped raining but for how long? If it stops I'll be rushing the airport surfacing. That will be an interesting job with a lot of equipment.

I will shoot [dynamite] the devil out of a red-rock hilltop in the field near the old Dobie [the Castro adobe on Oak Knoll Creek, near San Simeon Bay]. Then I will move the shovel in with as many trucks as it will handle.

For a real surface I feel that I will have to set up a crusher and bunkers. A fine red rock well rolled and tamped should make a very fine surface, if placed on top of a well rolled coarse sub-grade.

On the field I will have both cats spreading and moving dirt as we intend to do some grading. Then there will be the rolling and blading. I could really use you on that job and think you would like to take a good share of the layout and responsibility. . . .

By the way they rented a Ford tri-motor for the past two months, while they are overhauling the big one [the Douglas]. Well our hangar was about 6 inches too short for it. It got too wet to take off so it has stood there in the rain for weeks. However, as it is aluminum it does not seem to suffer even in the slightest.

Perhaps you heard that the chief had ordered a new Volti [Vultee] single motor job, six or eight passenger & pilots. I never heard of one but they say they are quite some plane. I hope it has the proper wing spread to fit our hangar, if not, then we get another job right soon.

. . .Wouldn't I love to take a trip to Jolon over our new road. I'll bet I couldn't get to the first creek without walking.

Three days later Loorz told Jim LeFeaver that, in talking to Hearst, he had learned the party didn't intend to leave San Simeon for at least a month:

He asked me when we were going to start on the outside pool, about the first of February? I mentioned that I thot it was his own choice to delay it a while as long as it is raining as it has been. He said, that would be O. K. as he was really in no hurry and would see me later about it. . . .

Mr. Hearst said he had received a very pleasant letter from Miss Morgan. Said she appeared to be having a very fine time. Said she should be in Southern Germany by this time. . . .

The boys taking care of the outside pool report some leakage now that was not noticeable at first. It has been so wet I haven't attempted to locate the trouble. We stopped heating the pool about two weeks ago and that is about the time it started leaking. I have an idea it may be where the slabs join, the old and new. It may need some pointing of the marble. Will let you know when I investigate.

It was Fred Stolte's turn on January 21 to get an update from Loorz:

Well it has been raining so much that things are still dripping wet even though the sun is out and we have a drying wind. It is too wet to start anything. . . .

Mac writes that they have a carver working on Wyntoon trim. Perhaps you knew about it. No further word has come about work up there. I suppose it would be nearly impossible to work up there anyway. . . .

Mr. Hearst is here and as you have read, is very busy writing and dictating. Boy he is working as hard as he ever did in his life. He seems to enjoy it for he is still very pleasant.

Did I thank you for the balance sheets? I'm glad to receive them. However, I note the usual size of accounts payable. I was hoping that would be lower. I think LeFeaver will be able to make a more generous payment this next week. . . .

If we [the F. C. Stolte Co.] can slide along this year as well as last we should be able to hold our heads up next year.

In writing to Loorz on January 22, Jim LeFeaver addressed the matter of accounts payable:

Am glad Mr. Hearst is not pressing to start at San Simeon because we really need the breathing spell for allowing our budget to recuperate. The marble and plumbing bills for the pool were very heavy, and besides Cardini's work amounted to considerable.

We would like to get these all well reduced before we start up again. . . .

We have had one letter from Miss Morgan and she said that at that time she already felt well repaid for the trip. We could not gather definitely as to the state of her health, but she does say that she is becoming enthusiastic about doing things, and to us that is a very good sign.

Stolte wrote back to Loorz that same day, January 22, saying, "Mr. LeFeaver has requested us to dig up some soft pine for carving [for Wyntoon]. The local market seems to be entirely out of this wood. So we shall send [our] truck to McCloud, and if possible, get some of our stock at our shop. If this is possible in 6 feet of snow."

Loorz himself was at the typewriter on the 22nd as well, writing to Mac McClure in San Francisco:

I knew you would be treated properly in the office. Mr. LeFeaver is quite aware that you are on the "in" with reference to Wyntoon so I'm certain he'll make it comfortable for you.

Talked to Mr. Hearst yesterday and he is still quite good natured and happy. Carey [Baldwin] wants another room added to the giraffe barn because it's too crowded for three especially since they are hoping that one will have a calf in April. She doesn't look it however. Anyway the possibility makes it interesting to W. R. and the addition will be forthcoming immediately.

A week later Loorz wrote to his "cat skinner," the heavy-equipment man Bud Sweeters:

The airport job which was in such a hurry has been postponed again for a while so you will have time to recuperate before swinging on to the shovel. In the meantime I am developing the quarry and shooting it up good so that you should have fun loading trucks.

We have enjoyed a couple of weeks of delightful weather. Just like spring. So much like it that I have felt like laying down and sleeping instead of working. They really have kept me quite busy sketching and figuring small jobs, like giraffe barn addition, poultry plant pens & shed, barn, corral and house alterations at Pico [Creek] etc. However, I have everything under control this morning. Finished the last sketches a few minutes ago.

He also wrote to his labor foreman, Frank Souza, that day—January 29—beginning with, "Enclosed find check—the three sweetest words in the English Language":

It certainly has been nice weather for work but the Chief says to wait until about March 1st. That pleases LeFeaver for they ran behind quite a little last fall. When they got Cardini's bill and Rankin's they were surprised at the amount it had grown.

Pete [Petersen], Elof [Gustafson] and [C. J.] Bobst have a few days work adding a room on the giraffe barn. They hope to have a baby giraffe and want a private stall for the mother. George Gillespie went to work Monday with two men. He will start a fence around the ridge below the reservoir where [Nigel] Keep is now planting pines. Val [Georges] is making fire-screens and that is about all there is doing.

Hearst himself entered the lists on February 2, writing in detail to Loorz:

[1.] I would like the things done first which we are going to need first.

There is now no use grading and surfacing the landing field until fall. We will not need the surfaced field until the rains come on, towards winter.

Of course there may be an opportunity to do the work before fall, and I do not object to that; but I do not want the work to interfere with the more pressing things.

2. The road to the other ranch we are going to need during the summer,—in fact from the spring on.

If you could work on that so as to get it ready for actual use by May first at the latest, that would be a useful thing to do.

The pool we are going to need in the summer.

If you could get that completed by May first, I would be very delighted.

I am merely using these as examples. Whatever we have to do let us do immediately if we can use it during the summer, and let us postpone until later the things which will not be needed until winter.

3. Before anything is done in the study I would like to talk with Mr. Solon. I want to discuss with him the desirability of leaving the arches as they are or modify them slightly to make them look more as if they were painted on stone than on wood.

I really do not know which I want to do, although I am inclined to the latter.

I do not know that we will do any other interior decoration until Miss Morgan gets back, but if we should attempt any, I would like it to be the three rooms over the billiard room.

I do not imagine that Miss Morgan will be back before the middle of April.

LOORZ AND HIS WIFE finally got away for a few days in early February, though more for a business trip than a vacation. They went to the Bay Area, where Loorz bought a rock crusher for the proposed paving of the airstrip and the Burnett Road. With the stork about to appear, as he had told George Wright, and with Hearst and his party staying on at San Simeon, those few days were as close as Loorz himself came to vacationing in 1935. (The rest of the family, however, went to Nevada that summer for a few weeks.) "I consider the trip really worth while," he told LeFeaver on February 11. "I haven't seen Mr. Hearst about the plant for he has a very big party, including some Vanderbilts I am told. They landed in the bay in a very large Amphibian and taxied right up on the sand thru quite heavy breakers just as simply as you please. Did San Simeon have a thrill that Saturday afternoon and turn out to see the sight?"

Loorz wrote to Jim LeFeaver again three days later, on February 14:

> Mr. Hearst has hardly left his rooms before 4:30 P. M. except one afternoon to ride down to see his new Vultee plane. It was on his way back that Mac got to see him for a very few minutes. Though I have several things to take up with him, even things that he asked me to get in touch with him about, I have not bothered him for he may not feel very well. Also the boys [Hearst's sons] are still here. Therefore, I can report nothing new to date.
>
> Pete [Petersen] & [Otto] Olson & [Dell] Clausen are back on the colonnades. [Frank] Frandolich & his helper are setting more marble on the temple. It actually rained last night and is still threatening so I will not rush the work for a while yet.
>
> Ray [Van Gorden] & mechanics have been plenty busy driving guests up and down the hill etc. We keep no regular drivers so we have to scramble when they ask for about six cars within 20 minutes.

And it was in writing to Jim LeFeaver on February 22 that Loorz provided us with further glimpses of San Simeon's social history—firsthand, revealing glimpses that till now have been hard to come by: "I have three cars waiting to take the remainder of the party to the airport where they will fly to L.A. Supposedly to see the Santa Anita Handicap. They expect to be back about Monday [the 25th]. This has been the longest continuous stay since I've been here." Loorz also told LeFeaver, "I'd like to hop in and complete the Study as soon as he departs for a while. I'd hate to have Miss Morgan come back and see it just as she left it." As for the trip to Santa Anita, Loorz told his parents on February 25, "Mr. Hearst and party went down to L. A. Friday to attend the races. They are expected to land in a few minutes, three or four airplanes."

From France, Julia Morgan sent Loorz a postcard dated February 26; the card depicted an enormous bell at the Cathedral of Chartres. "I have investigated dozens of bellfrys & their contents," she said. "This sample illustrates the fact that the hanging generally is not a *delicate* matter." She also said, "The car ate up the German chains in a jiffy,—(on the car) but otherwise it is a wonderful car—& the trip in character."

Miss Morgan's postcard was enroute from Europe when Loorz wrote to the painter Earl Caulkins, who was waiting out the off season in Paso Robles:

> I've just started up on this past Monday [February 25]. I brought Frank [Gyorgy] back on the job to do a little gilding and patching and I'm having to scratch my head to keep him busy. What is worse it looks like it is going to be a kind of skinny season for painters and decorators around here this summer.
>
> Solon has a little more changing to make in the Study ceiling to satisfy Mr. Hearst and if he would want you it would certainly be O. K. with me. However, you know that man, he thinks no one but Solon can do anything correctly, so that's that.
>
> . . . As far as Wyntoon (McCloud) is concerned there are no painters working. When they do I'll ask my partner to see that you get on. Of course, Miss Morgan has some old man in charge of painting and so far he's handled it alone.

The hilltop crew—the Hearst Camp crew—that Loorz put together during that last week of February consisted of twenty-three men, eighteen of whom were craftsmen, tradesmen, or laborers; the remaining five were a cook, a waiter, a janitor, a timekeeper, and Loorz himself. The Burnett Road crew, meanwhile, was its own entity, just as it had been the three previous seasons. King Walters had worked in Los Angeles instead in 1934, but he and Loorz still kept in touch. Loorz told Walters on February 27, "We started cleaning out the road on Monday and the boys will be way beyond the summit by tonight. I drove to the summit before they started and I don't know how much further I could have gone. We are only guessing that we have bad slides at the gorge for no one has been out. With good clean gutters like we had on this side we may not have as much trouble as we expect." The Wyntoon job also resumed during that last week of February. Stolte told Loorz on March 2 that Harry Thompson had gone up to McCloud and that Mac McClure had, too.

Hearst and his party remained at San Simeon. On March 4 Hearst sent Loorz a memo through Colonel Willicombe:

I must get the wild animals away from the immediate vicinity of the house. Therefore I would like to build the cat pits and the bear pits etc., this summer. The cat pits we will re-do as planned making six in all.

The bear pits can be made at the next bend [in the road] and can also be six in number. The cost of these latter need not be great. They need not be deep. Bears do not jump. Moreover people like to get reasonably close to them and feed them.

Suppose we plan this construction in detail and get an accurate idea of costs.

Loorz wrote to Stolte the same day, telling him, "Mr. Hearst is still here and feeling fine. Expect them to leave in a couple of weeks but who knows. Four of the [Hearst] boys have been here quite a bit lately. One left for S. F. today with our new Chrysler. Just when I get enough cars to handle the guests they come and take some away. Then I have to talk for another."

THE UNUSUAL, THE UNFORESEEN, the unexpected were forever cropping up in the lives of Hearst and those around him, as the George Loorz Papers so often reveal. On March 5 Loorz addressed just such a matter. R. F. Grady, an old friend of his in San Francisco, had got wind of Hearst's wanting to buy "all the Cast Models . . . in storage at the Palace of Fine Arts left from the old Fair"—the fair having been the Panama-Pacific International Exposition, which had been held in San Francisco in 1915 and in which Hearst and his mother, and Julia Morgan too, had played important roles. Loorz, though, knew nothing of the prospect. "In this case," he answered Grady, "you are one-up on me for I have never heard about the Cast Models from the Palace of Fine Arts. No doubt, Mr. Hearst will be interested and may even buy them as he does nearly everything he hears about but I wouldn't even hear about it until they gave me instructions to start hauling them." Grady's information proved accurate. Hearst bought the plaster models and shipped them to San Simeon—more crates for W. R. Williams to jostle in his beachfront warehouses. (The models did not see the light of day again until they were dispersed from those warehouses after Hearst's death in 1951.)

Loorz had recently heard from another old friend, Armand Brady, who had coyly written, "I see by the papers where Hearst is building several Tyrolean Castles up at McCloud. I want the one with the southern exposure for mine. So kid fix it up with Bill so I can take my one clean shirt and the old socks and go up there for the summer." Loorz answered Brady on March 8:

> Yes *we* are building several German style houses for Mr. Hearst at McCloud. They could be called castles since they are quite large compared to most homes. They are small compared to this institution. One of them has 13 bedrooms with bathrooms and Living Rooms. Note that I said we. That is the F. C. Stolte Co. is building them. You know, I hold just 50 shares of the company, Mr. Stolte 48 & our lawyer 2, a corporation. You see, by being the nice boy you taught me to be, I keep my fingers crossed and have managed to keep my partner & crew going quite well even from here. If Julia Morgan, Arch[itect] & Mr. Hearst live a few years more I should be well on the way. Do a little praying for me Armand or better still do a little *holding* for me for I have more faith in it. Isn't it terrible?

Hearst and his party finally pulled up stakes in late March, as Loorz explained to Jim LeFeaver on the 20th:

> Mr. Hearst is leaving today unless he changes his mind before this afternoon.
>
> In a general conversation regarding present work he asked for another metal warehouse right away. He really wants the concrete warehouse but the present plans call for wrecking the old one and we would have little extra space. We wouldn't have it right away and it would cost a lot more money.
>
> He wants to erect two but has agreed to one at a time and wait a little on the next one.
>
> I am practically ready for the steel in the colonnades. John [Vanderloo] has a few more panels to cast. I can hardly understand why they are not all ready since he started on January 7th. . . .
>
> He wants us to start a small crew and pour a few more beams at the Pergola. Fortunately we have 100 bird heads cast and three men will make a big showing. He suggests we order at least 200 columns for the summer but I think he'll be pleased with 100. It would cost quite a little to get footings for the 200 in addition to the beams.

He hopes we can have the Study completed by his return. We should do it complete with painting with proper crew. He does not want to change the beams now. He bought new rugs that just match the ceiling and so we may not have to touch them—ho—ho. . . .

. . . I intend to put all carpenters (four) in the Study in the morning. Pete [Petersen] is getting ready this afternoon. The thing I dislike most is to move furniture and cover it up.

Loorz wrote to his parents in Lovelock, Nevada, two days later, on March 22:

Mr. Hearst and party left us yesterday. The first time they have been away in five months. They will be back again in about five weeks. I think they will surely be back for his birthday April 29th. He always tries to be here xmas and his birthday and has ever since I've been here.

The day before he left I enjoyed an hour with him in the large Assembly Room. Marion Davies, young John and wife & Arthur Brisbane were in the room at the time. The day before that I sat in conference with Mr. Hearst, Young William, & Arthur Brisbane. It was interesting to say the least. He usually comes to my office but not feeling well he asked [me] to come in there. He has been awfully considerate of me and I like him for it.

Loorz pounded out two pages of tightly packed details for his good friend Arch Parks on March 23:

I drew up plans for an alteration of the Ford Building, W. T. Reid Co., in San Luis. My plans and bid were excepted [*sic*] and we will start work there in a short time. I sent all [the] dope to my partner and he will handle it. I don't want them to get anything on me here, that is regarding doing my own work on their time. I use plenty of their time writing and that doesn't seem to make so much difference. It seems that the most essential thing here is to be on the job, day and night, whether you actually produce or not. . . .

You see Arch I don't want all my eggs in one basket and suffer when they decide against me here. I'm prepared for it right now, though they are still awfully good to me.

Mr. Hearst was quite sick for two weeks. For about a week he didn't see anyone but Willicombe and took no phone calls. He had quite a fever but recovered rapidly. They left for L. A. last Tuesday after the longest continuous stay on the hill since it started. Five months all told in one stay. Talk about a happy household when they left. I thot the place was going to blow up the way those housekeepers were getting on each other's nerves. I saw smiles yesterday and day before that I haven't seen in weeks.

Carey Baldwin and Van Dormen are planning on a trip to Africa to observe animals in their native haunts, this summer. He asked for a leave of absence and they said O. K. Says he wants to take at least one real trip before he gets married. Of course, he hasn't found the girl or like the rest of us Arch, he couldn't wait.

Julia Morgan got back from Europe about the first of April. In the meantime, the stork arrived at the Loorzes' household; their third son, Bob, was born on March 26. Through his endless letters and phone calls, Loorz spread the happy news far and wide. The responses piled up. One of them came on April 4 from Mac McClure at Wyntoon:

Greetings to Robert Carl!—and congratulations to his parents. . . .

Our first month up here is ended and has shown considerable progress too. So much remains to be done, however, that we will hardly do more than get the inside work done by June. I understand that no extra money was *asked* for and an endeavor is being made to keep within scheduled expenditures—am I right? In any case we will be able to house a party by midsummer, and as I always expected we will probably rush up some temporary work [at] the last minute. Our interiors are coming fine. Much of the carving is already done and we have most of the paneling etc in place already. As you probably know, the moldings were run at Chico.

My trip to the city was to see J. M. and to go over all the changes with her. (The "office" had told her nothing but left all of the "pleasure" for me.) Of course she was a little surprised at some of the developments but took it all well enough, but had a lot of suggestions and criticisms, none of which will exactly speed up the work. She left last nite for L. A. and will probably be with you before you read this.

I think she looks very much better and am sure the trip helped her. However her improvement will prompt her to become very active again, I'm afraid, and will undo a lot of the good the trip may have done.

Mac was right about Julia Morgan's imminent arrival at San Simeon: she was there to confer with Loorz on Saturday, April 6. Loorz's minutes contained twenty-six entries, most of them concerning the Neptune Pool and the Gothic Study—for instance, "Arch[itect] to bring Mr. Solon down on next trip to start him on touching up and finishing Study paintings." A few other entries pertained to the indoor Roman Pool—for instance, "Set up trial floods for lighting the pool." Hearst was hoping they could provide that building with more dramatic lighting, not only in the surrounding room but also in the pool itself—under the water.

Soon after that Loorz heard from Fred Stolte, who wrote to him on April 10:

> Well, we are going full blast at Wyntoon and the budget is shot plenty.
>
> Asbestos roofing, power line equipment and high priced millwork all come at once. We send in two weeks of future costs so the office is quite well informed on the costs there.
>
> On the last trip north Miss Morgan said that she had received a rather anxious letter from Mr. LeFeaver, regarding the added costs. However, I fail to see where it can be cut, and continue to do the work as laid out. She mentioned that some material bills could be postponed. Perhaps we are accustomed to this?????
>
> Labor and material will average about $6000. per week for several weeks to come.

Stolte wrote again the next day, saying he had talked to Miss Morgan on April 9: "It seems the program remains the same, Gables & Brown Bear by June 1 or earlier."

Loorz wrote back immediately, telling Stolte he would be checking up on the Reid job in San Luis Obispo the next day. The refrain was all too familiar: "Boy it's the bunk the way they want things when they have no money." He also said, "I've got things going like wildfire here on the hilltop as well so you can bet I have plenty to think about. So many things I'm doing in a rush and I've had the rain [and] mud to contend with."

The weather remained a factor well into April, as a letter Loorz wrote to Julia Morgan on the 16th indicated:

> Well the rain is still falling and everything is wet. We have been unable to work on the Colonnade for several days. There is just a couple of more days on steel work and it will be ready to pour. However, because of the rain it has not been practical to haul the sand from Monterey. The gravel I have on hand for the job has been so wet that we cannot put it through our screens for grading. I hate to delay but———.

While it has been raining we have been able to make quite a little headway in the [Gothic] Study Towers, with all hands on that work.

ON APRIL 18 the Santa Maria architect Louis Crawford wrote to Loorz. Crawford was best known for his recent Santa Maria City Hall, built through the Public Works Administration; he had since begun designing schools in the greater area as P. W. A. jobs. The Arroyo Grande Grammar School was ready to be figured, and Crawford wondered if Loorz was interested. He was. Thus began a successful collaboration between Lou Crawford and the F. C. Stolte Co. that included the Arroyo Grande job and, soon after that, the grammar schools Crawford designed for Cambria and Morro Bay.

The Reid job in San Luis and the figuring of Crawford's Arroyo Grande School weren't the extent of Loorz's moonlighting in the spring of 1935. That same April 18 that Crawford wrote to Loorz saw Loorz writing to Stolte. "My labor foreman is building himself a home in Cambria," he said. "To help him out on his insurance I am handling the job in our name. He will pay us all the insurance etc. I'll send in a payroll each week. He is advancing me the money and I am paying [it out] so you will not have to send any money. Just make certain that the insurance is covered on the Frank Souza job, Cambria, Calif." The Souza house has been better known since the 1970s as the Grey Fox Inn (and more recently as Robin's), on the corner of Center Street and Burton Drive in downtown Cambria.

Loorz's reference to the Souza job appeared as a postscript in his letter of the 18th. The heart of that letter included the following: "I certainly am busy with Mr. Hearst expected this afternoon for the Easter week end. He phoned and sent a registered letter to inform me that he would be here so I suppose he will want me to be here personally on Saturday and Sunday for a while at least. Ho Ho, such is life out west." Loorz told his parents the next day, "Mr. Hearst and party are expected back tonight for the Easter week end. They are in L. A. at present working on another picture at Warner Brothers. We'll be glad to have them back for a few days to get some definite decisions on several things."

Julia Morgan was at San Simeon that Easter Sunday, and she apparently stayed overnight; Loorz's minutes contain a mere eleven entries, but they pertain to conferences held on both Sunday and Monday. "Work to begin on Billiard Room wing at early date," goes the third entry. "Floods thru diffused glass to be tried over Roman Pool; Mr. Hearst still desirous of underwater lighting," goes the eleventh entry.

Loorz wrote to Stolte that same Monday, April 22:

> Well they certainly have me busy on this hill. They told me to speed up and spend more money this month. I don't know where it is coming from for he did not give her any more and she doesn't realize that I have spent our share of the allotment.
>
> I think he just asked for a few more things and she is going to give him them even if she goes in the hole. Between you and me I'm not going to splurge too much. The pay checks are already getting behind.

Stolte answered Loorz on the 24th, saying, "The big spring drive is on it seems. What do you know about June 1? The Gables and Brown Bear are to be finished." He also asked if he should "go slow on expenses at McCloud." Loorz's reply was all business: "I know how rushed you are at Wyntoon and I know it will take a lot more of your time. You'll have to speed up a lot to do what he wants by June but do it whatever you do. Our very existence on the job depends on it."

Loorz reverted to his more accustomed form in writing to Mac McClure on May 7:

> Well here we are in the center of another of the yearly rushes just like you are. Only yours is a lot bigger right now I guess. However, I am rushing the [Gothic Study] tower rooms with walnut cases etc. Also there is a great rush down the hillside where they are making a 40 foot wide terrace. Another retaining wall that nears 20 feet at the highest point. There wasn't enough unfinished area on the hilltop so we take in some more. However it will make the place look like a real entrance and they may yet use it for that. At present it is intended to be a pedestrian and equestrian entrance and walkway between tight rows of orange trees.

Loorz wrote to Julia Morgan the same day, giving her similar details about the Gothic Study and also telling her about the progress at the Neptune Pool; his letter clarified that the new terrace and retaining wall he described to McClure were going in just below the big West Terrace. (The new "terrace" was more a hard-packed dirt pathway.)

Mac answered Loorz's letter of May 7 two days later:

> I am glad to know you are busy too. Miss Morgan usually drops a few hints about what is being done at the ranch and Santa Monica but the picture is still a trifle hazy. Yes—we are in it right up to our chins or rather over our eyes. I anticipate that from now until the arrival of W. R. there will be "no rest for the wicked." However I do see how we can, at least, have enough of the building done to accommodate them and that is really more than I sometimes hoped. The carved interiors are nearing something like completion and are fine, if I do say so.
>
> J. M. has just left us after a typical visit. I have a list of notes, mostly very small things, which we will have to get done "before Mr. H. thinks we are idiots,"—but all in all she is not too hard on us. If we could only do the essentials first and then do the "fiddling around later" it would be all right. However I suppose we will fiddle right up to the last week and then throw anything together in any way, shape, or manner.
>
> I am glad to know the "family" is well. I am also glad to hear (from J. M.) that you may come up later to build a bridge—we need the bridge and your moral support too.

The wet weather continued to hold sway at San Simeon. "We had another 4.83 inches of rain this last week and it certainly delays construction," Loorz told Hearst on May 10. "It is too wet to even start yet on the road. We cannot get into the beaches with our trucks to haul necessary gravel & sand for the warehouse foundation, pergola, wild duck pool or colonnades." But rain or shine the show went on—or at least the correspondence did. Loorz wrote to Stolte right after Julia Morgan's visit of Saturday, May 11:

> Miss Morgan was here yesterday and we had a very fine day. She was very happy even with Wyntoon. Mr. Hearst was just wonderful and I enjoyed talking to him in his room in his bathrobe at 9 P. M. last night after she left. He looks fine and is in [a] splendid mood. Very happy about their new connection with Warner Brothers Studio. They are really enjoying making this picture [*Page Miss Glory*].

Miss Morgan told me how they were getting behind in payments up there. I hope it has not become too much of a handicap. Down here with me I've already made them holler. Last week they asked me to rush a bit when I knew they could not afford to do it. They both knew I was right and I'm to go on as I see best. He said, "You just use your own judgment and give it to me when you think best."

WITH HEARST BACK in residence at San Simeon, the memoranda began flowing Loorz's way through Colonel Willicombe; May 21 brought the following:

Chief told me to-day to ask you to hurry the enlarging of the hangar, as the new plane will be here not later than the middle of June. . . .

Chief asks if there was any way of lengthening the field. I said I understood that was unlikely on account of the drop at one end. He said he thought that could be filled in, also that you could "put in a great big sewer pipe—say six feet in diameter which would carry off the water," and work it out that way.

May 24 brought further word from on high:

I told Chief you were hot after the mosquitoes and in fact had been after them for ten days and would give them the final sock in [a] day or so. He said okey, never mind the expert; but he suggested that we ought to start after them every year as soon as they start breeding, in fact before they have a chance to breed, and clean up and oil up to head them off. I suggest that you put them on your schedule for regular attention whether Chief is coming to ranch or not.

Willicombe had a chance to catch up on other business when Hearst and Loorz inspected the Burnett Road on May 28; the next day, Loorz told Mac about the trip:

I spent a good part of the afternoon yesterday with W. R. on a little drive to the Nacimiento. Just the two of us and we became quite chummy before we got back. He hopes to fly up there [to Wyntoon] with Miss Morgan tomorrow. If so, he'll be there before this reaches you. He is in a very good humor and may be so happy with the place that he will not change quite as much as you expect him to.

I think I can talk him out of the bridge trip as much as I would like to come up. I don't think the office would enjoy me making the trip for that purpose. Anyway, my [Nacimiento River] bridge stood over the winter and he thot it was O. K. when he saw it for the first time yesterday. I have built another the past week and will build a few more as we can afford it. Now that I have the cob-webs brushed away on my designing it goes pretty fast. With all the men I am working on the various units I have really very little time for figuring and designing, however. . . .

Mac business on the outside looks a lot better. I'm going to try the Arroyo Grande School, a P. W. A. job. If I come out O. K. I'll open an office right here and take on anything I can get within the surrounding country. I can employ a couple of good responsible men without shirking on this job. Now is the time to get started for there will be lots of money spent in the next few years and why should I wait. Maybe I'm ambitious and foolish for I really would like to take it easier. However, I feel that I can do it and make good so why not try. Then maybe I can quit this answering the whistle daily etc.

Loorz's letter was enroute to Mac when Fred Stolte sat down to peck out a few lines from Wyntoon on the evening of May 30:

Just to let you know that we are still on the job here. We are laying floor in the Gables at 8:30 P. M. Also the painters are staining woodwork, so that we may be a little further completed for tomorrow. A rumor is around that Mr. Hearst is visiting tomorrow.

The power line is in good shape to finish. We are stringing wire, about 3 miles complete. Logs are being hauled to the mill, and [the] trench is being dug for the under ground cable. About a week should see juice on the line.

George and Harry have been working like Trojans in fact all the gang are going places.

Mac seems quite happy this year and is mixing some with the boys.

I have been here almost a week and still lots to do, however I surely enjoy the work. Always enough trouble to keep from getting lonesome????

Loorz gave his parents another glimpse of the idolized San Simeon in writing to them on June 5:

Just a little interesting was the fact that I had to drive some guests yesterday in a hurry in my own car. They were George Hearst, Jean Harlow and Bill Powell. They were very pleasant and full of fun. They had just returned from an aeroplane flight. It happened to be

Bill Powell's first plane ride. Miss Harlow said, "That is a surprise." George said, "I'll tell you a surprise for you. The pilot on that plane was the one that flew you to Arizona when you married your last husband." She said, "He was? I thot he was familiar but I really didn't recognize him. What's more he stood up with us." "Of course," she said, "he had on dark glasses but I should have recognized the mustache." She and Bill seem very close friends.

ON JUNE 12 Loorz informed Stolte that he planned to designate San Simeon—mostly the Loorzes' house, that is—as a branch office of the F. C. Stolte Co. Stolte replied on the 14th, saying, "I believe your chance[s] of profit are much better there than in Oakland. So here's good luck to the branch office." What more impressive way for Loorz to operate that branch than to treat his local associates to a glimpse of the Hearst place? "Why not make your first visit to the hilltop here right soon?" he asked the Santa Maria architect Louis Crawford on June 19. "Any day would do and the earlier in the morning the better. We can see so much more before the guests start wandering about, about 11 A. M. Just let me know. I feel sure that you will want to see the place several times for there is a lot to it." Crawford must have fallen off his drafting stool when he read that.

The P. W. A. that Loorz, Crawford, and others in the building industry were tapping into was a brainchild of course of the Roosevelt Administration—the very administration Hearst helped put in the White House in 1932. Ironically, the same day Loorz invited Crawford to San Simeon, June 19, President Roosevelt took Congressional action that soon led to the Revenue Act of 1935, or the "wealth tax." Roosevelt was, in effect, pointing a finger at Hearst, who was already passing through the most controversial period in his picturesque, often stormy life. (Hearst's meeting with Hitler in August 1934, for one thing, had backfired badly on Hearst—and is still backfiring on him today.) The growing rift between Roosevelt and Hearst quickly deepened once the Revenue Act was passed. The Hearst press railed against the Roosevelt Administration and the New Deal from then on. George Loorz, meanwhile, may have supported Upton Sinclair in

1934, but he seemed as inclined as Hearst was to lampoon the powers in Washington. On June 27 Loorz heard from Colonel Willicombe. "I am returning the New Deal statistics," Willicombe told him, "which are very funny. Thanks for giving me a look at them":

Population of U. S.	124,000,000
Eligible for Townsend Pension	50,000,000
Balance	74,000,000
Prohibited from working under Child Act and Working for the Government	60,000,000
Balance	14,000,000
Unemployed	13,999,998
Leaving to produce all the Nation's Goods	2

YOU and ME—and I'M ALL TIRED OUT.

Loorz and Willicombe's chuckle came a few days before Hearst's long-anticipated trip to Wyntoon—the one for which Fred Stolte, Mac McClure, George Wright, Harry Thompson, and the rest of the crew had been scrambling to get ready all season. Mac wrote to Loorz on June 29 under a dateline of "Wyntoon—Sat eve":

Am taking a few minutes off for a breathing spell and in order to get my mind off this hectic whirl I will drop you a few lines. . . .

F. C. [Stolte] is here and doing his darnedest to get things ready for the visit. As far as we know the chief arrives tomorrow but I feel that he will not for another day or two.

This last week has been one of the worst I have ever put in. Personally I do not think it worth such an effort. We have worked until midnight for five nights running—and now as I write this I can see J. M. tugging and lugging porch and lawn chairs herself, but I am too tired and calloused to go out and either stop her or help her. All of the rooms have been furnished and refurnished about four times—curtains changed and rugs rolled out and rolled up again until we were cock-eyed—So let the Chief come soon, says I—at least it will put a stop to this, whatever else may be in store for us. We had a full car load of antiques arrive today and J. M. and I spent the entire day at the depot at McCloud personally investigating the subtle colors of rugs etc—while our furniture movers sat on their fannys at the job because there was no one to direct them—Of course when she came out at four o'clock she was wrathy because so little had been done.

For two or three days I have been biting my lips and counting [to] ten to keep from expressing myself but have managed to keep silent so far. Perhaps if we can get through this the next will not be so bad.— If she would only allow us to do our stuff and plan our own work and program.

Well Geo—don't think this is "getting me down" because after all we may only work until midnight again and then we can have the rest of Saturday off—Whee!

Mac was indeed weary—he wasn't exaggerating when he described the long hours the crew had been working. The electrician Louis Schallich told a similar tale in writing to Loorz on July 8, a few days after Hearst and his party arrived:

Should have written you a letter from here before but in the past month this place has been a mad house. We have been working day and night and everyday. . . .

As usual the most important work on the project has been the plumbing and steam work. Same old Rankin still talks with his hands. He is the most kidded man on the job and has to like it. "Society Jim" is his new nick name.

The guests are about the same as at San Simeon and act about the same also.

Saturday evening [July 6] Miss Davies had a theater party showing her latest picture at Dunsmuir. All the guests Mr. Hearst etc. were there. The whole town was lined up before the theater to get an eye full of the movies people. This was a treat to the home folks but to us it was just another picture. . . .

No doubt, with the big pay roll up here, it has cut your force down at San Simeon. . . .

We are working now from 10 AM. until 630 P. which are nice hours after a month of from 7 AM. until midnight.

Things *had* slowed down at San Simeon, enough for the sculptor L. Cardini, for instance, to relax at Adams Springs in Lake County. "I have good time here in the mountain," he scrawled on a postcard Loorz received. Loorz of course had plenty of things to do; there were always letters to write and outside jobs to figure in addition to supervising the work that crept along at San Simeon. One of his letters went out to Fred Stolte on July 11:

> After talking with you about the Wyntoon accounts and going over the books I found it hard to sleep. Especially when I hadn't even paid my men for five weeks down here. Therefore, I told Miss Morgan with tears in my eyes that we couldn't do it. We'd either have to have cash right away or shut down. There was no use waiting as much as I dislike saying it. But since the most they can give you is $15,000 per month, it would take 4 months for them to pay up if you didn't do 1¢ of work during that period.
>
> She agreed with me and shook my hand sympathetically. She said, she didn't dream it was that much behind or she wouldn't have allowed it. So she wrote to see what Mr. Hearst wished to do about it without quoting us at all. There is no reason why he cannot give her a lump sum as has been promised for some time. . . .
>
> Fred I think the depression is over. I think we should go back on scale. I think we ought to try to work in some young carpenters for foremen. I think we ought to try to get both the Corlett job and the Clark job which are close together.
>
> I think it would be better to chuck Wyntoon unless one or both of us are there [in Oakland] to give personal attention to all of our clients. . . . I know local Architects think we have too much business to give proper attention or service and maybe they are right. Wyntoon might die tomorrow but the building business is going to be bigger and better right now and for some time to come. Maybe I'm too enthusiastic but in that case it is fun to be wrong.

The "Corlett job and the Clark job" referred to Will Corlett and to Birge Clark, both of whom were Bay Area architects. Corlett's Theta Chi Chapter House at Stanford University was out for bid and so was Clark's Phi Delta Gamma House, likewise at Stanford. The F. C. Stolte Co. was the low bidder on the Corlett job and may also have been on the Clark job. Another job Loorz secured that July was Julia Morgan's alteration of the Edward C. Bull residence on Union Street in San Francisco.

Stolte wrote to Loorz on July 16, the same day the bids were opened on the Corlett job: "Harry phoned last eve and said Mr. Hearst wanted a 13 room addition to [The] Gables to start Monday." He assured Loorz he would see to it that Hearst came forward with "a substantial payment" before any such work was undertaken.

On July 20, Loorz hammered out another richly detailed letter to Arch Parks in Gilroy:

> Wyntoon has proved quite a nice job but—as usual—we let them get into us for many many thousand and now we are holding the sack. They just rushed the place like mad for two months getting ready for the chief without regard for the amount being spent. So it was just close to 60 grand ten days ago when I went up to the city and checked over our books. . . .
>
> We are leveling the airport [at San Simeon]. You remember the two bumps at each end of the main runway, well we are making the whole field nearly level. We intend to move about 50,000 yards of earth before we finish. We bought a 50 diesel caterpillar and an 8 yard carryall and does it move dirt. I have just three men working. One skinner works from 4 A. M. until noon and then one works until 8 P. M. The foreman works during the 8 hrs of the day, sets all stakes and directs and uses the road cat to rip up the surface for the carryall.

Loorz wrote that same day to Louis Schallich, who was back in San Francisco after his stint at Wyntoon:

> By golly Louis we are certainly cut down to rock bottom at this place. Pete is the only carpenter on the hill. Gyorgy has been off for a month or more. Val Georges is gone and only about half the labor crew. . . .
>
> This place is certainly lonesome, nothing going on in the Castle at all. Just working on retaining walls below west terrace and finishing up the colonnade balustrade and paving. With a small crew it certainly goes slowly. . . .
>
> Oh yes, since they kicked Jimmie out at Wyntoon he says he will be down here Monday to install the new burner in the donkey boiler. So I'll hear all about the dope at Wyntoon and find out whether you really behaved or not. I'll know all about it first hand. I'm greasing up my arms so that I can talk his language.

Loorz wrote to Mac McClure on July 22, telling him that "Smiling Jimmie" Rankin had arrived at San Simeon that morning. "Now that we have someone to kid we are O. K. Ought to be lots of fun after the quietude that has prevailed around here for the past two weeks. Honest it seems like a morgue. Even worse for the stiffs in a morgue don't complain of heat, work, slow pay etc."

WHEN LOORZ'S WIFE and three sons went to Nevada that July, Loorz invited Carl Daniels to stay with him. Daniels had supervised the Reid job in San Luis Obispo for the F. C. Stolte Co. and was about to start the Arroyo Grande Grammar School. Loorz mentioned Carl Daniels in writing to his family on August 1—and he mentioned a good deal more in the same letter:

Carl came in shortly after I got home last night and I suggested we go to the pines [the Cambria Pines Lodge]. We did and found it to be the yearly banquet of the Chamber of Commerce that we attended last year. They insisted that we eat with them and worse, they called upon me as Mr. Hearst's Superintendent to say something about Mr. Hearst or his place. Oh boy, it was the wrong time to ask me to say anything for it was the most remote thing from my mind. Then too I had overheard Mr. Fox and others talking in undertones about how Mr. Hearst didn't pay much taxes etc and I was really peevish.

I merely got up and thanked them for the compliment and said that "Being connected to Mr. Hearst's organization as I am, I hear so much about him and even overheard remarks this evening that [would] concern him. I'm not going to take time to tell you of his many fine qualities for it [is] too serious for [an] evening such as this. I will only say that I wish you could know him as I know him and I'm certain you would feel the same as I do. Not because I look to him for my support and livelihood for my own business nets me more but in several years of association I have always known him to be a perfect gentleman."

The second I started I knew I had hit an unusually serious key as their faces registered it plainly. When I sat down I almost regretted that I had mentioned it for there was none of the laughter that had been prevalent. 'Twas only for a moment and Doc Lowell, chairman, said "Mr. Loorz is perfectly right. I too know him well and I cannot say too much for Mr. Hearst as a man and as a real value to this community." He said it beautifully and it was impressive. . . .

At the conclusion of the banquet several strangers came to me and even shook my hand and said they were glad to hear me say what I did.

Loorz and Daniels were asked to dinner by several of their neighbors in San Simeon that August, as Loorz told his wife on the 6th:

Well the entertainment still goes on. Last night Bud [Sweeters] invited us over to a venison barbecue out on the point. We didn't go out until 7 PM and they were just ready to eat. Lots of good meat, salad, chili beans and pie. It was very good and Carl and I ate ravenously. Then we sat around the fire and talked aeroplanes and hunting, then John Reilly got his mouth organ and Bud the guitar and they entertained us for an hour and we went home.

I expect Miss Morgan today. Wish I had more completed to show her but I just can't do it with the number of men I have at present. She wants as much as possible to show Mr. Hearst when he returns which may be very soon.

Morgan evidently cancelled her trip to San Simeon; but she wrote to Loorz from San Francisco the next day, August 7, saying, "Mr. Hearst says he would *very much* like to see 'something different' on the Hill when he gets back. I told him I did not see how he could expect anything *excitingly different*, given our program, but that we were steadily pushing the [Neptune] pool area."

Hearst's version of what Morgan told Loorz was contained in a memo from Colonel Willicombe, dated August 8: "Chief instructed me to-day to send you a reminder that when you finish the airport, he does not want any more road building or fence making or other added expense incurred, but to confine operations to the regular program, including the pergola as part of that program." Another instance of mixed signals? Perhaps it was; if so, Loorz wasn't unduly surprised.

Loorz concluded a birthday letter to his mother in Nevada on August 12 with these words: "It is very hot here on the hilltop but not like it is there I suppose. You feel it just as much though since it is so damp. But it is always nice when I drive down home to San Simeon. It was just simply a perfect day yesterday. Hundreds of people were out on the beach and pier and in boats. We seldom have very many way up here on this coast. I can expect a lot of company when that road finally gets thru." The road Loorz meant was the coast highway from San Simeon to Carmel, perched along the steep slopes of the Santa Lucia Range through the Big Sur country. The road had been under construction since the early 1920s; though the bridging of a last few canyons remained to be done, the road was open by 1935 to local traffic as far north as

Big Creek, halfway to Carmel. Loorz and Carl Daniels had a harrowing experience in driving on that road one evening, as Loorz recounted for Fred Stolte:

> Now for the thriller, night before last we went up the coast (50 miles) to do a gratis job. The Women's Club of Cambria are going to erect a memorial to the senator responsible for getting this coast road started and asked me if I would visit the site and make a working drawing out of their sketches.
>
> Well coming back about 8:30 at about 40 miles per hour in low ratio, as we rounded a slight curve a couple of horses loose on the road, were startled by our headlights & one jumped right out in front of the machine. Carl was driving. He put on the brakes & veered to the left to try to miss him, which he did but we were then headed for and only a few feet from an embankment. So he jerked the wheel to the right as hard as he could to pull back, it came back alright but it was too sharp and with new tires on the rear that wouldn't slide, over we went.
>
> Now, here's one for the records. We turned completely over until we were right side up. We got out kicked the glass off the road turned around and were on our way home in less than three minutes.

The Rigdon Memorial Park that Loorz designed was established in honor of Senator Elmer Rigdon of Cambria, the "Father of the Roosevelt Highway." (The Roosevelt Highway has since become the Cabrillo Highway or, more simply, Highway 1.) The Rigdon Memorial is a mile south of Big Creek, alongside a rivulet the Women's Club named "El Senator Creek." A drinking fountain and a small grove of trees mark the spot today.

Another job that came to Loorz's attention that summer was the Santa Ynez Valley Union High School, designed by E. Keith Lockard of Santa Barbara. Loorz heard about the job from a hardware supplier but too late to submit a bid. "We are now operating from Mr. Hearst's place at McCloud," he told the hardware man on August 13, "to Arroyo Grande. Now that we have opened an office here we might figure as far south as Santa Maria but not further, I believe." Lockard, however, was also the architect of some buildings at Santa Maria Junior College, a job Loorz would land in 1936.

HEARST AND HIS PARTY remained at Wyntoon throughout July and well into August. Mac McClure gave Loorz another inside glimpse from that estate on August 15:

> No doubt you are pretty well informed on "news from the firing line" however here is my contribution, for what it may be worth.
>
> This has been a very tough session and apparently it isn't getting much better. My duties are so numerous and involves so many angles that I am about swamped trying to keep up with them. The ware-housing is assuming large proportions, and I wonder very much how I am going to keep the cataloging, etc ahead of the arrivals. (Our fourth carload is on its way I understand.)
>
> Our main activity, at present, is planning future work. As usual, all sorts of pretentious schemes are being worked out, and before I am half through with one, a new idea is sprung.
>
> The worst condition to face is the necessity of doing practically nothing in the face of constant orders to start this or that project "immediately." These orders are usually followed up by petulant enquirys as to "why we didn't get some men and get things moving." I have resolved to make no mention of finance to him and apparently whatever anyone else may have said has had little effect. I hate to have him think I am ineffectual and stalling when the real reason for non-action is something else, however.
>
> Just now we are starting a large terrace development at The Gables. It is a large project and will take time and money (perhaps $20,000). Mr. H. insisted we start now and at Miss M.'s suggestion we are using [caretaker Eugene] Kower's road crew and funds for part of the work. I am not too sure this will be a successful arrangement.
>
> In general, however, we are worrying through in some way or another and I imagine everything will work out without too much trouble. There is no sign of a break yet as far as the party leaving is concerned. . . .
>
> It's a great life and as J. M. says a sense of humor is a valuable asset. Sometimes I think she is very much fed up with the outfit too.

It was during that summer of 1935, while Hearst and his party were in residence, that *Fortune* magazine prepared a feature that remains the most detailed coverage of Wyntoon in printed form. Simply entitled "Hearst," the feature appeared in the October 1935 issue of *Fortune*, replete with photographs and detailed text—and, ironically, with claims that the Hearst empire was financially as sound as could be. (Hearst's opponents said the feature had been concocted to keep investors bullish on Hearst stock, lest Hearst's finances decline even further.) One photograph showed Hearst lounging in a garden chair, the very kind of chair Mac had watched Julia Morgan lug about. Concocted or otherwise, the *Fortune* feature remains an invaluable fund of information on Wyntoon, surpassed only by the George Loorz Papers.

Loorz answered Mac's letter of August 15 a week later, having heard by then from Willicombe that the party would be leaving Wyntoon on the 28th:

> You are quite right about Miss Morgan, she is decidedly fed up. Things have gone quite smoothly here and she uses the day of her visits here mostly for leisurely wandering around moving a lamp here and a nic-nac there discussing Wyntoon, Beach House and personalities. Her visits have really been enjoyable and have helped to break the monotony of things around here. If something doesn't break before long to excite us a little bit I'll have to shut down for a week. Not one but many of my boys show the signs of it. It is always more exciting and interesting to my crews when the party is around. They seem to have more of a goal to work for. An occasional glimpse of the chief or some other celebrity helps them to forget their enforced isolation.

Morgan was at San Simeon, in fact, on the very day Loorz wrote to Mac, August 22; Loorz's minutes amounted to a modest eleven entries, which pertained mostly to those old standbys, the Gothic Study and the Neptune Pool. "Mr. Solon to arrange to be completed by Thursday," he noted on the Study. "Mr. Hearst's unexpected call Tuesday found the room clean but not furnished but he appeared to be pleased with Mr. Solon's work." For the Neptune Pool he noted, "Mr. Cardini to antique Temple stone, new, making lighter by a little rather than darker than the antique"; and, "Cardini brought extra men down for a few days to carve out caps and end panels of colonnades. The carved wreaths look much more alive."

L. Cardini's work on the Roman temple would soon include the incorporation of a Renaissance sculpture group in the upper part of the temple; the group was of Neptune and the Nereids and, like the old temple, had entered the Hearst Collection in 1922. "Cut out in cardboard the shapes of the Neptune group in the North Terrace pool," went Loorz's minutes of September 5; "have Mr. Solon quickly chalk in the statue shapes and place them on the Temple Pediment for inspection. (Mr. Hearst saw them and liked them, hopes you will be able to make some adjustment so they will be suitable, Neptune, as you expected is a little too high but some alteration or recessing might be done.)" Loorz's next entry from that September meeting with Miss Morgan also concerned the Neptune Pool: "Place the two trial columns in the new locations after extending them three feet. (Mr. Hearst seemed to be pleased with these also.)" Had two such columns been permanently installed, the pool would have looked distinctly different. The columns would have flanked the Roman temple—would have occupied the open spaces between the temple and the north and south colonnades. These free-standing objects would have been nearly four feet wide at their bases, twenty-five feet in height, and higher still through the sculptures that were going to surmount them. The effect would have been pure World's Fair—a dreamy throwback to the San Francisco of 1915 or even the Chicago of 1893.

THAT FIRST WEEK of September 1935 was one that Loorz's second son, Bill, spent in San Luis Obispo General Hospital. "Bill has been sort of sick at his stomach for the past three days," Loorz had told his parents on August 27. "Too much party Saturday night and picnic Sunday. He eats so much watermelon and drinks too much lemonade." But Bill had appendicitis, not just a stomach ache; and he underwent surgery on September 1. Miss Morgan wrote to him on September 6, as soon as she got back from San Simeon:

San Francisco
Cal—
Our Office

Dear Bill—

I have looked around just now desperately to see if I could find something here you would like, as there have been so many people calling today I could not get out to find you a surprise— I found a case of books—& will send you another tomorrow as more than one will make the envelope too thick to go in the mail chute here.

I hope they will roll you out on the porch so you can see the sky and hills—and when you see little stray clouds, just think they are my thoughts and good wishes out trying to find you and doing it—

With affectionate best wishes
Your friend Julia Morgan—

She wrote to Bill in a similar vein at least three other times that month.

George Wright wrote to Loorz from Wyntoon on September 19. "Our crew is cut down to the bone," he said, "and even yet we can't get used to it after the rush and push of a short time ago. We have been finishing up the 'left-overs,' but that is nearly caught up now. I presume that the interior of the Turrets [the eventual Cinderella House] or Angel House will be next on the program, but as yet no details are out."

Loorz himself wrote to the carpenter Elof Gustafson that same day. "Mr. Hearst has come and gone and all is again quiet and serene here on the hill," he said. "He didn't bother us in construction but did change a few more things about the household and the garden. We will look for him back in about three weeks." He also wrote to Fred Stolte, saying he supposed Stolte would "be at Wyntoon for a few days with the chief returning [there]." And in writing to Charlie Badley the next day, September 11, Loorz said, "Anyway things are going nicely here around the pool, a grand rush with marble setters and cement workmen. All else quiet on the front. Mr. Hearst [is] back in Wyntoon with his lady friend."

Harry Thompson wrote to Loorz from Wyntoon on September 23:

My crew is almost down to nothing as you probably know and with Mac away on vacation and the party over it seems rather dead around here. Wouldn't be surprised if we didn't fold up soon for this year.

Went fishing yesterday, caught a mess of beauties 12 inches and better, just getting good again.

Julia Morgan was back at San Simeon that last week of September; she kept Loorz busy making notes on the Neptune Pool, among other projects. "Cardini to carve shell background and portion to drape around Neptune figure as outlined in chalk," he noted for the Roman temple. "Transfer chalk outlines to cardboard before removing ashlar to save layout as approved by Mr. Hearst and Architect"; and, "John [Vanderloo] to proceed with casting of Temple back wall as per approved sample. Try to get a little more yellow tone to black sand background, similar to [granite] columns. Do not rub down quite as much as sample."

Loorz provided his parents with numerous details, as usual, in writing to them on October 2:

> This government school job [Arroyo Grande] has a lot of red-tape connected with it. It is a good thing I can type and can make out reports. It would keep an unexperienced person busy continually getting reports out for them that don't mean a thing. . . . Anyway, we hope it comes out as we plan with a nice profit otherwise it will just be a lot of grief for some more education.
>
> Our other work around the bay district is going nicely. Some complaints now and then but in the main all is well. We have lots of work and I think we could get a lot more if we could afford it and tried. Everything we have and can borrow is tied up in the work now so we can't do any more. . . .
>
> Mr. Hearst and party were here for a couple of weeks but have departed again. Suppose they will be back over the week end. He still seems satisfied with my work. Hope so, another year or two here wouldn't hurt but I feel certain I could make more if I left right now. However, the outdoor life here is splendid for my health and that is something.

Loorz wrote in equal detail to Julia Morgan on October 4:

> Mr. Cardini is getting along nicely with the statues [for the temple]. He has three of them cut down and two of them raised to position to fit. I believe they will work out alright. Neptune's head might be a little close to the cornice above but that can be judged better when all three are in position and the shell modelling [is] in back. If necessary it can be brought out just a little and the plaster brought out to it. It is only a matter of an inch or so and I don't feel it would make much difference.
>
> We are setting the Temple stone and it looks very good to me. It varies a little from the samples but the variation is not far either way and should be an advantage and can be brought together if necessary. He [John Vanderloo] is making good headway on that and the balustrade casting. . . .

Now here's something that I am sorry came up but I don't know what is best to do about it. Just before Mr. Hearst left he called me and asked how much longer it would take to complete the airport and I said approximately two weeks. He said, he wanted to bring that crew up [the hill] and get right to work on the Pergola. Said he wanted to keep right at it until it was finished because it has been dragging so long. He asked how many more columns we needed and asked me to order them so that we would have them when the bases were ready. I know this [air]port work is unfairly on another account and that your present budget could not stand the suggested work on the Pergola. Please tell me what do to.

Hearst was back at San Simeon a few days later, as Loorz told Jim LeFeaver on October 9:

Mr. Hearst walked into the office in splendid spirits about five last night and we spent an hour of building and creating new projects. An airport on a hilltop above the fog was one. Oh boy, it would be an expensive project if it goes ahead. Sooner or later he will do something.

In thirty minutes he moved the zoo, constructed new bear grottos and divided the present ones for cats. He levelled animal hill out here. We tore down the shop and lowered a dozen oaktrees in groups of five making tremendous concrete boxes, excavating under them and letting the trees right down into position. Moving one tree at a time is a big job [but to] move a close group of about five is still bigger. Anyway he laughed a lot and seemed happy so we will put it down as a successful interview.

Loorz gave Stolte a variation on the same story when he wrote to him the next day. "Mr. Hearst came in the office night before last about 5 o'clock and we talked for an hour and a half. We went over the political situation, taxation, War and things in general besides tearing down arenas, constructing bear pits, airports etc. Boy he was in a good humor and laughed heartily and even told simple jokes." Loorz also said that Julia Morgan was slated to arrive that morning and that he would therefore be having "a filled day." His notes from that meeting were confined to a single page. The first entry, under "Neptune Pool Area," was as follows: "Cardini to proceed with new shell and drapery arrangement at Temple gable if Mr. Hearst approves. (Mr. Hearst saw the layout and came in to say that he did not want it. Said it was O. K. to leave the low shell but no more [than that] as he preferred just the plain statues [Neptune and the Nereids].)" Morgan corrected Loorz's entry, noting, "O. K. But this means working the plain back filler off the even face [of the temple]."

LOORZ KEPT PROCEEDING cautiously, but steadily, with his "outside" work, lest some spoilsport cry foul. His caution, his sense of timing, his undeniable competence proved a winning formula. On October 14 he told Carl Daniels that the Hearst Ranch management in San Francisco was about to engage the F. C. Stolte Co. for "the Barns and paddocks at Pico [Creek]," a portion of the ranch lying between San Simeon and Cambria. That wasn't all. Julia Morgan had recently invited Loorz to bid on some Hearst Radio transmitting stations in the Bay Area. Morgan also had a job coming up in Oakland, an addition to her Kings Daughters Home. Loorz and Stolte hoped they would get that job. They did.

But more success meant more work for Loorz, who had just turned thirty-seven. "It looks like the ranch is going to give us a contract on some barns and paddocks at the horse ranch," he told Stolte on October 22. "I had the plans all drawn and gave them a figure and all was acceptable but they decided to add more to it, make the rooms on the end of it two stories high etc. All of which means I have to draw it over again and get out new figures. You said it when I took on drawing plans and specifications as well as contracting and superintending I took a big bite."

The efforts of L. Cardini, John Vanderloo, and other artisans to finish the Neptune Pool remained at the fore throughout October. Loorz's notes from his meeting with Julia Morgan on the 28th began with this entry: "Have cardboard put in openings of rear wall of Temple and sketch on stone similar to ashlar being placed. (Mr. Hearst saw and liked these spaces filled in, very much. John is proceeding to cash ashlar for filling.)" And five entries later: "Make a long straight handle for the trident of Neptune and make an offset hand holder to fit in the present hand."

The rains that hampered work throughout the early months of 1935 returned to San Simeon that fall. Loorz told Morgan on November 5:

If the rain does not bother us further we will be able to have the present set of 100 columns in place by November 27th. That is on the Pergola.

We will be able to place about 25 columns per week thereafter *if* it doesn't rain. We will need 122 more columns to complete the work.

As for completing the Neptune Pool, a good deal more remained to be done, as Loorz indicated in that same letter: "I have both compressors going steadily at the pool, mainly taking down the statue pool walls preparatory to changing them to the new details."

That wasn't the only change pending at San Simeon, or on the greater Hearst Ranch, as Morgan's letter of November 6 indicated:

If you can arrange to take me over to Jolon Friday, please do so. In any case I will be down then, and will be over earlier than my usual time—to make the usable day longer.

We have plans for the work there, but find changes have been made that may not be worth keeping,—apparently not.

Loorz's notes from that meeting of the 8th contained a simple entry concerning Morgan's letter: "Hold work at Jolon until new studys are submitted to Mr. Hearst for approval."

Heart's approval of those studies—or his rejection of them—may have had to wait a while, for he had gone to New York, where he stayed in his own Ritz Tower Hotel. Hearst had more pressing things on his mind that November—Roosevelt's "wealth tax," for one—but he didn't forget about San Simeon entirely. Loorz got two telegrams from him on the 16th, both of them brief and pointed. "Please proceed with one grotto—then with the other," went the first message. "Please proceed promptly as soon as possible with new Kennels," went the second one.

Loorz wrote to Fred Stolte on November 22, telling him about his outside work as well as the work at San Simeon. In the former regard a prosaic but important job was in the offing—the Santa Maria Sewage Plant:

It looks like there is money to be made in that kind of thing, here in the middle of the state where the jobs are a little too small to interest real builders. Maybe a couple of low bids from us will scare them out of here entirely.

Things certainly look good here and I guess I might just as well throw my shoulders back, my chin out and fight it out for about six months.

Fred I'm certainly glad George Wright is with me. He is detailing all the steel for the Grotto additions and is doing a good job of it. He has taken over the responsibility of the Pergola layout. I also had to use him to help me with this [Santa Maria] estimate.

I would rather have him than anyone I've worked with because he does just what you tell him, just how you want it, quickly and neatly.

Loorz closed by saying of himself and Stolte, "Sometimes I think both of us were very lucky we met up, what do you think?"

Stolte replied the next day, November 23, "Yes the dutch combination still seems to be working O. K. I have often thought of our first job together, at 12th & Franklin [in Oakland] and whether Mr. Fate had anything to do with it all."

Loorz wrote to Hearst at the Ritz Tower in New York on December 2:

According to instructions from Miss Morgan we are planning on stopping the work on the hilltop on December 15th.

By that time we will have the new kennels completed and be well along on the divisions of the Grotto but cannot be completed. Shall I keep that crew which is working on the Hilltop Fund on until the Grotto can be used again?

In the rush on these two units I have slowed up the work on the Pergola. Will proceed with this work as men are released from the two units mentioned. Shall we stop this work on December 15th?

There is such a demand for mechanics on the outside that I hesitate to lay off about five of our best men. I'm certain they will receive employment immediately and may not be available when we need them in the spring. I refer in particular to such very skilled men as our ironworker, ornamental plasterer, marble mason & mantel expert.

I assure you this is not a dream for I have had a good deal of difficulty to get carpenters for our grotto work and I had to raise from $7.20 per day to $8.00.

Prices have advanced from 10 to 20% on nearly all supplies within the past two months.

Colonel Willicombe answered Loorz on Hearst's behalf. "Replying your letter second," he wired, "Chief says yes finish grotto, also keep on with pergola until finished, and keep skilled workmen you mention and keep them busy."

That was on December 6. In the meantime, Julia Morgan conferred with Loorz at San Simeon on December 2, a visit that yielded twelve entries in Loorz's notes, all of them under the single heading "Miscellaneous." For the Neptune Pool he noted, "In general all new concrete work in the Neptune area that cannot be completed with marble coverings, plaster, cast cement etc will be covered with white plaster scratch coats for the winter. All to look tidy and white."

LOORZ WAS TOO CONSCIENTIOUS a man to be unconcerned about the potential conflict his outside work posed. He must have been losing sleep as a result, for he poured his heart out in a long letter to Julia Morgan on December 4:

> Before I discuss the following Miss Morgan, you must know that my feelings and regards for you and Mr. Hearst is far more than just business associations. I both admire you and feel that you are one of my closest personal friends and as dear to me as my own family. I enjoy the trust and confidence that you both have expressed in your dealings with me.
>
> As I have mentioned before I am well aware that besides being generously compensated for my work here I have learned a lot that will be of extreme value to me. In addition I have developed an appreciation of some of the finer things in art that will give me much happiness.
>
> Now, Miss Morgan, it is unfortunate that Mr. Stolte cannot operate efficiently or satisfactorily, construction for my clients this far South. I must always take the responsibility of figuring work of any consequence either here or up there. Otherwise we either do not do the work in open competition or the gamble is too great. . . .
>
> I have handled three jobs in this district during the past six months. The net profit to us when those jobs are completed should be at least $6,000. Fortunately I have a very good man [Carl Daniels] who runs the largest job [Arroyo Grande] and does all the contact work. However, I let the sub-contracts and sign all the checks, almost 100% by mail. My average time away from the hilltop during a whole month is two afternoons. I have actually been on the Arroyo

Grande School but twice and it is nearing completion. There would have been a good deal more profit in the jobs if I had been free to follow them up more closely. You know how things go ahead much more promptly and smoothly when you can keep continuous and close contact on your jobs.

I have felt that it has been absolutely necessary for me to be on this job 44 hours per week. With the responsibilities that take a good deal of my attention on Saturday afternoons and Sundays, I have averaged more than that. You know that phone calls and requests come as frequently on Sundays as on week days either from Mr. Willicombe or Mr. Hearst. . . .

As you well know my responsibilities include the following in addition to construction: chauffeuring and private cars, trucking & transportation, trapping and furs, water supply and maintenance, new roads and upkeep, gate repairs (a broken gate on Sunday means a call and getting a man somewhere to repair [it] as they cannot be left open), household repairs and upkeep (often calls for men on holidays). Chauffeurs in any number are called at any time and since I keep and pay no regular chauffeurs who loaf while waiting it takes a little quick thinking at times to meet the demand. . . .

Miss Morgan I am confident that with times as they are I can do a lot better by taking contracts by several times than I can earn here. However, I do love my work on this hilltop with you and Mr. Hearst. . . .

On the other hand the opportunity right here in this County is such that I feel I can make as much as $20,000 in the coming year on P. W. A. contracts. I know well that you would not ask me to give up this opportunity. If you feel that you would not care to break in a new man I feel certain that I could arrange someway to carry on somewhat as I have during the past few months. If it could be understood that I could be away a little more than I have I could open an office in one of the neighboring towns, put this man of mine there and handle it. That would keep the name San Simeon out of it.

The George Loorz Papers contain no reply from Julia Morgan; in fact, not until Loorz and Stolte corresponded on the subject more than two weeks later did it resurface.

For the moment it was more newsworthy, albeit sadly, that Loorz fired George Wright on Monday, December 9. Wright, whose drinking had always worried the teetotaling Stolte and sometimes even the affable Loorz, had overindulged on the weekend and missed work Monday morning. He wrote to

Loorz that evening from the Anderson Hotel in San Luis Obispo, rankled that Loorz had dismissed him in writing rather than in person:

> But don't expect a list of alibis. There will be none. I only repeat that I explained why I wasn't able to be on deck this morning. Had I known at the time what was coming, I would certainly never have mentioned it. . . .
>
> Naturally, my pride was hurt, but I'll get over that. I lived rather well before I knew the F. C. S. Co. existed, and I'll not go into a decline now. But I was disappointed in your method. Everybody has unpleasant duties to perform at times. When I am put to it, I dread it of course, but I never fail to look my man in the eye when I tell him. It is so disappointing to see some one you have always respected loose stature. So you inadvertently put us both on the same plane. And that's a laugh to end it all with.

Maybe Loorz *had* acted hastily—maybe the pressure *was* getting to him. But he had to go on; the Chief would be returning soon from New York.

Loorz wrote to Julia Morgan on December 13 in that very regard:

> Mr. Hearst arrived early yesterday and went straight to the pool area. He seemed to be well pleased with it. Especially mentioned the treatment at the upper pool.
>
> He then walked over by the back of C house. He noticed the [marble] lions and beckoned me and said, "Of course these won't stay here." Apparently he will want them back in the East room.
>
> He then walked all thru the house with Mr. Williams [the warehouse man]. He was more than delighted with the Doges and the Library. He certainly remarked about all the nice new things you had there. Little, if any, missed his eye. Seemed real thrilled about everything. That should be some compensation for your late work the other night.
>
> The water is going back in the pool. It was nearly cleaned when he came out and I asked him if he wanted the water back in. I said it was already [*sic*]. They, Miss Davies and he discussed it, and decided that it would look better with the water in it even if they didn't use it. . . .
>
> I will let a few men off this Saturday and will be able to make considerable more showing by keeping the Pool crew for a few days next week.

Hearst wrote to Loorz two days later, not about what he had seen on his homecoming tour but about conditions in Hearst Camp:

> I think the little cabins that the working people occupy can stand a good deal of improvement. First, suppose you take a force of men and put the cabins themselves in first-class shape.
>
> Put heavier floors on so there will not be so much leakage of air; fix the roofs if they need it; and make the place as comfortable and as agreeable as possible.
>
> Then please get new beds—iron or brass—and please get new sheets and blankets throughout of a good kind.
>
> The blankets can still be gray blankets, if those are preferred; but they should be heavy, warm, woolen ones of the best class.
>
> Get rugs for the floor—carpet rugs of course—and make the places as nice as possible.
>
> How about baths and showers? Would it not be well to put a toilet, basin and shower between each two cabins, so that the men can have access to these bathrooms without going into the outer air?
>
> I feel that we ought to do these things and I would rather do this before we resume our own construction.
>
> If we started a crew the first of January, we could have things pretty well done by the time the men get back.

On December 17, George Wright (sounding more like his old self) wrote to Loorz again, this time from the San Carlos Hotel in downtown Los Angeles:

> I was a little bitter when I left, so I was bent on heading as far south as possible. I have always had a yen to go to Mexico City and I thought that would put as many miles as possible between us.
>
> But I stopped here in Los Angeles, had some good laughs, and regained my sense of humor. I think this is a good place to hang my hat; so I'll stay, if I can get located.
>
> Now the request. In seeking the position of chief engineer and general manager of several firms it is necessary to give the names of your employers for the past forty odd years—and the reason for leaving. Should they write you regarding me, may I ask that you do not overstress the point that I was dismissed for degeneracy, drunkenness, disrespect, moral turpitude, and the various other charges you have booked against me? . . .
>
> No I wasn't with Thelma Todd at the time.

The situation Loorz aired in his long letter to Julia Morgan on December 4 finally cropped up again in a letter he wrote to Stolte on the 21st:

> Fred you will be surprised to hear that I have asked Miss Morgan [to] relieve me on this job when convenient, no rush. I made her a proposition, if she wished me to run it and be here always when she or Mr. Hearst are here with an assistant on the job at all times O. K. However, I said, if she thot she had to have someone here steady I'd stay and work with him and show him all I know about the job. She didn't have the heart to speak to Mr. Hearst about it her last visit. We shall see. It would be nice if I could get it like [you have it at] Wyntoon but as it is it is like being in the army.

Stolte answered promptly, on December 23:

> Your decision to arrange for a discharge from a steady diet comes not entirely unexpected. I had been wanting to talk to you of this as I felt you were loading up yourself with a lot of work, with all the outside jobs, and I have been of very little help there.
>
> It had been on my mind to suggest a trade of jobs, to give you a change of climate etc., if no other arrangement could be made.
>
> There seems to be a lot of work coming out for figures in the new year. So we should be able to do as much work in 1936 as in this year. The jobs from $50,000 up have very little competition.

Happy news came Loorz's way from George Wright, who wrote from Los Angeles on Christmas Day that he had found work with an engineering company the previous week. "I think that when you discharged me, you actually kicked me upstairs. So I am well pleased with the whole business."

The Loorzes spent the holiday at home with their three sons; a few of the men from Hearst Camp joined them for dinner. The group was entertained by the toys Julia Morgan had sent, as Loorz recounted for her the next day:

> The little electric Questions and Answers you sent to Don proved to be the high spot of the well filled toy room.
>
> We all stretched our imaginations and recalled our schooling trying to answer questions all the way from Jokes to Chemistry. Don plying the questions continually. . . .
>
> We thank you also for the other toys and the ginger bread men and the nick-nacks. Things you can obtain in few places and that always

catch the eye. Though Bobby is a bit too young to know what it is all about, he has certainly been interested in the xmas tree and the numerous pieces of paper. So much so that we have had to halt his traffic on the kitty-car until things are removed. He rolls right up to the tree and starts dismantling. His mother caught him with two broken [ornaments] and a bit of stain on his lips. We found nothing inside his mouth so apparently she just reached him in time. She had placed chairs around the tree laying down but he forcefully shoved the chairs back into the branches until he could reach the colorful ornaments.

In closing, Loorz said a few words about the hilltop:

The pool area looks fine with the statue bases all covered with marble, the niche completed and the two portions of railing up either side at the lower end of the Neptune stairs. The weather has been fine and I think they used the pool for Mr. Hearst insisted that they bring it up to 75 degrees which meant two all night runs [of the boilers].

Except for a light rain on December 26, the mild weather lasted a few more days, until a heavy storm blew in on the 29th. As Loorz told Miss Morgan on the 27th:

We had a nice fresh rain last night. Only about 1/3 inch of rain but enough to keep things green and still be very good weather for the party.

All seem to be enjoying it. There is a lot of horse-back riding, hiking and tennis playing that is unusual at this time of year.

NINETEEN THIRTY-SIX

1936

JUST A FEW LINES to let you know that Mr. Hearst and party expect to leave here today," Loorz wrote Julia Morgan on January 2, 1936. "Whether it is to stay away for quite a while or just break up a very large party I am not certain. Since it is a little earlier than anticipated you can draw your own conclusions."

He also told Morgan, "The weather looks threatening again so we may be quite uncomfortable with the little work we are doing in the grotto etc."

Loorz wrote to Hearst at the *Los Angeles Examiner* on January 7, with details of work they had discussed during the fall:

> In completing the first set of improved rooms for the help I am not certain just how nice you wish them. They look real nice with the new wood finish but of course would look better painted. This I will do unless you write differently. . . .
>
> I have not completed my figures on the proposed excavation below the Grotto. Will present them soon.
>
> If the rain, holds off another day, we will have practically all of the footings poured for the remaining columns of the Pergola. . . .
>
> Weather permitting I intend to start hauling the remaining columns right away. This will keep the White [truck] busy for three weeks without any other hauling.
>
> I approximated the cost of the original division of the grotto with grills at $3000. This will cost more because we had to dig real deep with footings in the old fill I was not aware of at the time of the estimate. Also Mr. Baldwin has wisely requested a number of drains etc that I did not include.

Hearst answered on January 9. He devoted most of his reply to the improvements in Hearst Camp, but he also said, "The added cost on the animal pits will be satisfactory."

Julia Morgan also wrote to Loorz on January 9. "I think we had better set out to *finish* entirely the room directly over the billiard room," she began.

"There is a Gothic stone doorway on the order of the ones alongside the mantel in [the] billiard room, that could be copied by your clever plasterer as he did there. As the windows come practically to the cornice at top and have no elaborate trim, just a Gothic moulding is needed."

Morgan told Loorz what else they would need for the architectural decoration of the room. "Present plan is to be down Monday," she concluded, "unless it is a set in storm. Will be coming from Monterey."

Morgan made it to San Simeon that Monday, January 13; her visit prompted fourteen entries in Loorz's notes for the room formally named Billiard Room Wing Room #1. (The Billiard Room Wing consists of the Billiard Room on the first floor and its three surmounting bedrooms. The nomenclature, though simple enough, can be confusing: "Room #1" refers to the bedroom on the second floor, "Room #2" to the bedroom on the third floor, and "Room #3" to the bedroom on the fourth floor. At any rate, the four-story Billiard Room Wing connects the larger Recreation wing—or the New Wing, as it was later renamed—with the older, central portion of Casa Grande.) "Use [Spanish] corbels as selected to do the ceiling," went one of Loorz's notes for Room #1. "Check with Mr. Williams to see if there are plenty available." His other entries included these: "Check to see if there is available beams left over from [Gothic] Study for this room"; "Use stone doorway selected for the bathroom or closet and have the others cast of proper width"; "Antique oak carved doorway [is] to be used as sample from which to carve new proper doors."

Loorz wrote to Hearst in Los Angeles two days later, saying, "Miss Morgan has given me complete details for the room over the Billiard Room and we are already concentrating upon it." He also told Hearst, "She said you had not mentioned the bowling allies [*sic*]." (Hearst was planning to install bowling lanes in the basement underneath the Theater, which adjoins the Billiard Room.) But the rainy weather was more the subject of Loorz's letter. "The road [up the hill] held up pretty well under the $7^{1}/_{2}$ inch rain we had in four days," he said.

Loorz wrote to Julia Morgan the next day, January 16, about Room #1 in the Billiard Wing and about the bear grottoes he was trying to finish on the slope of Orchard Hill, a mile west of the castle. Loorz said, "If all goes well I should have the grotto nearly completed [before my vacation] and perhaps he would let me wait until I returned to start dividing the next one. (He seems real anxious to get them divided and the beast removed from the top of the hill.) However he will surely need a lot more pens or must dispose of a lot more animals for the six pens will help little."

That month of January was a busy one for Loorz, as he mentioned to his friend Bill Hollister, the County Assessor in San Luis Obispo. "I have myself up to my neck in work and can't see my way clear yet," Loorz said on the 16th. "On top of that I'm inviting more with the bidding on these coast schools [Cambria, Cayucos, Morro Bay], Santa Maria Hospital addition and the Lompoc Veterans Memorial building."

With Julia Morgan slated to make another Monday visit (January 27), Loorz briefed her ahead of time on some of the problems to be solved. The new room in the Billiard Wing posed its share, as did the Neptune Pool. "One other consideration is that our outside pool is apparently leaking much too much," he told her. "I think it is because it was empty so long it opened up at the junction of the old and new floor slabs. As soon as we know the party is not to be here for a period we can drain [it] and point up the marble. I say this because the household have some guests coming in today and of course, they expect Mr. Hearst but have had no notification to that effect."

Morgan told him during their meeting to go ahead and drain the pool and to point up the marble as a precaution against further leakage. She also told him, in Loorz's paraphrase, to "erect the remaining garages and tear down the gypsie camp of miscellaneous structures near the lath house in the garden department." This new year would see much work of that more utilitarian kind at San Simeon; Hearst, of course, had written to Loorz about Hearst Camp in December. "I am thrilled at the idea of having our camp cleaned up and painted," Loorz told Miss Morgan on January 30. "I have regretted for a long time that it has been necessary to have the men live as they have."

Lazer Nusbaum, an architect in the Morgan office, wrote to Loorz on February 5. "Dick," as he was usually called, told Loorz he was sending him "the detail drawing of doors for 2nd floor Gothic Bed Room"—meaning Room #1 in the Billiard Room Wing. "I hear that you are leaving for your vacation, soon," he said. "Apparently you and I are the winter sparrows of this outfit."

LOORZ AND HIS WIFE, with their youngest son in tow, headed south on their vacation—to the same Gilman Hot Springs they had enjoyed in 1934. But they were unlucky enough to have continual rain, and then the trip was cut short by a death in Mrs. Loorz's family in Nevada. "If I went into detail and told you everything that has happened to our little lot during this vacation," Loorz told Julia Morgan on February 20, "you wouldn't believe [it]. It would be too ironical and extra ordinary." He assured her, though, that he wasn't "worried about anything"; he was glad to be forced to stay home, at long last. "Instead of feeling that I'm losing my vacation," he continued, "I'm really grateful that I can be at home and really take care of my own boys, without feeling that I'm shirking the job on the hill." Loorz hoped he could fix up his house after his wife returned from Nevada; he had a lot else on his mind, too, as he told Miss Morgan:

> I'm going to start right here with your permission. The floors, rugs and house linoleum here are worn out. They are no longer nice and are very hard to keep up. This is true also of the living room set for the coverings I put on two years ago are getting dirty from little boys hands etc.
>
> Now Miss Morgan, have you ever had a chance to speak with Mr. Hearst about my work on the outside? If you think we can very

frankly make suitable arrangements between us wherein I can spend just a portion of two or three days a month away from the job to look over the outside work. If finally with some such arrangement you still want me to stay on the hill, I would like to stay. . . .

Fred really wants to come down and take a lot of the responsibility of the local work on the Cambria and Morro Schools and two Santa Maria jobs. That could not be for he could not give Wyntoon the personal attention it will need. Again with the contracts all signed and trades sub-let as they are the man who is running our work down here is perhaps more capable than either of us. I should really have little to do about it.

The "ironical and extra ordinary" continued for Loorz. He next found himself practically immobilized by an ear infection for three weeks. On March 13 he wrote to Julia Morgan:

Though I have handled my correspondence and been on the phone continuously talking to Ray [Van Gorden], Pete [Petersen] and others of our boys on the hill, I do not feel that I have earned my salary. The trouble is non-compensative so it [is] not more than right that I should be omitted from the payroll for one week at least. That is providing they will let me go back on Monday which I am hoping. If not, I cannot expect pay for next week either. It is a big salary and I want to earn it always.

I hope to see you on Monday [March 16] and decide definitely on corbels & beams for 2nd floor [Room #1] bathroom ceiling and for the wood finish in the dressing room. No work is being done on these at present. How is Mr. [F. M.] Lorenz coming on the doors? That reminds me I must order some olive knuckle butts to hang those doors with, also some locks and handles. I'd like to have this room in a more or less completed and cleaned state for Mr. Hearst to visit.

In correspondence with him thru Willicombe, Mr. Hearst has permitted [us] to stop work on the next grotto, has again said go ahead with the next cottage for the help and general improvement of helps quarters. . . .

Understand that Mr. Hearst is returning today or soon. Hope to have things please him so that he will appreciate that we have been doing something. I wonder how he liked our new steps and the jars on the posts at the West entrance [by the Neptune Pool].

As for Loorz's asking Morgan on February 20 whether she had talked to Hearst about his outside work and whether she thought suitable arrangements could be made in his behalf, the letter he wrote to his brother on March 24 comes the closest to supplying the answer: "Even though I turned in my resignation here in the face of my outside work, they have asked me to go on taking what time off I needed to take care of my own work. However, they may tire of that before long and oust me."

Hearst was back in residence by then and was still keeping the more humdrum jobs in mind, right along with the more fascinating ones. "Mr. Hearst says to run the new help's house parallel with the others," Colonel Willicombe notified Loorz on March 27, "do not angle it back."

The Colonel explained, "The reason for this is in order to keep space for an extension of the incoming drive, which Miss Morgan expects to make soon."

Loorz spoke of his outside work, and of his work at San Simeon, in writing to his parents on April 2:

> The rain and government delays have held up some of the school jobs a little too much for me to make any progress or profit but I refuse to worry for they will go ahead sometime, then everything will be O. K. . . .
>
> Things are booming here on the hill again. Mr. Hearst and party are here and that means we must keep on our toes and keep lots of things moving. However, that is when I enjoy the place most so I'm not complaining. . . .
>
> We had a few days of rain and cold wind but it has been lovely for a couple of days. Weather men and old timers warn me against a coming storm very shortly so I don't know what to do. I have a crew of men way back in the hills on the [Burnett] road. If it rains real hard they'll have difficulty getting out. They have plenty to eat so it doesn't matter anyway.

On April 11, Loorz brought Julia Morgan up to date on things at San Simeon:

> The panels in the Temple looked well balanced when raised to the member of the cap molds you indicated so John [Vanderloo] is proceeding with his molds for casting. The little raised member as a border adds a lot to the panels.
>
> We can leave the pool today, Saturday with both sets of steps leading down completed except for cleaning of the marble. . . .

It certainly has been difficult to make any good showing with the large party here. We cannot do hardly anything until 10 o'clock and then have to be careful until 11. Of course, we work in the shop preparing etc but it does not show. We understand that the party is leaving Monday so we should swing into it with earnest intentions next week.

Shall we plan on imitation stone on the walls of the 3rd floor as on the 2nd over the Billiard Room? We are not up to it but will be soon. The stone doorways are set completely. We are now lathing though we cannot complete [it] until we receive the sash. . . .

Certain packages arrived from May Co. in Los Angeles. Peter rabbit will tell the tale tomorrow morning. It is difficult to guess to whom we are grateful.

The weather has been just wonderful and I think Mr. Hearst has enjoyed his visit here a lot. . . .

The usual spring excitement of mosquitoes, grassing filling washes etc helps to keep variety on the jobs, together with the continual helps quarters, animal fences & quarters, gates, culverts, roads, howling coyotes and trapping. Then too there is the ever increasing and more than occasional hunt for one or another of the *Dashunds* (you know over modelled sausages). We have sounded two general alarms this week to round up some special pet.

I forgot to mention much excitement arranging chauffeurs and cars for two picnics this week and a rush order to have all trails cleared of branches and slides for equestrians etc. None of them small jobs when done to satisfaction.

I think they intend going to Jolon today over a hastily cleared and yet muddy road (in spots). A rush to clear landing field on other side for planes to bring them back. Then, no doubt, Mac has told you that he [Hearst] sees no reason why we don't send men over right away to alter the rooms as intended. He told this to Mac and not to me.

About the Burnett Road and the Milpitas Hacienda at Jolon, Loorz wrote on April 14 to Millard Hendricks, who had been part of the Burnett crew each season since 1932:

The three Barkers [brothers] have been out there two weeks and have the road in pretty fair shape. Only one really big slide and that just below the gorge. I drove from the Milpitas house to the hilltop in 1 hr. 15 min. yesterday morning. Not bad eh!

Mr. Hearst and about 40 guests drove over last Saturday for a fine Spanish picnic with 20 Spanish entertainers at Milpitas. All had a lovely time and most of them flew back.

OF COURSE 1936 was an election year, something Loorz and especially Hearst were well aware of. The garrulous Loorz ventured into that subject in writing to Harry DeHaes, late of the Hearst zoo staff, who was traveling in Belgium:

> Well the Chief has spent a lot of time here lately. Seems to enjoy it a lot. Has been in a real good humor which is strange consider[ing] how bitter he has been with the administration as regards income taxes etc. He certainly has been hitting Roosevelt hard in his editorials. However, let me predict another victory for Roosevelt. Let me add, that though I differ a lot with some of the plans that have been inaugurated by this administration it has done a lot of good and can do more if given another four years. I don't think they'll put us on the rocks as predicted by their enemies.

George Wright wrote to Loorz from Los Angeles on April 20. He thought he would have been north by then on behalf of the Paddock Engineering Co. but instead he had been "shipped to Palm Springs to build a pool":

> I knocked that job out in a hurry and brought back a cost sheet that showed a damned good percentage. . . .
>
> I expect to knock off several pool jobs at Palm Springs this summer. By the time I get them built I will think back about the days on the Burnett Road in July and August and will wonder how we kept from freezing to death. At least there is no poison oak on the desert. And that is something.

Dear old George, he really *had* regained his sense of humor.

Loorz answered Wright on April 23, saying he'd be glad to see him and "lip over some dainty scandal and gossip a bit"; then he brought Wright up to date:

> I have the Santa Maria J. C. going strong and also the Morro School. Haven't started the Cambria School as yet for the old Government hasn't sent them any money. I won't start until someone assures me that the old long green is forth-coming.
>
> We are going again at Wyntoon. They are in the act of putting a bridge at the [Bavarian] village. Still figuring and discussing the airport. Planned to be graded 400 x 4000 feet and paved 100 x 4000. If it takes six inches of stone to hold on that dry ash it will cost a pretty penny and Oh me is it worth it for a couple of landings a year.
>
> With all this work on the hill and my outside work George I am tied down continuously. Most every week end I take a trip around the [area and] imagine I'm checking things.

The subject of Wyntoon is all but missing from the Loorz Papers through the early months of 1936; and not until April 30 did Mac McClure contribute another of his letters from that alpine hideaway:

> Miss Morgan was here once during my absence and also last Monday. She seems "nervous" that things are moving so slowly and at the present rate of progress it surely looks like the Turrets [Cinderella House] would not be anywhere near ready by July 1st. However let "nature" take its course, says I, and in the meantime I am trying to save some money.
>
> Everything else is about as usual. The weather is Spring-like but wet and rainy.
>
> The bridge is not started yet—nor is Bridge house, or the servants' chalet. J. M. wanted to move the Bridge axis together with all foundations now in, but gave it up when she was here.

Loorz learned more about Wyntoon from James Rankin, who wrote to him on May 8 from his vacation house in Ben Lomond, near Santa Cruz:

> We finished the work to be done for the present at Wyntoon and pulled out but it won't be long before they will be ready for us again up there. . . .
>
> Fishing here is about as usual—very small and I guess an average of five inch would be about right—and to think the boys wrote me from McCloud that they were catching them twenty-four inches. I guess seeing would be believing. I do know that I had a piece of salmon that was from a fish much larger than that—but I bought it at Santa Cruz.

Loorz's meeting with Julia Morgan on Tuesday, May 12, was evidently a corker—his notes filled three pages comprising no less than fifty entries. The first of those entries appeared under "Neptune Pool Area": "Have John Vanderloo's crew & setters concentrate at this section trying to get it completed promptly. Make only necessary castings for work in Billiard room wing. Postpone work on outside windows [in that wing] except where forms are made and will be wasted."

San Simeon's many loose ends could be a sore subject, and we needn't look far to find someone who viewed them in that way. Colonel Willicombe wrote to Loorz from Los Angeles on May 19:

Mr. Hearst instructs me to ask you to have the wooden beams put in place in the pergola. He would like them put in place first on the older portion, and then would like the pergola "completed in other ways and made a finished job."

Mr. Keep states that the grape vines are growing at such an amazing rate that it is difficult to train them without the beams; also having to crowd the runners together, we are losing the effect the vines would give if they could be trained along the beams as they should be.

Your usual prompt attention appreciated.

Willicombe's letter crossed with one that Loorz wrote to him on the same day, May 19:

I find it advisable for me to write to you regarding the plague of rodents we are having here on the hilltop.

The orchard is literally crawling with the animals now coming in from the outside where the grass is drying up. Mr. [Ed] March in the garden is almost helpless. As soon as the party left and the dogs [were] penned he put out dozens of small traps and they catch nearly 100 per day but they are not keeping even.

They are destroying his young plants as fast as he plants them. In his lath house they destroy 15 to 20 flats per day, that is 750 to 1000 [plants] each day.

The men that are trapping and poisoning varmint [coyotes] have them quite under control. We do not see many tracks or signs. Would you discuss it with Mr. Hearst and see if it would not be advisable to have these two men go to work poisoning in the fields. Perhaps the varmint were an important factor in destroying the field mice.

Hearst's reply of the 20th, along with Loorz's letter of the 19th, appeared in Edmond D. Coblentz's compilation of 1952, *William Randolph Hearst: A Portrait in His Own Words*:

Ok—bring in the executioner.

I do not think the plague is due to absence of "varmints." Every once in awhile there is a plague of something or other—locusts or grasshoppers or frogs or rats or politicians—something to afflict us.

It has been so in all recorded time—and the politicians are the worst.

If we ever get rid of them, let us institute a special Passover.

As for the pergola, Loorz told Hearst that same May 20 that he was "pleased to order the wooden beams." He went on to say, "We have stood up all the columns we have on hand and have ordered 22 more to complete [the layout] clear around. All are plumbed and anchored. We are casting a few bird heads [for the ends of the concrete beams] each week without putting on an extra crew in the molders shop. We have already poured about 22 more concrete beams and have bird heads on hand to pour perhaps that many more." He also remarked that Nigel Keep had "the Pergola cleaner and nicer than ever."

HEARST CAME UP from Los Angeles for a weekend stay later in May; Loorz gave Julia Morgan the details on June 3:

Though he arrived Friday evening [May 29], he had not even visited our rooms [in the Billiard Room Wing] until he visited me Monday morning at 10 A. M. We walked thru hastily as he was in a hurry to get away on the plane.

It appears that Mr. Gomez [Alfred Gomes] gets another greenhouse right away, larger and wider. Mr. March gets one for Orchids that are apparently ordered from South America etc. Anyway the order of the day is bigger and better greenhouses.

I might just add that during the two days the party was here, when we could have no traps and poison in the garden the rodents removed some 2500 small plants. It is so discouraging to Mr. March. I marvel at the number of times he has grown and replanted as fast as they are taken. . . .

In our hasty trip thru the three rooms [of the Billiard Wing] and the Beauty Parlor, he made few remarks. He liked the 1st floor [Room #1] very well except for the light. Thot it might still be advisable to have the extra window.

The second floor [Room #2] impressed him as it did you. It had lots of light and was real nice, he stated. He liked the mantel installation very much and made no suggestion of any changes at all.

The 4th floor [Room #3] had lots of light. He thot he might like the wood ceiling a little darker than the sample. We had the first coat of stain on but not all the glaze. It was just mentioned and I think when it is all pulled together he will like it.

He was very much pleased with the Beauty Parlor and I told him the linoleum as designed was on the way. He thot the hair dresser should like it very much.

He then asked me what progress we were making on the Pergola and seemed satisfied and wanted us to keep right on until completion.

He didn't have time to walk down to the Pool Area but asked me what we had done. Apparently he had not walked down there during the stay. He dismissed himself in haste stating he would be back again on Friday [June 5] and would go over the things more carefully. In the meantime, I was to get as much information on hothouses as possible.

During 1936, and most likely after that quick tour of the Billiard Room Wing, Hearst wrote the following to Loorz on some blank Western Union forms:

I want more light in the new rooms than Miss Morgan gives us. It will save time and money to have the lights put in at the beginning instead of later.

In the lower of the three small rooms now nearing completion there is one lantern. There should be four or six.

I do not like the table in that room. It is too big and it is poor quality. We have a great number of good ones why not use one.

We should also have one or two bed side tables in *all* such rooms.

We must get another window in that room [Room #1] no matter whether it is symetrical [*sic*] or not. It needs light in the day time as well as at night.

Please see that there are many connections for lights in every room.

This is a mania with me. I like a room that you can see your way around in.

The question of light—or of excessive dimness—had cropped up before. Hearst seemed to like things brighter than Julia Morgan did; perhaps she was more the brooding medievalist than he was, after all.

The Billiard Room Wing was likewise the main topic of a letter Miss Morgan sent Loorz on June 9:

Mr. Hearst asked last night if we did not have old wood available for the soffit boards of the new rooms. I explained, but take it that he is not content with the "finish."

Would you think it well of my hunting some old French furniture man who has done "faking" in [his] youth, to come up and just make old wood. It takes endless time and patience, and is not the right training for our carpenters.

Mac McClure

The Recreation Wing, Casa Grande (renamed the New Wing)

We are to put a foreman on at Wyntoon and take care of the work there, but the steel should be ordered & on hand before "operations" begin.

Loorz replied that Morgan's idea of the furniture man was a good one, provided she could get "the right man." Then he hammered out the usual wealth of detail, this time concerning Hearst's expectations for the months ahead. "He wants the Pergola all completed this fall and enjoyed a little ride around thru it," began the most interesting paragraph. "He said, 'See Miss Morgan about the Fair Molds for Fountains, Bulls, and Various Statuary on a grand scale, for the various points of the Pergola and especially the entrance.'" (The "Fair Molds" were the plaster models Hearst bought in 1935 from the old Panama-Pacific Exposition in San Francisco.) What a sight *that* would have been—had Hearst's idea been realized.

Hearst was about to absent himself from California for the rest of 1936 and make himself a "non-resident" exempt from the state income tax. He had plenty of other places where he could hang his hat, of course, and plenty of better ways in which he could spend the money at stake. On June 13 Loorz wrote to his best carpenter, Pete Petersen, who was taking the cure at Dr. Halder's Hot Springs in Calistoga:

Mr. Hearst has requested the following while he is away on his European trip:
four greenhouses,
two animal shelters,
Pergola completed,
two more helps cottages,
rebuilt office across the road similar to cottages,
grotto partitions,
widen turn-around with new concrete wall etc.
All of this besides Miss Morgan's work and she has certainly laid out a program too large for the budget unless he increases it.

The distinction between "Miss Morgan's work" and the other jobs Loorz outlined to Petersen was this: the former came under the old Hilltop Fund whereas the latter came under the new Hearst Sunical Building Fund. (The Hearst empire was renowned for its administrative intricacies.) The distinction is important in our trying to unravel the following, which Loorz wrote on July 6 to Hearst in New York:

Has there been any change in the program for the miscellaneous structures [the ones Loorz outlined to Pete Petersen] . . . .

With Wyntoon getting more of Miss Morgan's budget, progress on North terrace steps, rails and paving, and rooms in Billiard and Recreation wing[s], will slow up somewhat.

Jolon alterations started this date. With everything laid out quite complete and Mr. [William] Murray [of the Hearst Sunical office, San Francisco] prepared to advance funds this should all be completed within two months.

Do you desire the above structures to be paid for thru the Hilltop Fund Account?

Hearst answered in the margin: "No let Murray pay for them."

The next day, July 7, Loorz again wrote to Hearst in New York:

In dealing with Miss Morgan, looking up plans, sketches, literature and information on Spanish & Mexican buildings, I am familiar with your proposed building program in the Grand Canyon.

Mr. Hearst I feel that I am in a position to handle that work for you as promptly, intelligently and economically, if not more so, than any other builder.

I would like you to consider my application for the work on any basis most suitable to you, namely; lump sum contract, [or] net cost plus reasonable commission or salary. . . .

Lump sum contracts are seldom, if ever, satisfactory unless complete plans, details and specifications can be prepared without any anticipated changes. I am quite certain that it is more expensive than *cost plus reasonable percentage and equipment rental.*

On open competititive contracts on the outside, from Santa Maria north thruout the state, we have been able to obtain over $300,000 of work at an average of 10% so far this year. Without the element of *gamble* we would be pleased to do the work for a commission of 5% net, if you preferred to do it that way.

Hearst's holdings at the Grand Canyon dated from 1913, the year he bought out a mining company at Grandview Point on the South Rim. Julia Morgan built a "cabin" for him at Grandview in 1914; but he had long since planned a more imposing structure—a more Hearstian structure—for that property. (Mac McClure, it will be recalled, told Loorz in May 1933 that Jim LeFeaver had said Morgan's office "would have to collect for the Arizona house"—that is, for their more recent efforts, which were entirely confined to paper.) Hearst's proposal for the Grand Canyon never got past the paper, but in 1936 its chances of realization had yet to be ruled out.

Hearst answered Loorz on July 13, his New York letterhead bearing the names of the twenty-eight newspapers he owned in those mighty, though increasingly beleaguered days:

> I would greatly like to have you do whatever work is done at the Grand Canyon. I feel sure that you could do it to our complete satisfaction, and more reasonably than we could have it done in any other way.
>
> I have read your letters and agree with everything you said. Consequently I will write Miss Morgan immediately and urge that you be given this work to do on the basis you mention—cost plus a commission of five percent, net.
>
> The work at Grand Canyon must be done economically. I am not prepared to spend a lot of money there any more than I was prepared to spend a large sum of money for the [landing] field at Wyntoon.
>
> I have not made any field at Wyntoon in consequence, and I would like you to have an opportunity to estimate on that and see what you could do. Perhaps we could get the cost down to some possible sum.

On July 24 Loorz sent Julia Morgan a copy of the proposal he had sent Hearst on the 7th; despite Hearst's encouraging response of the 13th, some confusion had cropped up in the matter:

> I mailed it to him with this note clipped on. "If you think this is unreasonable and not in order please send it back. I could get away from this job enough to organize and direct the Grand Canyon work without seriously affecting the progress here on the hill."
>
> I hadn't the slightest idea Mr. Hearst did not connect me with Wyntoon and Mr. Stolte. I have talked to him a lot about Wyntoon, especially the airport and the bridge, since the time you told me you had mentioned to him that I was interested with Mr. Stolte.
>
> Also I have talked to Mr. Willicombe about "My Partner" and "my man Harry Thompson" both of whom he liked, several times. I have also talked to Mr. Willicombe briefly mentioning our schools and other contracts here.
>
> Perhaps my mention of salary might have confused him. However, Miss Morgan salary or otherwise it is all F. C. Stolte Co. I get

$100 per week from you and Fred gets $100 per week from our company. When he got but $75 per week I put the difference of my salary in the company. Frankly Miss Morgan almost every cent I possess is in the company.

I hope this helps to correct a misunderstanding and I hope you agree with me when I say that "I feel that I can be a lot of help to you on the Grand Canyon Work." I think you can save many trips down there by talking it over with me here on the hill. At other times it might be convenient for us to drive down together or from there to the nearest station.

The confusion, the misunderstanding, was really of no consequence, for Loorz remained indispensable to Hearst and Morgan. In fact, he had spent part of the previous day, July 23, with Miss Morgan at Jolon, a session that yielded abundant notes under "Milpitas Ranch Job"; he also made notes that day under "Neptune Area," "Billiard Room Wing," and—a new heading—"Recreation Wing." With the work in the Billiard Room Wing well along, the adjoining Recreation Wing would be the next big job tackled within Casa Grande. Loorz also made some entries under "Miscellaneous," one of them saying that Val Georges, the resident ironworker at San Simeon, was "to make up a total of 15 sets of large door hinges as per antique samples for Wyntoon (For Brown Bear)."

Loorz and Julia Morgan were at Jolon at least twice during August 1936, according to the "Architect's Interviews" preserved in the Loorz Papers; Loorz himself was probably there several other times. In writing to the San Luis Obispo contractor Ted Maino on August 8, Loorz indicated that he had recently been at Jolon "all day." (Maino was the successful bidder, over the F. C. Stolte Co., on Lou Crawford's Cayucos School.)

THE LOORZ PAPERS run on the thin side through the late summer of 1936; however, the letters are as revealing as ever when they turn up. On September 5, for instance, Loorz told his parents, "Mr. Hearst is still in Europe and we do not expect him back for a couple of months. In the meantime as always we are rushing to have as much work completed for him to enjoy when he returns as is possible with the available funds. He is not spending as much as in the past, that is, on this particular place." Then on September 17 he wrote to Louis Reesing in Menlo Park; Reesing was Ed March's predecessor as head gardener and had quit in protest the year before, his patience with the hilltop administration having worn thin:

> Let me share with you your celebration of [your] relief from serfdom, on this the 1st anniversary of your departure from this Bastile on the hill. You are not now fully aware of the anguish and mental unpleasantness you have missed during this past twelvemonth.
>
> I'm expecting Miss Morgan today and the usual concern regarding probable approvals and criticisms still runs thru my mind. I am more concerned this time since I learned from My Partner, via the phone last night, that she comes bearing word that construction is to shut down. He had just received such notice for Wyntoon. To what extent I cannot anticipate but I do know that I am already cut down until it is hopeless for me to try to make a real showing on this vast hilltop. . . .
>
> Business is very good here in my own business. I started another job Monday and will start another Saturday. Have figures in on several more and oh boy it would really be fine if they let me out here, at least while prosperity lasts.

Sure enough, the word was that both San Simeon and Wyntoon were to shut down on the first of October. (Hearst had cabled Morgan from Germany on August 31 to that effect.) Loorz wrote to Julia Morgan on September 21, acknowledging that he would shut down on the 1st but with "the following exceptions":

> I will remain on to complete Jolon, to carry on the camp activities, supervise the use of our large amount of equipment & to supervise the erection of a Lord & Burnham greenhouse expected any day and purchased by the [Hearst Sunical] ranch building fund. . . .
>
> I plan on keeping Alex Rankin as I don't see how this place can operate without him. . . . As I mentioned I consider him the most handy all around man on the hill. . . .
>
> We will be able to use Mr. Gyorgy and helper for the work at Jolon and as you suggested whoever else from our regular men that fit in.
>
> Word comes from Jack Adams [the telegrapher] this morning that Mr. Hearst can be expected very very soon. Thinks he may be

already on his way. Unofficial and Jack very excitable, might have no more information than you have. . . .

I have not forgotten that you would like me to complete the rail at Neptune Dressing Rooms if it is necessary to keep John Van[derloo] and one helper and Frank Frandolich on a few days extra to complete.

I'm going to town today to try to raise more plasterers for Jolon so I can bring our man back to rush some of the small but important items thru by October 1st.

Of course where Wyntoon was concerned, no one else could tell the tale quite like Mac McClure, who finally came through for Loorz on September 23:

Better late than not at all—so here's the letter I intended to write all year.

According to schedule we will be out of here a week from today. This is somewhat earlier than we expected but no-one is very sorry. As far as the job goes, we will be leaving it in about as good shape as we would later. The Pinnacles (otherwise known as Cinderella House) will be nearly done but not quite. The "Chalet" (which is a building for servants quarters) is also 90% done and turned out fine, and the new Bridge House will be all framed and [its] roof papered. This later building is the one that moved across the river. Incidentally it was a great improvement to move it. We all thought it ought to have been there in the first place but it was M. D. who talked W. R. into the idea as it spoiled the down river view from the Brown Bear House (their suite).

We are curious to know just what the shut down may mean— My interpretation is that he has a bad case of jitters over European and Domestic politics. Perhaps he plans a lengthy shut-down but I doubt it.

It will be interesting to know just what status the Grand Canyon job is in. As far as I know he expected it to move but then he didn't give any orders to do so.

He approved the sketches I made and seemed to be finished with me so I wired J. M. if I should ask him anything about a definite start or get any other data but was told to come back without discussing such items—and here we are. It is a peculiar set up and has possibilities for much trouble (foregoing paragraph confidential).

This ends my fourth year at Wyntoon— I hope there is not another, but it hasn't been too unpleasant. I have enjoyed the association with Fred and Harry very much and am only tired of the place and not the people.

Maybe next year will see us looking into the Grand Canyon and again may be it won't.

My plans (or rather J. M.'s) are for me to take my vacation and then work in [her] office until W. R. returns. If I get some time off I may build a small house in Santa Monica. Otherwise "all is quiet on the Northern front" and I hope that the battles at San Simeon are leaving you unscarred.

LOORZ HEARD FROM another McClure on September 30—from Maurice McClure (no relation to Warren "Mac" McClure), who had just entered the College of Engineering at Berkeley. Maurice McClure had worked at San Simeon from 1926 to 1933; more recently he had worked for the F. C. Stolte Co. on the Cambria Grammar School, a job run by Frank Gendrich of San Luis Obispo. (Gendrich, according to McClure, had most likely been the superintendent in 1929 and 1930 on a job whose details are obscure—Hearst's Milpitas Hacienda.) "Rumor has it that the Stolte Co. has some more work in Yosemite," McClure told Loorz. "If this is true—Congratulations! And let us hope that it proves *profitable.*"

On October 10 Loorz confirmed for Maurice McClure what the latter had heard:

We have a very fine job or jobs at Yosemite. Three three-story hotel buildings. Two of them 33-room dormitories and one two-room apartment hotel. We have a large crew on and making great headway. Wyntoon closed down so we brought Harry Thompson down to run the job and he certainly is doing his stuff.

We are also low bidders on [Hearst Radio] K. Y. A.'s new broadcasting station in S. F.

Loorz went on to address the question of politics, which McClure had raised in his letter:

Believe me it has become increasingly difficult for me to express my political opinions. Miss Morgan and her office force keep feeling me out and mentioning how impractical and wasteful the present administration is. I make no commitments but I certainly don't make statements I don't believe.

My honest opinion is that we are going to have good times no matter who is elected. I also feel that income tax is here to stay. I also feel that the so called communists of our country except for a few radicals that we have always had are fine type men struggling to free themselves from relief and charity rolls. Quite an honorable thing I believe.

Loorz wrote to Julia Morgan in the meantime, on the day of the shutdown—October 1:

The construction crew this morning is Ray Van Gorden, Alex Rankin (mostly on ranch payroll for few days) the Cook and one waiter and yours truly.

The place looks more cleaned up and completed especially around Neptune Pool than we have ever seen it.

The whole crew has been paid off . . . .

As you stated I will bring Frank Frandolich back as soon as the marble coping arrives [for the Neptune Pool].

Frank Gyorgy and [Mickey] Brennan worked fast and a little overtime and completed placing Miss Day's paintings on the dressing room ceiling [in one of the Billiard Wing bedrooms]. She said the Frieze would be shipped today [Thursday] or Friday. . . .

Brot the plasterers back from Jolon last Saturday and they are back there again this morning. . . .

Main terrace lower north steps completed except for polishing marble risers. When too foggy to wax, waxer can spend time polishing if O. K. They look fine.

New addition on recreation wing stripped and cleaned. . . .

Placed the green tile in the 4th floor bathroom [Billiard Wing Room #3]. . . .

Iron grill placed in window outside Billiard Room hallway.

Small wall between [north] duplex [tower] and recreation wing tower placed and sample of tile [put] on it. Looked at it from way down the road and it certainly makes the needed tie.

Loorz dashed off some similar details the next day for Jud Smelser, a close friend of Mac McClure's who had worked intermittently at San Simeon and Wyntoon:

Well things are almost maddening around here right now. The construction payroll consists of Ray Van, Alex Rankin, the cook one waiter and myself.

On Hearst Sunical greenhouse I have Pete [Petersen], Frank Souza and Joe Galbraith.

On Jolon doors I have four carpenters in the shop.

Up here around the office and around the Pool area where we have had so much activity it is so quiet I feel like screaming. Personally I am expected to stay only until Jolon is completed unless we hear to the contrary from Mr. Hearst in the meantime. . . .

We are starting strong at Yosemite so If you wish I could send you there. Harry Thompson with Fred's able assistance will be Super and is on the job today.

I had a nice letter from Mac but I don't know where to answer to. I suppose the best way would be to write thru the office in S. F. I would like to see him just now as I have several possibilities that we might sketch up together.

Miss Morgan will be here today and we will make that trip to Jolon etc. Wonder what headaches are in store for me. Wish things were more definite as there is certainly lots of work outside if I was free to get it.

Loorz may have felt like screaming, and he may have felt excessively confined at San Simeon, but he hadn't lost his humor altogether. On October 6 he returned his tickets to the University of California for the upcoming football game between Berkeley and UCLA.

"I would like further to cancel my order for other tickets for this season," he said.

"My reason for this cancellation is that an extended voyage to the West Indies makes it inconvenient for visiting football games."

Instead of leaving for the Caribbean, Loorz went into another meeting with Julia Morgan on Friday, October 7. Under "Hilltop Miscellaneous" he noted, "Disconnect elevator (New one) to insure safety for present attendants and show operation to Mr. Hearst when he arrives." That had been another one of those utilitarian projects in 1936—the installation of an elevator in the Recreation Wing, or the New Wing as it was later renamed.

Jud Smelser wrote back to Loorz on October 16, giving him Mac McClure's address on 6th Street in Santa Monica. "I think he is doing a hide-out but his office may have this address," he said. "He hasn't said but that is usually the way that he handles his time off."

Smelser added a postscript: "I read in a recent *Time* that W. R. H. American newspaper tycoon recently purchased seventy grand of Flemish and English Art in Amsterdam. I think we have been sold down the river in the interest of art. Having always been an admirer of art I guess I shouldn't feel bitter."

Loorz wrote to the Oakland plumber James Rankin the next day; he greeted him by using his middle name, Fleming, and joked that he had taken "10 years to find out that name":

> Well I thot it wise to advise you regarding the wheres and the whyfor's around these parts. First let it be understood that no one knows anything and everybody is guessing and yours is as good as mine.
>
> However, this I can tell you. I am going to complete the Jolon job and the greenhouse. I intend to complete the heating installation but since they are a little behind in the money I have not yet asked you to go ahead. . . .
>
> As far as Jolon is concerned, that all goes thru Miss Morgan's office. [William] Murray gives the money to her and she pays it out like on Hearst Construction. . . .
>
> Well Jimmie (Fleming) business is still very very good for Fred and me and we know it has been with you. I know further that over 60 of my own relatives are far better off than three years ago. I know we are all more happy and hopeful. Then is it right that they should try to scare us so much?
>
> Every year Jimmie are we going to let Big Business scare us to death and make us change? How can candidates be so wonderful at the beginning and so bad in the end? It just means to me that no one can satisfy them. I like this fellow [Alf] Landon [the Republican candidate for President] but I don't think Roosevelt [is] as bad as they paint him. . . .
>
> I'm afraid we'll have another Silent Cal in the person of Mr. Landon. I think that is why they picked him. They don't want someone that does things of his own accord. . . .
>
> Well Jimmie I know you are back on the old Elephant cart where you belong by nature and creed but give us the benefit of the doubt and please don't say we are un-American. What Motto could be more Worthwhile (if not American) than "Government for the benefit of the greater number"?
>
> Oh Hell Jim come on down and we'll talk it over. They've got me so scared that I'm apt to vote for Landon. Also I'm certain things will go on nicely and prosperity will remain regardless for some time to come. Both are fine upright, religious, God fearing men. Roosevelt has shown that he is not a man-fearing man.

Loorz may have been wavering on the question of Alf Landon, but the Governor of Kansas had one supporter he could always count on—William Randolph Hearst. In his role as the nation's soothsayer, Hearst had already made it known that the November election would result in a "Landonslide." He was dead wrong, of course, but the slogan was priceless.

Loorz wrote to Mac McClure at his Santa Monica "hideout" on October 23:

> I'm expecting Miss Morgan today. Glad she is coming for she hasn't been here for three weeks, though I saw her two weeks ago when we bid on the K. Y. A. new broadcasting station thru her office. By the way we are low on that at $21,000, but it was so much more money than a similar building they are just erecting in Los Angeles that they have not yet permitted us to go ahead. . . .
>
> Let me explain that, in the fact that they were given a plan of the other units that have been constructed and asked to adjust it to fit local conditions but make it look just the same as Mr. Hearst wanted them to standardize all of the stations.
>
> Well they didn't want to copy the plan outright without apologies to the Architects so they wrote and explained. The L. A. Architects wrote back, "Oh don't mind just go ahead, we did the same thing we copied it from some other plans from the East." LeFeaver was telling me this and got a real kick out of it.

ONE THING LOORZ and Morgan discussed during her visit on October 23 was his new "W. R. H. Construction Proposal," which he put in writing for her on the 28th. Loorz's proposal called for his taking over "the complete management and financing and general supervision of construction of Mr. Hearst's work at San Simeon and elsewhere at net cost plus 10% Commission":

> It is understood that I receive no salary as a part of the cost. My full compensation for personal supervision will be a part of the commission. . . .
>
> If awarded this work it is my intention to handle it all thru our F. C. Stolte Co. Branch Office at San Luis Obispo. I will maintain a home and reside in San Luis Obispo or in the house at San Simeon as you may desire so that I will be able to give a lot of personal

attention to operations on the hilltop and be able to meet you or Mr. Hearst in conference on short notice. . . .

Under this system or arrangement I would be free to give personal supervision to work at Wyntoon & Grand Canyon, if it goes ahead. Having worked with you and Mr. Hearst for nearly five years I should be able to more economically execute the work on these two projects with more satisfaction and less worry to you both.

The Loorz Papers contain no reply from Julia Morgan. But she and Loorz weighed the proposal. His letter to her of November 12 reflects some important modifications they had agreed upon. The ten-percent commission had dropped to five percent; to offset that adjustment, Loorz would keep drawing an annual salary of $5,200. The idea of handling the work through San Luis Obispo still held, but nothing was said of Loorz's moving to San Luis himself—though he mentioned the possibility elsewhere in his correspondence that fall. It remained, in any event, for Hearst to pass judgment on the matter.

Hearst had returned from Europe to New York by then, to his Ritz Tower Hotel in Manhattan and to the faint dust remaining from the "Landonslide" of November 3. He wired Loorz on the 6th, but not about proposals, not about politics: "Please build immediately another whole section of runways at Kennels." Fine, but how to pay for the work? Loorz wired back to Willicombe: "Please advise what funds to use in constructing new Kennels & runways as per Mr. H. telegram."

On November 19, a week after Loorz sent Morgan his modified proposal, she wrote to him from San Francisco; by then the ever-unfolding scenario had taken another turn:

Mr. Hearst writes he will not be back before the middle of January, and that work can go on at San Simeon in Spring but at Wyntoon not before summer. . . .

I am going east after Thanksgiving, will be gone about two weeks in all, and will not discuss any other questions until I see Mr. Hearst there.

How is Jolon progressing? Unless much needed, I do not plan to come again until back around the middle of December.

The scenario took still another turn, as Morgan indicated in writing to Loorz four days later:

Mr. Hearst's plans are evidently changing—i. e. developing,—and it looks now as though he would be back around the first of the year and want to see work going on.

He also says in his last letter that he wants to use Wyntoon Bridge House, Gables, etc, *early* in the year!

By the time he comes, he will probably have a definite program. He suggests you *superintend* Wyntoon, San Simeon, and The Canyon.

Well, that last point was good news, long-awaited news; but Loorz must have been wondering what the next day's mail would bring. With the quixotic Hearst as his patron, he had to be ready for anything, just as Julia Morgan had to be. On December 1, Colonel Willicombe wrote to Loorz from New York:

Carey Baldwin has reminded Chief that the apehouse is of cheap construction, difficult to keep at proper temperature for the young chimpanzee. As we do not want anything to happen to Mary's youngster, Chief directs me to tell you that he would like to have a new ape house built without delay. Perhaps you could airmail me a sketch and estimate and plan of location, etc.; that is if such procedure will not interfere with the new house being ready by the time the cold weather sets in. All Chief said was—

"Build new ape house."

Loorz had a detailed estimate in the mail by December 7, an estimate for a well-equipped ape house at $3,500. Hearst balked at the price, which prompted him to wire Loorz on the 12th: "DO NOT BUILD A NEW APE HOUSE REPAIR PRESENT APE HOUSE IF NECESSARY. PROVIDE ACCESSORY HEAT FROM OUTSIDE IF NECESSARY."

In writing on December 16 to the plasterer Dell Clausen, who had heard that Loorz was "thru on the hill," Loorz mentioned why he and Julia Morgan had opted for five percent, plus salary, on his new "W. R. H. Construction Proposal" of late October. It had simply been "so as not to make the commission sound too big" to Hearst. Loorz elaborated further:

She thinks I ought to continue to live here and personally supervise this place [in] what time I could spare from the others [Wyntoon and Grand Canyon] and my own business. Then I would keep a

Pinch-Hitter to fill in the gaps while I'm away. This I once mentioned to you, that I had you in mind. However, I didn't mention that to her and one day she said she had just the right young fellow in mind for my right bower. A young fellow from Los Angeles. So I said nothing at least until things are definitely settled. Mr. Hearst may be displeased with the whole set up and then the rumor you're hearing might come to pass. In which case I still do not need to worry. In fact, my overhead is far too great on my private work in this district and as much as my salary is here I could do most of it [myself]. . . .

My family are all quite well and happy and the wife is hoping that no more jobs come in to figure at least until after the Holidays. . . . Don, pathetically, with tears in his eyes, approached me the other evening with the remark, "All you do Daddy is Work, read the paper and go to bed."

Julia Morgan wrote to Loorz the next day, December 17:

Am just in from New York today [Thursday] and plan to be down for Monday.

We want to get the bed room just over the billiard room furnished. Will make a list tonight and send it to you, as well as to Mr. Williams.

Mr. Hearst seemed well and cheerful, but dubious about spending any more time in California this next year than the current year.

Morgan did not elaborate on Hearst's dubiousness, yet Loorz could read between the lines well enough. Taxation lay behind it—confiscatory taxation, as Hearst had explained to Morgan soon after the dastardly Roosevelt won his second term. Confiscatory taxation. The main reason for the sudden shutdown of October 1. But no matter what the future might hold in that regard, life went on at San Simeon, as Loorz told his parents on December 18:

Well here it is almost xmas and things all stirring for a fine holiday season. Went to the school play last night and enjoyed it. The boys did well though poor Bill left out two verses of his piece. He did not falter, none except those that knew the piece knew the difference. But it certainly made him nervous for the rest of his parts but he made no more mistakes.

Bobby still has a slight cold but is just as good as he can be. Sleeps until nearly 7:30 these mornings and is as always into everything. I think he will get a real kick out of xmas. . . .

It is still lonesome here on the hilltop with only a few men but a lot of odds and ends. There is nearly as much paper work as ever and the phone rings nearly as often.

We have just had a wonderful 3 inch rainfall and things are much brighter again. The farmers and cattle men around here were worried about the grass. In a day or so the grass will be up and hills all green. All we need here is rain anytime of the year and things get green. It certainly is God's country when you stop to think of it.

Julia Morgan had to cancel for Monday the 21st, and so Loorz sent her two pages of details on the work at Jolon and San Simeon. He closed with a personal note:

The boys were real pleased with the two very appropriate cards they received from [you from] Wyoming. Bill came running to show me when I got home that day. In the spirit of xmas, which is growing on them more and more now that they are older they each have asked if they could not send you something. I could not deny them this privilege especially since you have been so good to them.

NINETEEN THIRTY-SEVEN

1937

ON NEW YEAR'S DAY, 1937, Julia Morgan wrote to young Bill Loorz, thanking him for the Christmas present he had sent her:

That is the most remarkable pencil I ever saw— If one could not think out fine things to draw with all those colors ready to just jump onto the paper, it would only mean that you forgot to include a little wee brain to fasten on top the "supply" end— Now *that would be a good idea.* Then I could just sit back and dream, & hold the pencil loosely onto the paper, & pop-pop-pop-pop-in four colors the fine ideas would all be in lovely lines & color combinations on the paper!

It is a lovely gift and I appreciate it very much, your kind note also, & the exciting Christmas card.

The steady stream of business correspondence resumed soon after that. Young Bill's father wrote to Miss Morgan on January 7; he had just been to Jolon, had found things "looking very nice" at the Milpitas Hacienda, and had also seen the results of the latest storm:

Yesterday the snow laid on the ground nearly an inch thick at Milpitas until about noon. It remained on all the hillsides and in the ravines all day. It was real cold. . . .

It has been so wet and cold *here* that we haven't been able to do much. It was even too cold this sunshiny morning to place the cement finish around the marble inserts in front of the dressing rooms at Neptune Pool. Not too cold for the men but the wet cement would freeze up as soon as you spread it thin on the base.

We are still making rain repairs such as additional drains, recoating roofs, opening old drains etc.

The weather remained a factor for several more days, as Loorz explained on January 13 in writing to Miss Morgan again:

> Well things are going quietly on the hilltop with so very few men. It has been so cold and rainy that we haven't been able to do anything outside. It has actually been so cold that we have over 50 breaks in water pipes and Alex [Rankin] is kept real busy trying to get needed water. A lot of plants that have never suffered before have been damaged or actually ruined by the continued frost. . . .
>
> The weather was so cold that our [Neptune] pool shrunk again leaving a place for leaking between the old and new concrete. I have the boys repairing it again today. We want to have it right when Mr. Hearst gets here.

Hearst remained away till mid-February; Morgan, meanwhile, visited San Simeon for the first time in 1937 on January 21. She followed through on having said in December that Room #1 in the Billiard Room Wing should be furnished. "Mrs. Redelsperger [the head housekeeper] to put towels and dainties in bathroom to make it ready for immediate occupancy," went one of Loorz's entries regarding that room. He also noted that Morgan would be purchasing towel bars and other fittings for the six new bathrooms in the Milpitas Hacienda.

Loorz, of course, was keeping abreast of his outside work all the while, with Morgan's blessings (and evidently with Hearst's as well). Nineteen thirty-six had had its up and downs, though, as Loorz told his friend Jack Hall late in January:

> We are doing quite well. In fact, we had out biggest year in 1936 but I did not do a perfect job of it. I hit a couple of tough jobs that rolled me for a few thousands. It is the first time that I let things get away from me but with a tough architect, a tough job, and relief men of the poorest caliber and myself tied down here on the hilltop it is no wonder. Fortunately Jack I had several others down here and the partner had a lot up there so we had a very good net. In fact, Fred's greatest worry right now is to get out of income tax.

Loorz's reference to "relief men" concerned employees on one of his P. W. A. jobs. But whether the "tough architect" was Louis Crawford or Keith Lockard or someone else, and whether the "tough job" was the Cambria School or the Santa Maria Junior College—or yet another one—are questions not easily answered. The Loorz Papers are too elusive in the matter, despite several such references. What the Papers do reveal is that building schools could be profitable. The same day he wrote to Jack Hall, Loorz told Louis Schallich he was "figuring on a large school" at "$150,000 or so." The school was to be built in Avenal, a small town midway between Paso Robles and Fresno.

The stormy weather continued into February 1937, as Loorz told his parents soon after his mother visited San Simeon that winter:

> We have certainly had rain since you left. We had seven inches here on the hilltop in 36 hours. Roads washed out, small dams [on Burnett Creek] washed out and leaks everywhere about the castle. It is almost impossible to keep out water when it rains like that.
>
> Mr. Hearst is in Los Angeles and might be expected up here anytime and we must hurry to get as many leaks cleaned up and patched as possible. I certainly hope he comes soon as this place will seem more interesting. It has grown tiresome to me and I am unable to put pep into the work for myself or the men.

That was on February 8. The next day, in writing to Fred Stolte, Loorz said he wouldn't have time to "spread much bull," the mail being ready to go out. But he quickly told Stolte, "With the chief back in L. A. there is little doubt but that we will see him before long. Miss Morgan should be here in a day or so and I will try to find out anything that I can. I think she intends to call on him in L. A. soon and then come back up here to discuss plans."

In reality, Loorz thought Morgan might not be showing up for a while yet, for he sent her a typically detailed report on the 10th that covered the work at Jolon and San Simeon. "Anxiously awaiting orders to put on more men and increase production," he told her. "A lot of the boys out of work and apparently not too much in site [*sic*] for the next month or so."

Morgan replied from San Francisco the following day, February 11:

Thank you for the "report." I don't imagine Mr. Hearst will descend at Jolon under present conditions. But I would like the furniture "distributed" so that it can be quickly put in final place. You know it always requires some shifting, however planned.

Mr. [F. M.] Lorenz has 12 pieces of the 4th floor carvings [for Billiard Wing Room #3], two finished on both sides, plus the original—also all the door panels—of course no doors.

He goes onto the *complete doors* for the 3rd [floor (Room #2)].

It sounds as though the odds and ends were being caught up with pretty well. Many thanks.

The curtains for the 2nd floor [Room #1] are neutral—but I could get nothing without dyeing and thought if O. K. would get Mr. Gyorgy to make a sample of the pink of the room, and bring the curtains back and have dyed. It will be much cheaper than having the fringe and material dyed separately.

No word from Mr. Hearst as yet—but we can go ahead with all the work over the Billiard Room—and perhaps even get it done!

THAT FEBRUARY SAW still more stormy weather, indeed violent weather, which Loorz described to Morgan on the 15th:

We have just gone thru the worst storm and blow that I have witnessed on the hilltop. In fact, none but Mr. [Manuel] Sebastian seem to be able to remember such a storm and that was in '89. Anyway it did us considerable damage Miss Morgan. It blew out glass and forced water thru sash that have never leaked before.

I kept men on dipping up in the recreation wing to avoid damage down in the Theater. The household stayed on duty doing the same thing in the houses and castle so that except for broken glass and even sash I think there will be no serious results.

Our chimney or flew [*sic*] blew off our kitchen in camp. Many large branches were blown off the Oaks and the garden is a mess. It whipped the vines bare. The poor palms in the East Patio never had many branches and today they have none so I wonder if they can live.

The water that comes down the chimneys alone does a lot of damage in storms as big as this one. This is particularly true in the guest houses. . . .

It is not unkind for me to say that I am pleased Mr. Hearst and guests were not here during this storm.

But Hearst and the party weren't far behind. They arrived at San Simeon on the 18th, having been away for nearly nine months. "Mr. Hearst is here on the hill and things are going more interesting and exciting," Loorz told his sister, Iva, on the 19th. "It always means more work but that is just what I like. We are also having better weather for a change and we are very grateful for that."

Despite Hearst's financial difficulties, he was full of ideas for projects, as Loorz told Julia Morgan on February 24:

> As usual when Mr. Hearst is here he wants a lot of work done. Because financial conditions are as they appeared when you were here I have habitually inquired about it. I find this to be absolutely necessary and to get his written approval when on his private account or the ranch account.
>
> So yesterday he asked me to start right away widening the road from the Pergola to the hilltop and get the concrete wall in [along China Hill] as he mentioned before. This is naturally on [the] construction [account] so I mentioned that I was increasing the crew cautiously as I understood that the available funds had been reduced from last year. He said, "If Miss Morgan needs more money she can ask for it for I want this wall and all the rooms in the recreation wing completed." I hope he does not change his mind. . . .
>
> He seems so anxious to have something real active going that I intended starting the shovel crew this morning. However, we are in the midst of a terrible storm and I'll have to wait perhaps until Monday [March 1].

Loorz also wrote to James Rankin and to Fred Stolte on February 24. He told Rankin about the Recreation Wing, and then he concluded with, "Anyway we are happy to have Mr. Hearst with us again, to know that he looks well and seems quite happy. He was sorry to see what havoc the frost has done to the garden but is quite reconciled to it and laughed heartily about the strange California weather." Loorz had more, though, to tell Stolte:

> Now about Mr. Hearst. He just called me up to his room and announced that they had just had a catastrophe. He pointed out a broken plate glass on a storm door and laughed.
>
> He has been in real good humor and is, of course, in the building business proper, at least in conversation. However, when Miss Morgan

was here Saturday [February 20], she said he wanted things but actually had cut down the budget by more than half for both places. That was in accordance with a letter from New York.

However, yesterday he asked me to get busy right away and do some work. I told him I had been informed that the budget had been cut and I would have to be cautious. He said, "If Miss Morgan wants more money she can ask for it, I want that [concrete wall] done and all these rooms in this wing soon."

So if he holds to the reduced budget there will be very little at Wyntoon this year perhaps $40,000 total. Let's hope he enjoys himself so much here that he'll get the bug and build voluminously. No doubt you agree with me about it. For the present I am supposed to spend all of the budget here until you start up there then we'll split [the money].

Loorz and his men got going on the Recreation Wing before the month was out. The Recreation Wing consisted of three large floors overlying the ground-floor Theater. Except for the installation of the elevator at its west end in 1936, the Wing had seen little or no work since 1934, the year the crew temporarily finished several rooms for Hearst's birthday party. The masonite and plasterboard were still in place from 1934; they were about to give way to materials befitting the grandeur of San Simeon. The second and third floors of the Wing were conventional enough spatially, but the fourth floor was more complex, with its corresponding West Tower and East Tower suites. Some of the first work done in the Recreation Wing in 1937 was concentrated in these uppermost rooms. Loorz informed Julia Morgan on Sunday, February 28, that he would have "two more carpenters on the West Tower Room on Monday." He also told her:

I would like at least to do as much of the rough work in the East Tower as possible before we finish the West tower so we can use the elevator for the bulk of the materials, especially for mantel work and plastering.

Mr. Williams is getting the rest of the Salamanca Ceiling materials out [of the warehouse] today and will have them here for me the first thing Monday morning.

(The Salamanca ceiling was one of many Spanish ceilings Hearst had bought from Arthur Byne—the same Madrid antiquarian who sold him the monastery that lay behind the "big job" once proposed for Wyntoon.)

Morgan answered on March 1, telling Loorz, "As the ceiling for the West Tower is not in California, Mr. Hearst agreed we had better do other rooms at this time." She would therefore "bring down a list of the ceilings for the first floor of rooms"—meaning those immediately above the Theater. Morgan, for whatever reason, erred in saying the Salamanca ceiling was not in California. It was in fact there, and W. R. Williams delivered it to the job that very day, as Loorz said he would. The ceiling figured in Loorz's notes of his meeting with Julia Morgan on March 3. "Put up three sides of antique ceiling just as dismantled with short side toward the fireplace," he said of the Salamanca ceiling and the West Tower. "Will adjust long side to suit then." He also noted that he was to "remove all present temporary partitions on 2nd floor and prepare to install permanent partitions" and that he was to "select antique windows for Patio side [south side of Wing] and make sufficient copies for North side."

MARCH 4, 1937, marked the fiftieth anniversary of William Randolph Hearst's life in newspaper publishing. Loorz was at the typewriter as usual on that historic day, this time writing to Frances Apperson; Mrs. Apperson's husband, Randolph, a first cousin of Hearst, had succeeded Arch Parks in 1934 as superintendent of the Hearst Ranch:

> Are we happy to have Mr. Hearst back and things moving again. Even though they want some things faster than available labor and materials make it possible.
>
> Among the many proposed projects is a long Spanish type bunk house for the ranch which Randy [Mr. Apperson] no doubt mentioned. It looks dandy to me, so does the cost. I hope you like it and if not I don't know what you can do about it but use your influence through Randy. Just to show my cleverness I'll sketch below what I remember of it as I glanced at it for a minute or two yesterday where Mr. Hearst and Miss Morgan had been mulling over it.

Loorz made his sketch under the words *HERE'S THE EFFORT*, a sketch closely resembling the Bunkhouse—or the

Hearst Sunical Men's Quarters by formal name—that Loorz and his crew began building a month later.

To Randy and Fran Apperson was accorded the privilege of living in the spacious Ranch House, which Hearst's father, George Hearst, built in the 1870s on the coastal plain below the castle. The new Bunkhouse was slated to be built a few hundred yards away. The Appersons were delighted with the improvements Hearst was about to make in 1937 on the ranch, not just on the hilltop.

As for the present work on the hill, Loorz brought Julia Morgan up to date on March 9:

> With the shovel operating and the partitions coming out on the second floor [of the Recreation Wing] and some action in general Mr. Hearst seems quite happy. He comes out often and goes around with keen interest in everything.
>
> He's anxious to get us started on the concrete wall and was satisfied that our program included the wall completed on the south side by the end of this year. He is going to talk to you about an entrance to China Hill and I will leave plenty of space for same until it is settled. He wants us to go right on with the grading however on the North side at this time including the terracing.
>
> He has personally gone over the terracing, approving the removal of certain trees.

China Hill, so named for the "Chinese House" Hearst once planned for it, was just across the hilltop entrance drive from the Neptune Pool. The proposed retaining wall would parallel the entrance and the exit drives, thus encircling China Hill. Though a minor effort architecturally, the wall would go far toward giving the Enchanted Hill a more dressed-up, nearly finished look. And now that Hearst had been building at San Simeon for almost twenty years, he was increasingly keen on tying up as many loose ends as possible—hence the recent work on the pergola, the Billiard Room Wing, the Recreation Wing, the terraces by the Neptune Pool, and so on.

Loorz concluded his March 9 letter to Julia Morgan by mentioning the Salamanca ceiling in the West Tower of the Recreation Wing: "That antique ceiling was in quite a shape and it will take quite a little labor repairing before we can actually raise it. I have sent for one more of our old Antique experienced carpenters to work with the man on it."

Except for a quick trip he made to Los Angeles, Hearst stayed at San Simeon from mid-February through mid-March. Just before he left to go back to Los Angeles again, he sent Loorz several letters and memoranda; the one dated March 14 took the cake:

> What would it cost to have the elevator—the old one—go up another story and reach the Celestial Suite?
>
> I would like to do this if not too expensive. . . .
>
> I spoke to Miss Morgan about chimneys and flues. She agrees to everything.
>
> We will cut down the main chimney to where it was before, and during some long absence we will move the big fireplace in the living room [the Assembly Room?] out a foot. That will be very advantageous.
>
> We will enlarge the flues in the new theatre wing [the Recreation Wing], and we will put in new flues for new fireplaces on first and second bedroom floors.
>
> These flues can SURELY be made right.
>
> The flue of the East Room fireplace MUST positively be reconstructed all the way up. The sooner you do this the better. You can begin NOW. We will be leaving this week.
>
> Tear everything apart and put in a BIG flue so we can make the East Room fireplace like it was meant to be.

Hearst again pursued the problem of the smoking fireplace the next day:

> I would like to have a fireplace in the East Room like we have in the Billiard Room—a real fireplace, all open, carrying a big fire, and never smoking. To do this we need a big flue and sufficient projection.
>
> It is very simple, but we cannot get it by wishing for it.
>
> We have got to construct.

Loorz must have been reeling by then. Fortunately, he sent the letters on to Julia Morgan for her perusal; she wrote back on March 22, saying that she would support him:

> The East room flue is exactly the size of the Billiard room flue and symmetrically placed in the flue stack. The difference is that the East room fireplace is located about 12 feet from the chimney stack, due to several changes in the location of this chimney before "your day," and consequent complications. I will see if a new chimney

cannot be built some way at a less distance from the fireplace, and will go into the problem once more with Mr. Hearst and see what solution he would approve, taking the responsibility for the few days delay if necessary.

Loorz wrote to Hearst in Los Angles on March 26, not about fireplaces but about "the old black ostrich" at the zoo. The ostrich was notoriously violent and had attacked a carpenter working on the animal shelters; the carpenter, in self defense, had struck the bird dead with a two-by-four. Hearst was known for his love of animals—and for his deploring of any cruelty toward them. What on earth, Loorz must have thought, would he say in this instance? Hearst answered on the 29th:

As long as the ostrich did not hurt the MAN there is nothing to worry about.

However, we should endeavor to cure ugly birds and animals, and I think the best way is to shoot them in the prat with a charge of rock salt.

Animals are like humans—they are ugly when they think they can get away with it. A little severe discipline naturally convinces them that they can NOT get away with it.

The severity is not cruel. It would have saved this ostrich's life.

When the men are working in places exposed to attack, I suggest that you send a watchman along with a shot gun containing a small charge of rock salt.

I think it will do the trick.

Hearst added a detached line at the bottom: "$3,000 is not too much for the elevator"—Loorz having told him on the 26th that his proposed raising of the elevator to the Celestial Suite would probably cost that much.

Julia Morgan was at San Simeon the day Hearst answered Loorz, March 29. Loorz compiled two pages of notes, some of which can be cited here under the headings he used:

CHINA HILL WALL

1. Curves at beginning near Neptune Temple to be symmetrical with Center Line thru pool axis.
2. Height and shape of curve to be carefully adjusted to tentative layout of stakes by Architect.
5. Wall to continue around curve at the mentioned axis line for the present and removed, if necessary when future development occurs.

BILLIARD ROOM FOURTH FLOOR [Billiard Wing Room #3]

7. Mr. [John] Glang to exercise extreme caution in antiqueing the balance of the carvings in this room. Work very much overdone. Attempt to restore some of the finer lines.

RECREATION WING

10. Ceiling of West tower very good. Exercise caution about exposed nailing.
21. Mr. Williams to hunt out tile ceiling "Sevillian" as received in 25 cases [in] 1926 photo 2420. (Mr. Williams states he can locate no invoices or shipping information from which to locate same.)
22. Mr. Williams says he will have no trouble finding "Blazonceil" [ceiling] or whatever it was as it was received in the past two years. . . .
24. Send back to warehouse ceiling originally selected for [Third Floor, Room] #4 still crated.
25. Send back uncrated ceiling. (Note that this ceiling has many large nail holes in it some in the carving itself from the manner in which it was crated and the beams cleated together.)

MISCELLANEOUS

27. As Wyntoon will not start up until after 1st of May O. K. to spend some over $15,000 [of the present monthly budget] and get some of the Garden wall poured.
29. Proceed to remove the brick at the top of the opening back to four inches in the East Room mantle.
31. Arch[itect] to send photographs of largest possible mantels to go into new rooms [of Recreation Wing].

Having allotted a monthly budget of $15,000 for San Simeon, Hearst was back in the building game with a vengeance. Still, he could be quick to blow the whistle. On March 31 Loorz told his local Stolte man Carl Daniels, "They rushed thru plans for the [Grand] Canyon but when Mr. Hearst heard they ran $180,000 (Miss Morgan's estimate not mine) he went up in the air. Much too much says he. Sorry, for if it had run a little over $100,000 I think we would have started there May first with a bang."

The "Sevillian" tile ceiling, which Hearst likewise bought from Arthur Byne and which Loorz mentioned in his notes of March 29, turned up without undue delay. Loorz told Morgan on April 2, "Mr. Williams has located the tile ceiling and is going to bring it up right away." A week later, in speaking of the Recreation Wing's Room #3 and Room #6—between which the Sevillian ceiling was divided—he told her, "The tile ceilings are going in nicely. A little fudging here and there to make carving come out on centers etc but no damage to anything. All subject to shifting if you wish." He also told her in that letter of April 6 that he could start digging the footings for the new Hearst Sunical Bunkhouse on the 12th.

THE WORK ON THE HILLTOP and elsewhere on the ranch continued briskly. On April 12 Loorz told the former gardener Louis Reesing, who lay dying in Menlo Park, "The way we have started out this year, it really looks like we are going to do more actual construction and completing than we have since I have been here." He wrote to his parents in a similar vein on the 14th, saying, "There never has been a time when I have had more to do on this hill. However, I like that because I can give lots of men work (I have them already) and both Mr. Hearst & Miss Morgan are leaving me more and more to my ideas. In that way I am able to make good headway which makes everybody concerned very happy." He wrote to Julia Morgan on the 15th, likewise in that spirit. "We are making headway now and everyone is happy about it," he said. "However," he cautioned, "I fear I'll have to put on the brakes for a while as the limit is not far off." He also said, "Carpenters are making good headway on the tile [Sevillian] ceilings so I intend to start on Tarazona [another Arthur Byne ceiling] to see if we can figure it out."

The odd, the droll, sometimes the absurd are interwoven through this stretch of the George Loorz Papers, just as they are through so many other stretches. "We had to build a fancy crate and ship the elephant to L. A. on hurried notice," Loorz told Bill Murray of Hearst Sunical on April 29. "Mr. Willicombe told me to do it, the Chief's orders. The cost of same will be near $140. A bit expensive but done safely and well. How many bales of alfalfa would that pay for?"

Loorz mentioned the same episode in writing to Louis Reesing on May 1: "At last Louis, you have so often heard, on this hilltop about getting rid of the zoo. Well the elephant was given to the L. A. zoo the other day and though she is only one animal she was a good portion by tonnage." Above all, Loorz was trying to cheer Reesing, who was in his final days and was hoping Loorz could reach his bedside before the end came. Loorz tossed off another entertaining paragraph for Signe Reesing to read her husband: "Jim Rankin is back on the job so I have quite a little amusement. He and I get together and wave the dukes and swim along unmindful of things about us as though it were complete oblivion. It is good to get some of the old timers back and really go to town on the latest dirt. You know I was always pretty good with the shovel and I haven't decided whether it was more than a tie between us."

But back to the business at hand for Loorz et al. The Recreation Wing remained at the forefront, as Loorz's notes from Julia Morgan's visit of May 3 indicate. "Cathkingceil [yet another Arthur Byne ceiling] approved for [Second Floor] room #2," begins one of the notes; "addition of one section necessary. . . . Ceiling is on hand and in very good condition as regards painting." "Show other mantels to Mr. Hearst for approval for other rooms," begins another note. "He approved all as you selected. However, when photographs of three more came next day he liked two of them better and they are slightly smaller so all is well." And another, with a bit of rhyme to it: "Send sample moldings to Sam Berger from Antiques as directed for carving trim for rooms as selected."

Hearst was back in residence for most of May 1937. He wrote to Loorz on the 9th about those same "Ghosts of La Cuesta Encantada" they had gone after in 1934:

> I cannot sleep in my room on account of rattlings on the roof or in the towers when the wind blows.
>
> I will have to abandon my apartment or you will have to find some way of removing these noise-makers.
>
> I have often asked your help and you have often tried to comply, but there has been no betterment. In fact, the noises seem to be worse than ever. They sound like the tin thunder in a theatre.
>
> Please remove everything that is loose and that can possibly rattle.

Please take out the screens, and take down the bells, and take out all scaffolding and encumbrances of any kind.

We must stop these noises if we have to reconstruct the roof and the towers.

A carpenter going up on the roof for fifteen minutes some fine evening (when the wind is NOT blowing) gets us nowhere.

We will have to approach the matter thoughtfully and carefully.

Hearst then said he had "looked over the [China Hill] wall and considered the height of eight feet"; he thought that was "the RIGHT HEIGHT" for it:

We have an eight foot wall at the [Warner Brothers] studio and it is fine.

An eight foot wall here will not cut off anything worth seeing.

We will advance the planting to the wall and the high wall will be GREAT for the roses.

Saturday, May 15, was far from the last time Julia Morgan visited San Simeon. Yet it was the last of her visits to contribute an "Architect's Interview" to the George Loorz Papers. The first of the twenty-eight entries pertained to the Recreation Wing's "Cathkingceil," so named by Arthur Byne for the "Catholic Kings" of Old Spain, Ferdinand and Isabella. Loorz noted, "Ceiling in Room #2 to be added to by splicing out girders and adding another section of panels at either end & sides with two half girders or less, in accordance with Arch[itect]'s sketch. To mix new and old panels when installing." Loorz also noted, "Raise concrete wall at China Hill gradually up to 8 ft. height at lower end of present wall where bank is higher"; "Be prepared to curtail total expenditure on the hilltop to about $10,000 [per month] on or about the first of June, do not cut down just now and make as much showing as possible"; "Have Val [Georges] make some escutcheon plates for handles of Wyntoon doors that have long narrow iron hinges sent up a few weeks ago and send to Mac." Mac McClure and the others at Wyntoon made up a "fine little crew," Morgan said in some notes she gave Loorz during that last interview of May 15. "Wyntoon is cut to $5000 per month," she also said in her notes, "finishing [Servants'] Chalet, tea house, & so far as possible, exterior of Bridge House—with present crew—The material is largely on hand."

ON MAY 16 Signe Reesing wrote to Loorz from Menlo Park. "Louis gets a big kick out of your lighthearted letters," she said, "and he is looking forward to your promised visit, with a twinkle in his Eye he said: do not wait 'too long.'"

Loorz sent Reesing another letter two days later:

> By Golly, Louis, it looks like I'm not going to be able to get away from here without just stealing away and say nothing to anyone. We have been waiting and waiting for the party to leave and day by day they postpone leaving without even asking my permission. . . .
>
> I continue to have occasional battles with my little lady friend. So far I am ahead of the game but only because I keep a chip on my shoulder. I hate to be that way but it is sincere. I will not put up with being slighted or continue to act like a monkey on a string so each time it comes up I ask to be let out. Someday they will call my bluff and perhaps I shall regret it but who knows. You could best advise me on that score [more] than anyone else. I mean that you must have put considerable thot on the subject and honestly, do you now consider that you did the very best thing when you resigned from this place with all its faults and virtues considered together?
>
> I said occasional battles for really both Mr. Hearst and Miss Morgan have been lovely to me and it is only on rare occasions that we lose our sweet dispositions. All three of us have more patience with age.

All kidding aside, Loorz was no doubt serious in saying that Julia Morgan wore his patience thin at times, what with her merciless attention to detail and her compulsive need to accommodate Hearst's every whim. Hearst himself could be equally demanding. The previous day, May 17, he had written to Loorz, "I think we have the wrong system of lighting on the tennis courts." Whereupon he followed with the usual suggestions and pronouncements. Good heavens, Loorz must have thought, what will he come up with next?

But for every thunderbolt there was a gentle breeze. Hearst told Loorz on May 20:

> In order to finish men's bunk house on schedule, we can use men from hill top and cut down proportionately here. I want the men to have their house.
>
> We have so much house here that we can wait.

Loorz wrote to Hearst at his hilltop office on May 22, a

Saturday. He asked to be gone Monday "for urgent personal business in King City" (he had a grammar school to "sign up" there). And he needed to continue to Menlo Park—to see Louis Reesing before it was too late. Hearst fielded his mail seven days a week, rain or shine; Loorz heard back later that Saturday, the reply consisting of Hearst's scrawls on Loorz's original. "O K to leave," went the first scrawl. "I am very sorry about Mr. Reesing," went another. Loorz had concluded his letter with, "I regret that you find it necessary to leave the hilltop, my work is so much more interesting and fun when you are here. I thank you for your cooperation, also that of Mr. Willicombe & Mr. Murray." Hearst said to that, "Thanks. I will be gone about a month."

Loorz saw Louis Reesing in Menlo Park on May 25, an experience he later recounted for Jim Rankin:

> I had a splendid talk with Louis the day before he died. I really must say that I enjoyed my visit and that the memories of that last conversation, in which he could not see me and could barely move his lips, will last permanently. I am pleased to say that he was mentally clear though slow because of weakness and dope. I am happy to say that though Louis had many strong convictions regarding life and religion in general and many of them far from conventional, he still stuck by them to the end. When I put the question to him his answer was, "No George I haven't changed, I still believe the same as I did, I have no regrets, I have no fear and I have no hopes."

The very day Loorz was at Reesing's bedside, Hearst informed Julia Morgan that San Simeon was in for another shutdown—a big shutdown. (Dire news had reached him from New York; his empire's debts now exceeded $100,000,000, and the creditors and stockholders could no longer be dodged.) Loorz knew Hearst had to leave San Simeon on short notice. But he knew nothing of the shutdown, or of the gravity of Hearst's situation, until after his trip to Menlo Park. "Naturally it has been quite a blow to most of our men," he told Julia Morgan on May 29. "Most of them already knew more about it than I did. Apparently it leaked out thru the household's copy of the letter. My family knew all about it when I got home last night. Ha Ha this kind of news travels fast."

Maurice McClure, who was just finishing his first year of engineering at Berkeley, wrote to Loorz on May 30; of course, he hadn't the faintest idea of the shock waves reverberating through San Simeon. "I hope that you and 'Papa Hearst' still love each other," he jokingly said, "and that everything goes well with you up there, because after all that is really a pretty good job in spite of its drawbacks."

Loorz took the jovial words in stride, and then he broke the news to McClure:

> Now, I want to state that I personally feel that Mr. Hearst and I are still the best of friends. In fact, I must say that we had a lot to do personally together during his last visit and it was very pleasant. He became more confident and personal in all of our conversations. He would josh with me and occasionally go so far as to laugh and tap me on the shoulder.
>
> However, Mr. Hearst and money seem to have parted company. If you were fortunate enough to read the *Time* about three weeks ago you would appreciate it fully. However, the fact is that the construction on the hilltop will shut down entirely for the first time. By entirely I mean we will even turn over the commissary to the ranch. I will leave the hilltop. His instructions are that I take the best of my men and complete the large bunk house started at the ranch at a *maximum* expenditure of *not more than* $3000 per month. However, Miss Morgan and I have talked it over and my own salary and other overhead is such a large portion of this that I intend to take most of the time for my own business and a vacation, yet keep it [the Bunkhouse] going by having materials on hand and dealing with the various subs. We will see. He said it was possible that we would start up again in three months but Miss Morgan says no—not this year again.
>
> Further drastic changes are, Albert and Mrs. Albert [Redelsperger] are to go to Wyntoon and Mr. Williams [is] to move into the castle to care for the antiques. At first they were out but he reconsidered and kept them for his visit to Wyntoon when he returns in a few weeks.
>
> The household is reduced to nearly half. The garden department is cut to half. The orchard crew is trimmed. Two watchmen are laid off. You'll be interested in knowing that Ray Swartley, Marks [Eubanks], Dally [Carpio], Lee [Wenzlick], Charlie Harris and a few more will remain.
>
> I have made arrangements with the ranch to have them keep Ray Van Gorden on to run the commissary up here for them and keep the remaining hands well fed. . . .

Now we just this morning started a new contract on the King City School. We should be just about ready for the steel and concrete work and a lot of wrecking about the time you get out. So before I get too many local men on I'd appreciate if you would report there for work. Frank Gendrich will run the job and Elof [Gustafson] will be leadoff man. Same old Cambria [Grammar School] wrecking crew. . . .
I am deeply grieved for such men as Gyorgy, Frandolich etc.

Grieved for the likes of Frank Gyorgy and Frank Frandolich, yes—for the older men who were to be thrown out of work by the shutdown. Loorz could be grateful now, as never before, that he had driven himself the last two years in establishing his outside work in the greater area. And still he remained invaluable to Hearst, and to Morgan, who wrote to him the same day he wrote to Maurice McClure, June 1. Morgan had received copies of two letters Hearst sent Randolph Apperson, the ranch superintendent:

I read it that Mr. Hearst expects you to carry the Ranch House [or rather the Bunkhouse] on the percentage basis of Wyntoon or Grand Canyon. If you will do so at whatever per cent you need,—it will keep all in touch.
I do *not* think Mr. Hearst intended to put this upon Mr. Apperson. Let us make this interpretation unless more direct word comes.

Some confusion was bound to accompany the big shutdown—witness Morgan's trying to clarify things for Loorz. It suffices to say that, with Hearst and Willicombe in New York, Julia Morgan, Bill Murray, Randy Apperson, and George Loorz were dealing with the local situation as best they could. Thus Loorz could write Willicombe on June 3 that he was "working in full cooperation" with Morgan and the others. "We fully appreciate the necessity of the shutdown," he continued, "and are attempting to do so in strict accordance with instructions."

LOORZ KEPT IN CLOSE TOUCH with Julia Morgan through the early part of June; he sent her the following details on the 4th:

The four days this week with my greatly reduced crew have been sufficient to clean up as we should properly do.

I will keep on a part of the force next week and think we can leave things in shape that will please everybody concerned. By that time all of the Pergola beams will be in place and that yard cleaned up.

The last poured section of the [China Hill] wall will be completed and cleaned up. I will have time to cover over the newly placed fields culverts to leave them safe.

We will leave the Billiard Room [Wing] bedrooms completed and I think very nice. . . .

The recreation wing is rapidly taking shape so that we can leave things tidy and arranged to proceed without loss of time when and if they do start again.

Morgan replied on Monday, June 7, saying, "I would like for us to clean up and leave the Hill this weekend—even if you have to 'bring up' help from below to do so." She also told Loorz, "Am still planning to meet you in King City on Friday, getting off the Daylight [train] from San Francisco. I will have to go south that night from somewhere."

Loorz sent Morgan further details on June 8, among which was this one: "Books being brought up to date and accounts being closed out. Records being burned as suggested. Should be able to leave hill entirely on Saturday. Can clean up balance of mail and small accounts from my house below." So at times Julia Morgan *did* burn records. (The story has long been told that she burned her own office records when she retired.) But was she acting symbolically in some way or more in the spirit of housekeeping? Probably the latter.

In another letter Loorz sent Morgan on June 8, he said, "It is already very lonesome here on the hill so many will be glad to leave in the next day or so. Only because they know they have to go anyway."

On June 9 Loorz wrote to Colonel Willicombe at the Ritz Tower, New York:

Unless I receive further notice I shall remain in San Simeon. I have fixed my present salary with Miss Morgan on the Bunkhouse work at $200 per month. It was $500. . . .

As per Miss [Jean] Henry's phone call, I will send in figures soon on dismantling the zoo. I shall submit a separate figure on the excavation in case that is desired.

I wish to report that two more sections of the wall were poured and completed with plaster. Looks like a finished job that far.

All rooms over the Billiard Room completed and ready for furniture. I think Miss Morgan intends to make selections for Mr. Williams to install.

All cars in good shape for Wyntoon. All new or good equipment and trucks being left operating in good shape. Two old trucks out of commission. . . .

Ray Van Gorden will perhaps enjoy a few months off the hill. However, if construction is not to be resumed for a long time, if ever, I'd like you to keep him in mind for a position of his kind [bookkeeper, etc.]. They do not make more loyal, capable or efficient men, as you no doubt are aware.

In the midst of the hubbub, Loorz's wife and sons left for a summer vacation in Nevada. Loorz wrote to themon June 12, the day after his Friday meeting with Julia Morgan:

I met Miss Morgan as per schedule at noon yesterday in King City. Worked all afternoon until 5 o'clock [at the Milpitas Hacienda, Jolon] moving furniture up and down stairs etc. Back and forth all alone and I was beginning to think, oh boy, the side when I get thru with this.

Well we left there about 5 o'clock and headed back thru the Burnett Road. All went well until we got half way between the two dams and the rear end went out. It was nearly seven o'clock then and I wanted to walk on in and send a car back for her but nothing doing. She said she was a good walker and if I'd let her put her finger in my rear pocket she'd like to walk as far as she could anyway. I agreed when she promised she'd let me know when she got too tired.

As would be expected with her, she walked right straight into camp with me. We arrived about 8 o'clock. We walked all that distance in about 1 hour and a half. On top of that she had only a cup of coffee and a bit of pie for lunch and I had a glass of milk and piece of pie. Strange to say I was not even particularly hungry until I started eating about 9 o'clock here on the hill.

After eating and a few minutes rest (not more than 15 minutes), we started the trek thru the rooms up and down stairs. She insisted on calling a taxi from [Steve Zegar's in] San Luis to take her in, wouldn't let me drive her in. So I followed Steve's car to the ranch house [the Bunkhouse] and we got out and went thru that just before midnight.

Except for the fact that I ate a big meal with coffee so late I felt fine. Too full to sleep properly so after a restless night I got up and went out in the garden at about 5:30. . . . With plenty of exercise and good habits I should be at least two years younger when I see you.

Mac McClure, Harry Thompson, and a few others were holding down the fort at Wyntoon all the while. Loorz heard from Mac three times that June. The letters were in Mac's typically graceful script, yet they were atypically devoted to humdrum details. (A painter named Fisher had argued with Thompson, who threatened to "raise hell" with Miss Morgan, and so on.) Mac concluded the first of those letters, dated June 15, by saying, "Everything else is pretty good—only waiting for the next 'surprise.'" He was referring to the big shutdown, presumably.

On June 15 as well, Loorz wrote to Fred Stolte. He told him, "We have a set of plans [to figure] on a state tennis court for the Polytechnic College in San Luis Obispo." He also mentioned having agreed with Hearst to stay on at San Simeon and supervise the Bunkhouse job. "I told him plainly that I would do this gladly in cooperation with his economy [program] if it did not last too long. If more than a few months I asked him to let me know so that I could move nearer my business and could increase the volume of my personal business. It is definitely understood that I am to be away as much as I desire on my own work to make up for the difference in loss of salary." So Loorz had secured the terms—more or less—that he had long sought concerning his outside work. The shutdown had finally brought the matter to a head.

Except for the job coming up at California Polytechnic, Loorz's outside work had recently shifted north. The King City Grammar School was one example. So was the Santa Rita School in Salinas, designed by the Monterey architect C. J. "Jerry" Ryland. And now Loorz was figuring another job in that area, the San Benito County Hospital in Hollister, designed by two other Monterey architects, Robert Stanton and Thomas Mulvin.

Loorz told his father on June 21 that he felt as though he were on vacation. "However," he said, "they call upon me at all times even now. Yesterday, Sunday, they called me from L. A. and wanted some important papers from the hilltop files. No one else was available who knew anything about them so I had to go up and send them along."

Loorz wrote to his wife and sons on the 22nd, telling them he had had a "good day of work on the job and in the office" the day before. "I had Jim Rankin come down last night and took him to the Pines for dinner and then to the movie *Waikiki Wedding.* I enjoyed Bing Crosby's songs and the show was entertaining but was strictly comedy."

He wrote to his wife alone a few days later, on June 26:

Tonight we have agreed to come to a Chamber of Commerce meeting or dinner [in Cambria] in honor of Gov. Merriam and his wife. He is supposed to show up today to open up the or rather accept the Rigdon Memorial.

Tomorrow the coast highway opens up and a good crowd is expected. They have asked Randy [Apperson] to be there at the opening ceremony and he has asked me to come along with him. The opening is to be celebrated somewhere about the half way point between Monterey and here. They are giving a barbecue there and I guess I should get in on it free. What a break for an old bachelor.

The Sebastians have been rushing a lot of things including new refrigerating units together so that they will be properly stocked for the anticipated crowd. I think it will help their business a lot but if they are not prepared to receive it they will make little from it. Manuel is wide awake, Pete is going ahead scornfully.

Loorz followed through on the 28th by recounting the highway ceremony for his family:

Yesterday [Sunday] and Saturday were very exciting days around these parts. You would scarcely know or feel the difference in San Simeon except for more traffic. However, at the [Cambria Pines] Lodge Saturday night we heard Mrs. Merriam say a few nice things of personal appreciation of the real friendly hospitality of this small community. . . . The Governor was not at this meeting but arrived at 2 A. M. that night and had breakfast there the next morning.

A short ceremony by the cross road at San Simeon at 10 A. M. yesterday where the governor cut the ribbons but made no comment. With Randy and Mr. Reid we followed the procession to the Rigdon Memorial where we listened to an impressive ceremony. The governor gave a nice talk as did several others. Mrs. [John] Marquart handled the program very well and made her own personal speech short. With the presence of Mrs. [Elmer] Rigdon in tears the unveiling of the fountain made it appear really as a monument to her deceased husband. Strange enough, though many might not know it, Gov. Merriam knew Mr. Rigdon well. He himself was in the Senate from Southern California in 1917 already. The governor makes a good talk and does it without notes and does it easily. He is a forceful talker and I feel quite favorably toward him. I think perhaps it was a very good thing for the state that he was elected rather than our friend Sinclair.

About this time I was hoping you and the boys were along to hear the leaders of our state but later I was glad. We had to stop the car in a line about 1 mile long when we arrived at the picnic grounds at Big Sur. We waited and waited and I finally walked on ahead to see what was happening. I found they were just starting their ceremonies on that end with another set of speeches and some rock blasting and drilling by the governor and Earl Lee Kelly. I walked back to the car and had Randy park it right there and walk on back down to hear the completion of the pageant and thence to the barbecue about 3/4 of a mile up the creek on the opposite side from our car. As I walked back to Randy passing this long line of stopped cars I was bombarded with questions from those impatiently waiting. They would start honking their cars. There were babies and even ladies in their cars crying. Some were suffering from the heat while others were just plain hungry and tired from sitting in their cars. It was then about 2:30, they had about an hour yet to wait and had had nothing since breakfast except of course those who were fortunate enough to have taken lunches.

Well with the pageant over we went to the barbecue on tickets Randy had been given by the state Chamber of Commerce Officials. We sat with a distinguished crowd some of whom were introduced and all of us very close to the Governor where he made an even better and longer speech. . . .

. . . It was well after 5 o'clock when we got away and was nearly 7:30 when we arrived home.

Loorz concluded that memorable letter to his family by saying, "It has been real foggy here on the coast for three days but they say hotter than the devil on the hilltop." What an image that evokes: the perfumed gardens, the blinding white terraces, the shimmering Neptune Pool, the imperial castle itself lying silent in the sun under a polished blue sky, with scarcely a soul to behold the grand spectacle, as though it were the abandoned stronghold of a Persian king. And below on the coastal plain, half hidden in the gray, the string of cars plying the new road—the road named in honor of Hearst's nemesis, Franklin Delano Roosevelt, the champion of the New Deal.

The opening of the new highway fascinated Loorz. The same day he wrote to his wife and sons, June 28, he addressed an equally long letter to his wife alone:

> There certainly is a lot of traffic by here now. A continuous line of cars just as on the other highway [U. S. 101]. The Sebastians have tripled their business I do believe. They want to rush some work in on toilets as they have only the one and that not very good. I really believe a lot of work will come out of the traffic by here. It is such a long trip from here to the next service place that they should do very well. Somehow it doesn't feel so isolated as before. It seems to me that in a jaunt I can be where things are active. I know I'll keep a closer eye on Monterey from now on. Carl [Daniels] can look after things in San Luis.

Loorz had begun that letter by saying, "Well we received another of those many surprises associated with this place. Mr. Hearst is supposed to be here Wednesday night [June 30]. Oh me, this will be fine for those on the Hilltop who are unhappy and still don't know what and when to do anything."

THE HIGHWAY CONTINUED to hold its fascination—and Hearst arrived as anticipated—as Loorz told his sons and parents on July 1:

> Cars are still going by by the dozen. I'll bet those that have business locations along the other highway certainly are noticing the loss. The Sebastians are very busy and have a fine gasoline business. Every business in Cambria is going great guns. They have to turn people away from the eating and sleeping houses and cabins. If I had a few extra thousands I would build a nice dining lodge with cabins in some nice spot between here and Monterey. It is so far between supply places that it would go well.
>
> People who have car trouble have to send word down by other cars and that is often as much as 50 miles. So naturally they have to wait quite a while. If I was Bud Sweeters I'd certainly look around for a likely sight [*sic*] for a service station and repair shop together with some cabins. I think with his mechanical ability he could clean up, if he got started right away before too many get into the business.

Mr. Hearst is back on the hill. Landed yesterday in the nice new plane. I haven't seen him and will not try to unless he calls me. He may want to start something right away if he sees me. If he did I would not be able to come up and get you [boys]. I'd like to wait until I get a few of these plans out of the way. Most of the work we are figuring is around Salinas.

Hearst's return to San Simeon was far from triumphal, as Loorz told Julia Morgan on July 2:

Now I haven't contacted Mr. Hearst. He knows I am here and can call if he wants me. I'll stick closely for a while so that I can be of whatever service he might desire.

However, Miss Morgan, from Randy I learn that Mr. Hearst is a pathetic, broken man. I don't want to bother you with this sad news. However, sad I feel that you want to know. Apparently his creditors are quite anxious to hurt him if they can. Further a government tax investigation seems eminently possible. Please let me repeat that I have heard only what Randy came down to confide in me last night.

I hope that Mr. Hearst is really not as badly off as he [Randy?] feels. We so often face difficulty with loss of confidence, oftimes needlessly so. I am so sorry for him. I am glad to hear that Randy reports Miss Davies to be very considerate of him, to be his only real comfort. They are here on the hilltop alone. She stole him away from New York as he seemed so worried and confined there that she feared he might not stand it. He was not out of the hotel once since he went back.

I hope further Miss Morgan that you will be provided with Funds to keep Wyntoon paid up and the Men's Quarters [the Bunkhouse] as well. I hope with things as they might be, that you will protect yourself. I know you would do all you can to help Mr. Hearst and share his burden. The truth is that all your own worries might not help him a bit. You have worried so for Mr. Hearst these many years that you should feel you have more than done your part. You should, therefore, obtain all funds due you, if possible and enjoy a little the results of your efforts.

Morgan answered Loorz on July 7:

Mr. Hearst called me last night—unfortunately the line connection was poor & my voice extra bad on acct of a cold— He wanted a to-date line-up at Wyntoon & said he would probably not come up before the end of the month— I wrote today telling him how fresh & spring like things were, & how I hoped he would come before the heat & dust took toll of its beauty—It would do him good I am sure—there is enough activity & much he has not seen at all— It is all I can think of doing—.

Loorz had said in his letter of the 2nd, "Please forgive me Miss Morgan, if I've been too personal. I feel free to talk this way Miss Morgan for I feel our friendship is real." Morgan closed her letter of the 7th with words of gratitude and reassurance: "Many thanks George—yes—we are *friends.*"

(As for Morgan's saying there was "enough activity" at Wyntoon, Mac McClure had written to Loorz on June 29, saying, "I suppose this job, too, will be 'folding up' before long. I look for it any day now. It seems a sad ending after the years of comparitive [*sic*] plenty, but I will be glad to be away from it when the time comes.")

Loorz's eye for a good business prospect extended to the new highway, even as he kept track of the Bunkhouse job and his outside work from his house in San Simeon. He wrote to his wife on July 7 in Nevada:

> I hope to go up to the hill this afternoon and check up on a few things. At the same time I hope to see Mr. Hearst. I really think I will ask him if he would lease me a piece of ground near San Simeon, on the Highway for a service station. It might be mean for me to attempt to take some of the Sebastian business but this is a free country. I talked to Randy about it and he wished me luck and would certainly recommend it if Mr. Hearst asks him. He'd like to keep more of the traffic on the highway [bypass] instead of thru San Simeon.

Loorz also wrote to Julia Morgan that day. "They have had a few guests [on the hill] over the holidays and not the movie crowd," he told her. "Reports come in that Mr. Hearst is feeling much better again and is pleased about the California [state income tax] nine month law. The governor's secretary and wife were among the guests." He also told her, "The highway has continued to be patronized at an unusual rate. No one in their wildest dreams had any idea it would be used so much. We are no longer isolated here in San Simeon."

Loorz's plan of running his own gas station apparently came to naught. But the letter he sent his wife on July 8 showed that soon others would be running their stations—to the benefit of the F. C. Stolte Co. :

> Oh boy, I have Carl [Daniels] and the whole gang here this morning working on everything imaginable. The demand for construction is suddenly taking wing in these parts. Besides the three jobs that go in in Salinas Saturday, we must get out sketches and figures on at least three service stations for different places up and down this road.
>
> It keeps me mumbling to myself to keep all hands posted so that we will make some fast accurate progress. No doubt we cannot lose out on all of it. I expect Cap Evans here this morning. He wants a service station, cabin arrangements and living quarters for his own family for a sight [*sic*] just above the [Piedras Blancas] lighthouse on the ocean side.

(The San Simeon branch of the F. C. Stolte Co. got the Evans job as well as some of the others Loorz mentioned.)

Loorz couldn't get that new highway off his mind. The scenery through Big Sur was breathtaking, and he loved to drive fast over the endless curves and grades. The sense of freedom was exhilarating. More and more he looked north, thought north, felt a homeward pull north. He told Julia Morgan on July 21, "I very often go to Salinas and King City now and along the new coast highway where I have a couple of small Service Stations under construction. Therefore, if you would enjoy it I'd be glad to pick you up at your place in Monterey and in two hours we would be here. If you don't make it this week why not plan it that way, or I can even call this week."

HEARST REMAINED AT San Simeon all the while—he hadn't gone to Wyntoon yet—and he naturally made his presence known to Loorz, Joseph Willicombe often acting as the intermediary. July 28 brought a message about the baby giraffe; July 30 brought one about those persistent noises in the Gothic Suite; July 31 brought news of Hearst's concern over coyotes and the safety of the zoo animals.

Loorz was the man Hearst and Willicombe typically turned to in these situations, yet his main job through the summer of

1937 was the superintending of the Bunkhouse. In writing to Julia Morgan about the job on August 11, he made an interesting comment regarding that normally reclusive woman: "Several people of Cambria have remarked that they were happy to see you in Cambria Pines and to seemingly enjoy it. They hope you will do it more often."

Morgan wrote to Loorz on August 16, saying, "Mr. Hearst flies to Wyntoon today." She also said that she would be going up the next night and that she would meet with Loorz at San Simeon and discuss the Bunkhouse on the 19th "if possible." The traveling about that Julia Morgan routinely did up and down California was remarkable. She was by no means young, having turned sixty-five early that year; but she was as spry as ever. She had to be. Besides, Hearst was nine years her senior—and *he* hadn't shown any lasting signs of slowing down.

The beckoning north, along with Hearst's declining fortunes, prompted Loorz to relocate, as he told the plasterer Dell Clausen on October 6:

> If this falls thru here with Mr. Hearst I am planning on moving into Monterey for permanent location. I had thot about San Luis Obispo for a long time but it is a dead place. Nothing but small buildings around this country. In Monterey I will be close to Salinas, Hollister, King City, etc. Besides I anticipate there will be lots of construction up and down this coast due to the new highway.
>
> I have gone up and down this coast so much the past month that it was easy for me to make the decision. Now that my family have become used to the sea coast I realize it will be difficult to keep them away from it for a very long [time]. . . .
>
> Drove around to King City yesterday and met Miss Morgan. Spent a very busy day rushing around furniture and curtains with her at Jolon. It looks real nice Dell. . . . We got back to the ranch bunk house about 5:30 and went over that. It certainly is a nice looking building Dell. Anyway the whole day was sort of fun again.

But Loorz didn't wait for things to fall through at San Simeon. In mid-October he went ahead and negotiated for a house on Franklin Street in Monterey Heights, almost directly across the street from the house Julia Morgan owned. The deal fizzled, but there were others for him to pursue in the area. His plans were still in abeyance when he wrote to Paul Polizzotto on the 22nd; Polizzotto was a friend of his from San Luis Obispo who was traveling in Italy:

> I am still in San Simeon as you see. Have not quite finished the Ranch Bunkhouse but soon will. It is real nice looking and I'm proud to have had so much to do with it. In other words Paul there is more of me in this house than in the big one on the hill.
>
> Money is still scarce on the Hilltop and little or no work except repairs is going on. I have handled it but it hasn't been necessary for me to go up the hill very often. When I do the place seems so lonesome with no workmen around.
>
> Mr. Hearst is still at Wyntoon, Mt. Shasta, and seems to be enjoying himself. Looks like he will remain there until after Thanksgiving. Then he will have to get out of the state for a month [to exempt himself from the income tax]. Then we hope he will return here to resume some kind of work. If he doesn't then I now think my future address will be Monterey, Calif.
>
> The wife and I and boys are going to Monterey tomorrow to look at some old residences. I think I will buy one. Then if things blow up here at any time I'll have a permanent address and some business headquarters other than in my bag.

The Loorzes' house-hunting trip that late October weekend bore fruit. They found a modest home in the Spanish style, quite like their home in San Simeon, but overlooking a far more historic bay. The house lay just beyond the Monterey city limits, at 203 Pine Avenue in Pacific Grove.

BACK AT SAN SIMEON, Loorz kept working on the Bunkhouse; of course, he also kept after his outside work, which continued its northerly shift. The Santa Cruz City Hall, for example, designed by Jerry Ryland of Monterey, was coming up for bid, and Loorz was preparing to submit figures. He got the job—and went on to handle it through the new Pacific Grove branch of the F. C. Stolte Co.

Though he had protected himself by buying the house in Pacific Grove, Loorz was still biting his nails over his arrangement with Hearst. He wrote to Julia Morgan in that regard on November 26:

I have been anxious to see you and talk to you and I am really worried about my work here. Somehow I do not feel that much work will be done on the hill in the near future. Up to now I have earned my way. Next week should see the end of work at the Men's Club House [the Bunkhouse]. . . .

As I have stated previously, I am very fond of my connection here on the hilltop. I am grateful for the privilege of working with you and Mr. Hearst. I want that connection to continue if it can be made to advantage to all of us. I would be pleased to remain here if Mr. Hearst could afford to proceed with sufficient budget to permit me to earn my $125 per week. As it is, that would be a wasteful luxury for Mr. Hearst and I would accept it as a charitable gift.

Miss Morgan, I have not written or talked to Mr. Hearst or Mr. Willicombe [about this] since construction shut down last spring. Mr. Hearst called for me once when he last spent a day here but I did not return until late that night and he flew away before I contacted him the next morning. Therefore, Miss Morgan with your permission I would like to pay Mr. Hearst a personal visit and discuss the above frankly and openly with him. I assure you I will not embarrass him or encourage him to make some expenditures he cannot afford.

You will agree that our firm could do with a little more efficient management around the bay district. I intend that it will be one of the most efficient firms in the Bay Area. My method of bringing that about will depend upon my own place of residence. I have procrastinated too long already.

Hearst had to absent himself from California during December 1937 to qualify as a non-resident under the new tax law. (He and the party repaired to the Hawaiian Islands that month.) Loorz's request of November 26 was shelved. On December 14 he wrote to Julia Morgan again. He was undecided about moving to Pacific Grove—he could rent that house for the time being, if need be—and he was also thinking of moving to Alameda, Fred Stolte having moved the main office there from Oakland in 1936:

I am sorry that I did not get a chance to see Mr. Hearst. The reason is that I think it advisable for me to move from San Simeon so that my boys can start the next semester in their new school. I am certain you have explained carefully to Mr. Hearst regarding this, but I did want to see him personally. I am unable to decide definitely where we will move depending of course upon the amount of work that might be done on the Hill. If it were at all possible that Mr. Hearst would resume construction on a fair scale later in the spring, I would move to Monterey, where I could reach the Hilltop within 2 hours notice at any time. From where I could make at least two weekly visits with ease. Where I could conveniently keep in close touch with you.

If the proposed construction would be very small, it might be better for me to move to Alameda.

I know that this decision must be my own, for I would not put either you or Mr. Hearst in a position to feel obligated to carry on a certain amount of work because of arrangements with me. I merely mention these things as thoughts that have occurred to me in making my new plans. . . .

It so happens that we just signed a contract for a Gymnasium at Campbell, [and] a City Hall at Santa Cruz. I feel that we have a splendid chance of being the low bidder on the King City Auditorium next Tuesday. Monterey would be a nice center from which to manage these jobs. Of course I must not forget the many possibilities offered by personal contacts with industrial heads around the Bay Area.

I must mention that one of my chief concerns holding me to San Simeon is because I have been able in no small way to take care of our mutual friends such as Frank Souza, Frank Gyorgy, Peter Petersen, [John] McFadden, Ray Van Gorden and Frank Frandolich.

George Loorz had indeed a big decision to make. And it was ultimately a decision that only he could make, not Julia Morgan or William Randolph Hearst. His papers are too spotty over the weeks ahead to disclose when he opted for Monterey—that is to say, for Pacific Grove. But that was his decision, a decision he made, at least in part, because he learned there *would* be some work at San Simeon in 1938. As he told his old friend George Wright on January 18 of that new year, "After the first of February I can be reached at 203 Pine Street [Avenue], Pacific Grove, where our office will be located. Will run the Hearst Construction from there."

Not quite three weeks later, on February 4, 1938, Hearst sent Loorz that glowing letter from San Simeon with which this narrative began:

I shall be very happy to have you refer anyone to me regarding the high quality of your construction work at San Simeon.

I have had the most complete satisfaction with everything that you have supervised and executed.

You have been most careful, not only about the quality of the construction, but about the cost.

I cannot imagine it possible for anyone to be more competent and conscientious, and I am glad to testify to that effect.

Loorz treasured that letter for the rest of his life, until he died in 1978. His wife treasured it too; and when she died in 1989, her sons found the letter among her personal effects, still in its original envelope.

EPILOGUE

LOORZ OFFICIALLY BEGAN operating from his house in Pacific Grove on Tuesday, February 1, 1938. That morning, Ray Van Gorden wrote to him from Hearst Camp:

> Well Miss Morgan was on the job yesterday. I was surprised at about noon by a phone call from the gate that she was on her way up. The wind was just howling and the rain was coming down in sheets. She was up with Pete [Petersen] for a couple of hours and went back to San Luis at about 5 P.M. Even John Vanderloo didn't get to see her. This morning everything is quiet and the storm is over until possibly tomorrow or the next day. I heard over the radio last night that the San Simeon [Big Sur] road had a big slide and was closed indefinitely. You got through just in time but it won't be so handy to come down weekly all the way around [on Highway 101].

So the saga continued to unfold. And it would continue to do so, not only in 1938 but also into the early 1940s, though by then the references to Hearst, Morgan, San Simeon, and Wyntoon would become increasingly scattered in the Loorz Papers.

Van Gorden next wrote to Loorz on February 7, mentioning that Julia Morgan had been on the hill again. "She seemed to be in wonderful spirits and spent quite a lot of time with Pete," he said. "Mr. Hearst isn't very active these days," he also said, "especially since the weather has been so miserable. He shows up for his lunch around 3 or 4 o'clock and then for dinner at about 9. I haven't seen him around the grounds for over a week."

But Hearst was active enough, and inspired enough, to authorize Julia Morgan to resume work on the Recreation

Wing—hence her two trips to San Simeon thus far in the winter of 1938. We may well ask—just as she and Loorz and Van Gorden surely asked—how Hearst could be pushing ahead. Somehow he had found the means, for the moment at least; that was all that mattered. Morgan wrote to Loorz on February 8, explaining the "setup" of things. "We are no longer a part of 'Sunical,'" she said, "but are to work directly under Mr. Hearst as employer." Then she added gloomily, "It is hard to tell what work will go on and to what extent, but it does not look as though there would be much done this year."

Loorz began making his weekly visits from Pacific Grove, the bad weather notwithstanding. ("It is raining and blowing like hell here today," Van Gorden told him on February 18.) Still, Loorz could tell Morgan the next day, "All hands seem to know what is wanted and are making progress on the ceiling and recreation [wing] rooms in accordance with your instructions." And so the work went, with a small crew, into March and April.

The focus soon shifted to Wyntoon, to which Loorz made a trip, a kind of reconnaissance, early in May 1938; he had last seen Wyntoon before he began his six-year stint at San Simeon. As the chauffeur Jud Smelser said in writing Loorz on May 6, "Everything seems to be doing nicely here [at San Simeon] except the coffers. God only knows what has happened to them of late they almost seem to be non-existent. . . . It looks like Wyntoon soon."

Why Wyntoon? Because Hearst thought he could stay there—and, never forget, because he thought he could *build* there—more economically than he could at San Simeon. Mac McClure and some others were already on hand, preparing for the Chief's arrival. Loorz wrote to Mac on May 8, right after he got back to Pacific Grove:

> Thanks for the report on available materials in the Bridge House. We will certainly use that material if we need it for it doesn't look like we'll get to do anything on the Bridge House this year. However, one never can tell with this organization. . . .
>
> Mr. Hearst was pleased to hear that we are doing something at Wyntoon. He wants it to go faster, however, and is willing to stop any department at San Simeon to do more up there. I see that we can

look forward to an increased budget for the time being at least. From the intonations in his voice I gather that he is making this budget with an ill-afforded gesture. Frankly he did not look too happy and well to me. Perhaps the reaction from an exciting party [in Santa Monica] on his birthday, together with the various and sundry ramifications that always accompany such parties. . . .

Mr. Hearst would like the two front towers [on Angel House] promptly but does not care if we don't even start those on the rear.

Loorz wrote an equally key letter to the McCloud River Lumber Co. that same day, May 8, spelling out some new arrangements:

We are resuming construction at Wyntoon on a small scale this year and will therefore be purchasing various materials.

From Mr. Kower [the caretaker], you will know that the F. C. Stolte Co. will not handle the work this year. Though I own half that company, I will manage the work as Superintendent of Construction, as an individual.

For economical reasons the small amount of work will be handled by transferring our San Simeon Crew.

To make certain there will be no mix-up in the billing etc. kindly keep all records entirely separate from the Hearst Sunical Account or the W. R. Hearst Private [Account] which will exist during Mr. Hearst's anticipated visit.

This account will therefore be known as the W. R. Hearst Construction [Account] c/o Geo. C. Loorz.

Mac answered Loorz on May 10. Veteran that he was of the Wyntoon wars, he knew the proposed resumption of work could fall through any minute. He said sarcastically, "[Willy] Pogany's men were back for a day last week to do some touching up on their [exterior mural] pictures. They thought they would all be back for a Summer's work soon!" By mailing his letter on the 11th, Mac had time for a belated postscript: "A letter from Miss Morgan this A. M. mentions an itemized program both here and at San Simeon."

Loorz got a similar letter from Julia Morgan, dated May 10:

It is decided that

1. Gyorgy is to paint at San Simeon all summer.
2. John Vanderloo and an apprentice helper, and Frank Frandolich and helper, are to cast and set stone at San Simeon all summer.

3. Ceiling and mantel work [in the Recreation Wing] is to stop with this week at San Simeon.
4. Petersen, plus those you arrange to send, are to go up as soon as possible to Wyntoon.
5. Enough more stone men are to be employed as needed to make all possible advancement on the two front Sleeping Beauty house [Angel House] turrets, and front entrance,—and from there go onto Bridge gate.
6. Mr. Hearst says bridge will have to be raised this Fall, which means looking out for necessary changes in the footings of the Bridge gate.
7. Thinking it over, if carpenters can be up early in week, they can start right in on turret framing, propping up, or cantering out, until stone work is up.
8. I will go up when sure the workers are up there.

With the usual variations—Loorz was asked, for instance, to reopen the Burnett Road after the heavy storms—the program Morgan outlined held true over the next few weeks. But then word came that both San Simeon and Wyntoon would shut down on the first of July. At San Simeon, one of the most interesting jobs ever attempted there took place in those waning days: the installation of four massive marble reliefs in the walls of the Assembly Room. "Frandy [Frandolich] and I have been sweating blood trying to make some headway," Ray Van Gorden told Loorz of that job on June 24. "I think after we have the first one in place the remainder will come a lot easier. . . . It is quite a job even to bring those statues [reliefs] into the Assembly Room. We have to cut all the anchors and then unrivet the cleats and change them into their new position. It all takes a lot of time."

AT WYNTOON, MEANWHILE, there was a reprieve: work would continue for the time being, according to the latest word from on high. Loorz wrote to Pete Petersen on July 3, "Well things change every day, don't they? It looks like you might be up there quite a while now. Miss Morgan thot it would be three or four weeks yet to do what Mr. Hearst still wants to do. However, I know as long as he is there you will have so many things to do besides work on the Angel House that you won't be able to accomplish much."

As for Loorz's role in the new scheme of things, his letter of July 5 to Joseph Willicombe is revealing:

> Please advise Mr. Hearst that after July 1st I will not be on any of his payrolls. However, I wish to assure him that I will continue to supervise the [Burnett] road improvements as economically as I know how. I will merely keep in touch on my regular visits to my other work in San Luis Obispo County. As the budget is small, I cannot work a crew continuously. I am using my own men to do this work.
>
> Further, though we have no real authority over the present work at Wyntoon we are assisting in the purchases, payrolls, etc., for the convenience of Miss Morgan and the men on the job. We will continue this service as desired until the work ceases.

Loorz wrote to Mac McClure a few days later. "It is really funny," he said, "my present connections with the Hearst organization. I'm meddling with your work up there and doing some road work at the ranch. I have no authority and I am on no pay roll. Call me what you will."

One man thrown out of work by the latest shutdown at San Simeon was Lo On, a Chinese cook. In late June Loorz had written to Lo On's countryman George Wu, saying, "Lo told me he was going to start a small Chop Suey joint in Cambria. If he does, I hope he makes good." Lo On wrote to Loorz on July 20 from Elko, Nevada; he had hired on with the Western Pacific Railroad and was cooking for 115 laborers at every meal. He told a poignant story:

> I am sorry I didn't see you before I leave the Camp. I have told Mr. Ray Van Gorden to give my regards and say good bye to you. I left the Hill Top Kitchen in the evening of June 15 to Cambria. I stay there one night and next day and went to San Luis Obispo then I went to San Francisco by train to my sister's house. Meantime my sister show me a letter from my house in China. My home was destroyed by Japanese bombs. I feel very depressed. So I don't feel like going back to Cambria to open the Chop Suey house, the business condition is very bad for me and I lost lots of money.

Loorz answered Lo On in Elko on July 29:

> Sorry to hear that your home was destroyed during the time of stress in China, Lo On, but I know that you are like all of your people and will not give up even though the odds may be great

against you. I, and the world as a whole, look upon the bombings with great distaste. However, Lo On, no matter what the Japanese might do, they will never be able to conquer the Chinese people because your people had had a civilization and culture of a very high order in the past and will again in the future. The invading countries might annex much of the Chinese territory, but it will always be China, even though ruled by another nation. This because the Chinese want to be, and will be, a distinct nationality.

So Loorz remained the confidant, the dear friend—and sometimes the father figure—to a wide array of correspondents, from a draftsman as highly placed as Mac McClure to a cook as humble as Lo On. The George Loorz Papers are much the richer for it.

Loorz may have been off the Hearst payroll as of July 1; but, on one occasion at least, he was called to Wyntoon just the same during August 1938. And he could usually count on Mac to keep him abreast of developments there. Mac wrote to him on September 1, for example, telling him, "[Willy] Pogany [the muralist] was sent home (for the season at least) the Tuesday after you were here." Mac added, "We don't know what our program is, if any, during Miss M.'s absence. (She sails to Europe in a week as you no doubt know.)"

Loorz and Ray Van Gorden were writing back and forth at this time in 1938. Van Gorden reported on August 31, "There isn't much activity in this neck of the woods with the mine closed down as well as the Camp. With the [county] election over Cambria will now lie down and die." Loorz answered on September 4, "I am a little like you are about Cambria and its slow death. However, I think with the increased use of the [coast] road which is inevitable they will gain as much as they lose from local industry. However, again, no town is as nice that is dependent upon transients as upon local industry." Van Gorden wrote Loorz again on September 7, adding a wry postscript: "They have discontinued the mail service to the Hill. Mr. Hearst must be broke."

Hearst was back at San Simeon by October. Small numbers of guests came and went. Hearst busied himself, as always, with the running of his newspapers. His top-heavy empire was in a kind of receivership, but he had retained editorial control of his papers; he was a newspaperman at heart, more than anything else. All manner of his assets—even newspapers—were being partly or, in some instances, entirely liquidated by 1938. Not the least among them were thousands of the art objects he owned. A man named C. C. Rounds had been sent out by the New York office to make inventories at San Simeon and Wyntoon; Rounds's counterpart in California was H. C. Forney, who worked out of Julia Morgan's office and whose wife, Lillian Forney, was Miss Morgan's secretary. Ray Van Gorden wrote Loorz on October 4:

> Mr. Forney was telling me that Mr. LeFeaver is now working for the Fair [the Golden Gate International Exposition] and that his wife [Mrs. Forney] is all that Miss Morgan has in her office.
>
> He was of the opinion that Mr. Hearst might never start [building] again but when I told him that Miss Morgan had written me that he probably would start in the spring again providing his business continued to improve, he said he meant that he would never start on a large scale. He is probably only guessing like the most of us must do.

LOORZ WAS AT SAN SIMEON at least once that October of 1938, the last time he was there until 1939. All the while, of course, he was hard at work building up the Pacific Grove branch of the F. C. Stolte Co. "As usual we have been rushing," he told his parents on October 8. "However, we now have some $300,000 worth of work. . . . We enjoy a real reputation as being one of, if not, the biggest contractors in the middle part of this state."

Mac McClure wrote to him on November 9 from West Los Angeles, a month after Wyntoon shut down for the season. "The program, as far as I am concerned, with Hearst work is most uncertain," he said. "Presumably there will be some work done up North next Summer, but if it is to be done on the cramped budget of last season, I don't want to be involved. As you know W. R. H. was not especially satisfied with results." Mac considered himself "free to look for other connections" now; he was thinking of building a duplex or triplex in Palo Alto "for income." He also knew he could hire on with Fred Stolte and George Loorz—should he decide, in fact, to break free of the Hearst connection for the first time since 1929. Mac would eventually go over to Stolte and Loorz, but it would take Pearl Harbor for him to do it.

On March 30, 1939, Loorz wrote to Alex Rankin, James Rankin's son:

> Mr. Willicombe calls occasionally and Mr. Apperson needs information from time to time so that I keep in fairly close touch with the Hilltop.
>
> Every now and then, an enquiry comes up that sounds like work is anticipated but I doubt very much that it will happen this year.

Loorz was almost wrong, for on April 4 Julia Morgan sent him the following notes on proposed "East Room Changes":

> As regards the moving back of the fireplace in the East Wing [the East Room]—it means:
>
> 1. Removing the present plumbing fixtures, pipe lines, etc., including providing entrance to men's toilet from Billiard Room stairway.
> 2. Taking down and resetting mantel and the 2 doorways.
> 3. Extending the (present design) marble pavement.
> 4. Making and carving the ceiling extension.
> 5. Decorating it.
> 6. Revamping doors to Billiard Room to conform to East Room.
> 7. Plastering new work.
> 8. Electrical changes.

Evidently the East Room fireplace had remained a chronic problem. It was just as evident that Hearst was keen on correcting the problem, regardless of the expense. "My guess is that it will cost between $15,000 & $20,000," Loorz told Julia Morgan on June 5, 1939. "'Tis honestly only a rash guess with a tendency to play safe and to include all possible costs." He also said, "For the sake of our mutual friends I would love to see some work start at San Simeon. However, this particular job in the East Room might include many many headaches. When completed Mr. Hearst would have a beautiful large room but I think the fireplace would still smoke."

How could Hearst even have been considering a job on that scale? A rumor was afoot that recently "15 million had come into the kitty" (so Ray Van Gorden told Loorz on May 4). Yet that was all it had proved to be—a rumor. Still, Hearst wasn't about to sit on his hands and be a model citizen. He had been sitting enough as it was.

In that same letter of June 5 in which Loorz discussed the East Room, he also told Morgan about his recent trip to San Simeon:

> I just returned this noon from two days on the hilltop. I went down in answer to a request from Mr. Hearst thru Mr. [Nigel] Keep. He wanted me to run a survey of China Hill and lay out a narrow Pergola Pathway around the hill. It is too far for him to walk to the present one [Orchard Hill] and walking on China Hill is now nearly impossible. He always walks around the hill [China Hill] now on the road which is both dangerous and not too pleasant. I'm certain it was just another air castle but enjoyed the two days in the sunshine and really worked hard to complete [it] so I could come back this morning.

Nothing ever came of the proposed work in the East Room or on China Hill, though the two days Loorz spent at San Simeon were enjoyable, as he said, and gave him a chance to see Mac, who was also there.

Mac wrote to Loorz from Wyntoon on July 13, 1939, telling him, "Pete arrived last evening and for the time being we will get along with a local helper." He mentioned that "the present work will consist of re-framing in Angel House."

Loorz wrote to Mac on November 1, saying he hoped that the work was "going along nicely" and that there would be "no winter shut down":

> Saw Miss Morgan a couple of weeks ago and she said she had been up there once. Didn't have much to say. Mentioned you were working on the Bend [the old Charles Wheeler place] as well as the Angel House. She looks better since her sister [-in-law, Mrs. Parmelee Morgan] passed away. She was terribly run down there for a while going to L. A. once or twice a week. She still goes to visit the little girl [her niece, Judith Avery Morgan], to make her think there is really still someone who cares. How many of us would inconvenience ourselves that much.

Mac answered on November 4, with a classic of a letter rivaling those he had written a few years earlier when Wyntoon was at its height:

It was good to hear from you after a long time— I guess the last time we had a visit was the day spent gathering fox tails on China Hill!

It has been quite a long Season here. For me at least, it has amounted to as much as other years. We started in on Angel House in July but were soon switched to The Bend where quite a nice alteration job is in progress.

Mr. Hearst has been quite contented—I think— He would like a little more action but he is getting all we can produce with 3 carpenters, 3 stone masons, and two laborers.

Jas. Rankin and Co. were called in two weeks ago to rough plumb a remodeled wing at The Bend and also to put in the pipes for steam heat. . . .

Mr. H., has been jumping around with his program, even more than usual. One day it is one thing and the next day another. I think he tries to get more out of us by heaping on the work. As it now stands, we will spend the rest of this year getting, what is now under way, closed in for the winter.

Miss Morgan came up the one time to check items on the [Hearst-Cosmopolitan] bungalow [at Twentieth Century Fox] I think. She had little to say about the work here. I have been more or less in touch with her right along and write to her for information now and then.

All in all this year is no better and no worse than usual. The whole outfit is "screwy" and the best thing one can do is to not let it "get" you down.

Mac said that, after spending the holidays in Detroit, he would be back in California early in 1940.

The weeks and months skipped ahead, 1940 proving a good deal less eventful than 1938 or 1939 where the Hearst work was concerned. A variation on the San Simeon and Wyntoon pattern came along in March 1940. Loorz told the carpenter Pete Petersen on the 16th that he was "figuring a job for Mr. Hearst in Los Angeles." He also said:

Suppose you heard that the Bridge at Wyntoon washed out. Logs got in front of the bridge and the whole flat was covered with two foot of water. A good deal of damage was done but mostly mud.

Mac went up to look things over. He said he didn't think Mr. Hearst could afford to go to Wyntoon this year. That sounds funny.

The job Loorz mentioned in Los Angeles proved to be an alteration of the Marion Davies house at 1700 Lexington Road, Beverly Hills. Loorz told his parents on March 30, "They took a figure from the man [Frank Hellenthal] who has done most of Mr. Hearst's work down there since I was down there in 1928. Well they thot he was a bit high on this one and called me in to figure [it] and I got it."

Loorz sent Pete Petersen to Beverly Hills to work on the Davies job, which ran through the spring and early summer of 1940; Mac McClure was also on the job. Loorz gave Petersen some written instructions on July 2, toward the end of the job: "As I said by phone, remove and carefully crate the fine mantel and have it stored at the Beach House [in Santa Monica]. Order your materials and construct the new mantel as soon as possible. Tell the painter to go ahead with the painting of the Patio and exterior garden walls clear around. Try to do it with the one coat job if possible."

Mac was back at Wyntoon soon after that—and so was Hearst, despite Mac's having said earlier in 1940 that he didn't think Hearst could afford to go there. Indeed, Mac told Loorz on August 20 that Hearst had him "going on the usual schemes, sketches etc."

As for Loorz and his Pacific Grove branch of the F. C. Stolte Co., the Marion Davies job, at roughly $25,000, was of only passing importance. In taking that job, Loorz was maintaining contact with Hearst; above all, he was doing Hearst and Miss Davies a favor; he knew from the outset that the long commute to Beverly Hills would be a nuisance. He had plenty of work closer to home—schools, residences, sewer plants, even a government contract or two. In fact, government work was about to become the staple of the F. C. Stolte Co. The era of preparedness, brought on by the recent outbreak of war in Europe, steered Loorz and Stolte toward defense contracts; Pearl Harbor reinforced that direction and kept the partners going that way into the mid-1940s. Their first big defense contract was that of Camp McQuaide, near Watsonville, which Loorz landed at nearly $500,000 in October 1940.

AT THE SAME TIME Loorz and Stolte were building up mightily, Hearst was still liquidating mightily. The northern portion of his greater San Simeon ranch—the portion that surrounded Jolon and Mission San Antonio, and that amounted to some 150,000 acres—went to the federal government late in 1940. The Milpitas Hacienda was part of the sale and became the showpiece of the new Hunter Liggett Military Reservation (now Fort Hunter Liggett). And to think Hearst had been remodeling the Milpitas Hacienda as recently as 1937! Hearst's Grand Canyon property had already been sold to the federal government, in 1939. So much for that dream. Its realization had seemed so close just a few years earlier.

Pete Petersen, like Mac McClure, went back to Wyntoon when the Marion Davies job ended. In his broken, almost illiterate hand, he wrote to Loorz on November 29, 1940: "[The Davies] sure was a long drawn out job. it is about the same here build it up today and change it to morrow." He added, "it is hard to say when Mr. Hearst will say stop just heard that he will stay til after Christmas." He also said the job boasted "only a verry few men."

Petersen and Mac apparently kept working at Wyntoon right into the winter of 1941. Petersen wrote to Loorz again on February 18 of that new year. He admitted, "I am not much at whriting but here goes." He said, "Mr. Hearst is going to Mexico next Monday [the 24th] what for I do not know but I hope that he will close up shop here and tell me to get the hell out off here." Petersen wrote again on February 25, saying they were working indoors on the heating system but were running short-handed— "cant get men to come up here." Hearst seems to have delayed his trip to Mexico. Petersen said in that same letter, "I dont know how long Mr. Hearst will stay here hope not to long and also that when he goes that he will close up the works here." The importance of these otherwise unimportant lines lies in their rarity: the Wyntoon of 1941 is barely documented in the George Loorz Papers or in any other archives pertaining to the subject. (Hearst eventually left for Mexico, where he still owned an enormous ranch in Chihuahua, the San Jose de Babicora.)

The San Simeon of 1941 is even more thinly documented

than the Wyntoon of that year. The winter of 1941 was exceedingly wet; Nigel Keep the orchard man told Loorz on April 23, "The Burnett Road is impassable," as was only to be expected. The decorator Frank Gyorgy regilded some of the exterior ironwork at San Simeon that spring. He wrote to Loorz on April 30, saying, "Since the party left here it feels like living in a cemetery what a difference now and when the [work?] was going on the hill top." Presumably Hearst and the party were heading back to Wyntoon by then.

Loorz was in touch with Joseph Willicombe at Wyntoon during the summer of 1941. The "Colonel" and his young wife, Jean (the former Jean Henry of his office staff), owned a house in Carmel Valley. They discussed its remodeling with Loorz but balked when he told them how much the work would cost. "That $17,000 settles it," said Willicombe on August 25, "and we have decided to wait until prices come down." He said he hoped that when conditions changed they could take up where they were leaving off with their plans. Conditions soon changed, of course—more than Willicombe or anyone else could have foreseen—come Sunday, December 7, and the bombing of Pearl Harbor.

Hearst was at Wyntoon on that fateful day. So was a small crew—evidently Pete Petersen, Mac McClure, Earl Tomasini, and a few others. Tomasini, a resident of Cayucos, had worked up at Wyntoon the past few years. He told Loorz on January 5, 1942: "We closed at Wyntoon on Dec. 21 and it seems like maybe there will be no more construction there in the future." Nothing short of World War II had been enough to commit Hearst to a lasting shutdown at that estate.

Later in January 1942, Loorz heard from a serviceman named George Cully, who was stationed in the Canal Zone. "Say Mr. Loorz," Cully said, "how about you getting a hook into this building program down here? You could really get your hooks into some nice cold cash if you want to." Loorz probably could have hooked into that program, but he already had his hooks into some very profitable government jobs in California. As he told Randy Apperson on March 10, "Last week we were the low bidder on a million and a half dollars worth of Government work at Pittsburg, California. Today we have about six million dollars worth of bids going in at Marysville. Therefore, our feet are way off of the ground and we are soaring in the clouds."

The F. C. Stolte Co. had other big contracts going that Loorz could have told Apperson about, most of them in California but some in Loorz's home state of Nevada. Contracts that large meant the company was employing thousands of people—was becoming one of the leading companies of its kind on the west coast. On October 1, 1942, the company shed its old name in favor of Stolte Inc., which it still goes by today. The company's wartime prosperity was typified by the year-end bonuses Loorz and Stolte paid in 1942. Carl Daniels, Elof Gustafson, Olin Weatherford, and Conrad Gamboni—a native of Cambria who moved north with Loorz in 1938 to be his secretary—were among those receiving $5,000 apiece. That was big money, of course, in 1942. In fact, Stolte Inc. was now prosperous enough to launch its own magazine that year—*Stolte Blueprint* it was called. One of the early issues had a picture of Mac McClure, who had at least temporarily left the Hearst fold to join the staff as a draftsman. That same issue included the other McClure—Maurice McClure—who had graduated from Berkeley in 1940 and was now on the payroll as an engineer. Jerry Ryland, the Monterey architect, was likewise on the payroll. So was Jim LeFeaver, late of Julia Morgan's office.

By 1943 Loorz was ready to pull up stakes in Pacific Grove and return to the Bay Area, at long last, to be closer to the main office of Stolte Inc. He had opted for Pacific Grove in 1938 mostly for Hearst's sake—to remain close to a job that never quite managed to get back on its feet after the big shutdown of 1937. Pacific Grove was a delightful town, but Loorz had outgrown it.

THE GEORGE LOORZ PAPERS continue into 1944. And then they stop. And they stop almost cold, with scarcely a letter, a telegram, a memorandum to break the silence from then on. True, the activities of Stolte Inc., and of Loorz himself, generated records without end. Loorz, for example, was president in 1950 of the Northern California chapter of

Associated General Contractors. Then in 1960, he and Mrs. Loorz visited Russia; upon returning, he distributed twelve pages of "Observations of European U.S.S.R." to his "fellow Stolteans." He remained active in the company until the 1970s. But the Loorz Papers as we know them—the quaint old letter boxes that Loorz himself kept—end in 1944.

Thus the burst of work for Hearst at San Simeon and Wyntoon from 1945 to 1948 is mostly undocumented, for the Julia Morgan Collection contains virtually nothing on that period either. A few issues of *Stolte Blueprint*, however, contain valuable information on those two jobs. The *Blueprint* of October 31, 1945, for instance, reported the following under "Cast Stone Shop Opened":

> Stolte Inc. is gratified to announce establishment of a cast stone and plaster shop at our 85th Avenue Yard [in Oakland]. Here, under the guidance of Superintendent Fred Jurgewitz, an experienced unit of artisans will model, mold, and cast a wide variety of objects both useful and ornamental.
>
> Fred's initial task will be the creation of ornamental plastics for the Hearst estate at Wyntoon. In addition to this, however, he will be open to orders from the general public—in fact, is keenly interested in expanding the use and appreciation of this type of work.

The *Stolte Blueprint* of December 21, 1945, contained articles on both San Simeon and Wyntoon. Hazel McClure contributed the one on San Simeon. Her husband, Maurice McClure (no relation to Mac McClure), was now the construction superintendent; he could rightfully be proud of that title. (McClure had left the family farm in Nebraska in 1925; had hired on as a day laborer at San Simeon in 1926; had begun high school in Santa Maria in 1933, as a man of twenty-eight; had begun his engineering studies at Berkeley in 1936; and had been a Stolte regular ever since he graduated in 1940.) Hazel McClure's article was entitled "Life Fit for a King at San Simeon Estate":

> Stolteans from various jobs are more and more heading for the Hearst estate at San Simeon. They've heard tell by now of how every day is finished off by a swim in the magnificent Roman plunge, heated to 80 degrees; of how employees are later invited to attend Mr. Hearst's private theater where a show is given nightly.

We've discovered low gear in order to wind our way through the zebras, yaks, oryx, kangaroos, camels, emus, llamas, and many other animals that roam freely over the hills.

As for personalities: Snuffy Layman is happy with his new loader. Otto Olson is still rushing to get 12 hours work into 8. John McFadden, in charge of electrical and stonework, is a handy man indeed. Roy Evans, he and his family well again, is getting those well known Stolte results.

Frank Wilson is pushing an eight-inch pipeline from the new reservoir on the Hearst ranch to the town of San Simeon for fire protection. Bill Igo is handling the pipe when the dozer is down.

Maurice McClure has his eye on the 73 dachsunds in Mr. Hearst's kennels. And him with two cocker spaniels already and the promise of a great dane next spring!

As for myself, I'm in the kitchen doubling for cook and helper who up and left us. Not boasting, you understand, but I drew and cut up 15 chickens and had them in the pan the other day in an hour and 20 minutes.

The pictures adjoining the San Simeon article showed Hazel McClure at the Neptune Pool, Gerald Franklin at the tennis courts, and Maurice McClure at Casa del Sol—all of them looking perfectly at home in their glamorous surroundings. A healthy dose of humor and good fun characterized each issue of *Stolte Blueprint*, and Hazel McClure's article fell squarely within that tradition.

The companion article in that *Blueprint* of December 21, 1945, was entitled "Wyntoon Has a Heat Wave in the Snow"; the author was identified as "Mr. X-mas":

It seems that one of our best men—a fellow named Morris Adams—was shaking like a palsy patient on one of the cold afternoons we've been having recently. Frank Gendrich felt sorry for him and told him to build a little fire in a firepot for himself and the other boys.

He did, but the fire didn't seem to warm him. Nobody knows what he did next to build up the fire. All any of us know is that suddenly the whole building felt like it was ablaze.

The building wasn't—but Morris was. What we saw of him, though, was a streak of fire as he zoomed past us in the direction of a snowdrift. When we pulled him out the seat of his pants was missing; the seat of his underwear was gone; part of his understanding was even impaired. . . .

It has snowed heavily here in the past 24 hours so that there are now about two and a half feet of snow on the ground. The roads are hard to navigate, since they are mostly steep and narrow.

Frank Gendrich, for example, slid into a ditch on his way down to the Bend this morning. With the help of a lot of the fellows, like Gustav Buck, Bill Gatschet, and Morris—whose arms are all right—we finally got the pickup back on the road. On the next trip Frank walked.

Frank Gendrich superintended the work at Wyntoon throughout the postwar period. He had been a Stolte regular since 1936, when he built the Cambria Grammar School; a few years before that, he quite possibly had superintended the work on Hearst's Milpitas Hacienda. Gendrich contributed a "Letter from Wyntoon" to a 1947 issue of *Stolte Blueprint*, dated December 25:

The Wyntoon crew is quite small at the present and there is not much of a story to be told, but the following might be of some interest to the Stolte fishermen anyway.

It's about the big one, a "Dolly Varden" trout 28 inches long, which did *not* get away. . . .

As this job is nearing its completion, I want to thank the Ranch Superintendent, Cal Shewmaker and his crew for the splendid assistance and cooperation extended to us during construction. . . .

And last but not least, let's extend our sincere thanks to our architect, Mr. Warren McClure, under whose able guidance and assistance we were able to do another Stolte job well, indeed.

An unsigned article entitled "San Simeon News" appeared in that same *Stolte Blueprint* of December 25, 1947:

There is very little to report from San Simeon in view of the fact that we have a very small crew at the present time.

Work on the Service Wing has been temporarily discontinued and Paul Gatschet, who was in charge of the construction of that wing, took his crew and departed to the Fairfield-Suisun Army Airbase to work with Elof [Gustafson] on the Hospital.

John McFadden, Frank Frandolich, Otto Olson, Gustav Buck and Wm. George are still buzzing away, trying to complete the finish work in the Recreation Wing. Jerry Franklin is still with us, handling miscellaneous jobs at Ranch and Hilltop.

Roy Evans, our labor foreman, with a crew of almost zero is still with us and finds plenty of activity to engage in.

Mr. [Camille] Solon, the interior decorator, departed recently to complete some decorating in his own home in Mill Valley. We are hoping for his quick return to our fold.

Ted Rathbun, our blacksmith, is learning that his trade embodies untold types of activity never before dreamed of. Ted is able to "take it" however, and we never hear a murmur of complaint.

Ray Carlson is still handling the architectural work here, while Warren McClure divides his time between the Los Angeles [Hearst-Davies house in Beverly Hills] and Wyntoon jobs. The "grapevine" tells us that Warren McClure is going to take a much needed vacation to Detroit, Michigan, and other points East in the very near future.

Warren McClure—the same "Mac" who exchanged so many memorable letters with George Loorz in the 1930s—soon had time to take his vacation. For the Hearst jobs at Wyntoon and San Simeon shut down in 1948, never to be resumed. William Randolph Hearst, the power behind it all, died at the age of eighty-eight in 1951. Julia Morgan, whose role was minimal during the late 1940s, died at the age of eighty-five in 1957. George Loorz was the next of those long-lived players to pass on; he died at the age of eighty in 1978. Fred Stolte outlived them all; he died at the age of ninety-three in 1983. Mac McClure was still living then, but the date of his death and the other details of his later years are vague.

THOUGH THEY FALL OUTSIDE the bounds of the George Loorz Papers, two letters Mac McClure wrote in the early 1980s throw much light on the period covered in *The Builders Behind the Castles*. He wrote the first of those letters on December 21, 1982, to Nellie Shewmaker, the widow of Cal Shewmaker, who succeeded Eugene Kower in 1942 as the caretaker of Wyntoon; Mac typed the letter, which contained several misspellings, as follows:

Soon after I arrived at San Simeon in Jan 1929 [1930] news arrived that the Phoebe Hearst Castle at Wyntoon had been totaled by a fire said to be of electrical source. The building was being remodeled slightly so that Mr. Hearst could visit it although he was at Santa Monica at the time. I recall how little the fire seemed to upset anyone. I learned afterword that it meant the fun of a new project.

I had come to Los Angeles in 1922—hoping to get movie studio work in designing historical architectural work in which I had some proficientry. I did not get far but did get access to Mr. Hearst through Mr. Thadeus Joy who was Miss Morgan's assistant. I recall working on a big Beverly Hills, house in Old English Tudor style which pleased Mr. Hearst and I was later sent to San Simeon where I arrived on the date to the castle fire at Wyntoon [January 29, 1930].

The relationship between Mr. Hearst and his architect was unique. His knowledge of art and style was enough to enable him to control to a great extent. Miss Morgan had the ability to steer projects into reasonable channels. Even so, Mr. Hearst wanted a draftsman's designer at hand whereever he was. At San Simeon he spent a part of every day in the architect's offices sometimes late at night, working out his idea with me.

Hard times and coming war time pinches made the San Simeon program greatly curtailed but it never stopped completely. The plans turned out were mostly all for Wyntoon.

The big development was the purchase of a ruined monastery in Spain which wa[s] brought to San Francisco at great expense—finally to be abandoned where the unreality of the situation dawned on all concerned.

The Bavarian Village of Old German architecture provided living quarters and the purchase of the Bend property a mile down river gave something new to work on.

In 1946-47 work on the Bend main building began to take shape. Mr. Hearst's health began to cause anziety—Miss Morgan felt that she could no longer maintain her office in San Francisco which she closed.

It was her arrangement to transfer my employment to the Hearst payroll. I think it was the winter of 1947 that the Bend main building was re-constructed from the foundation up by the Stolte Co. contractors of which George Loorz had been construction sup't at San Simeon. It was hard to get away from [the Hearst-Davies house in] Beverly Hills for me to travel north very often but the results were pretty good. Of all the buildings this one [was] primarily the design of W. R. Hearst. I regret that his failing health prevented him from seeing it. He did approve the photos.

Miss Morgan did not see it either.

You asked about Willie Pogany. He was a big time artist—He may have been with M.G.M. but usually in N.Y.C. The Pogany [mural] project took all the budget money one summer.

Doris Day preceded Pogany's time. I believe she is still living in San Francisco.

My writing is not what it used to be. —neither am I as I had a light stroke a year ago— Still can manage but not too good.

Mac's declining health had reduced his graceful script to a tortured scrawl, in which he wrote the second of those letters; this one went to Nellie and Cal Shewmaker's daughter, Shirley Shewmaker Wahl, on December 17, 1983. In writing to Mrs. Wahl, Mac told much the same story he had in the first letter but with some variations and additional details:

I came to California in the 20's, hoping to get work as a set designer. My previous efforts were that of architectural draftsman in the Detroit area. I didn't land a studio job but did meet Julia Morgan's assistant who was engaged in building an annex to Miss Davies Beach house in Santa Monica. Thad Joy was this assistant and [it] was through him I joined Miss Morgan's staff and agreed to go to San Simeon when the Santa Monica job ended.

I arrived at San Simeon in Jan 1930. I had very little to do with the Castle but from the start began working on schemes for re building the Wyntoon Castle which burned in the same month of Jan 1930.

It was also the year of the great financial crash which cramped expenditures for continuance [of] work even with seeming endless money supply but there were insurance funds to work with for a Wyntoon replacement.

About this time Mr. Hearst bought the Spanish monastery, or the usable parts, at least. It was an impulsive buy and a disaster as far as usable material for a Wyntoon new castle. The idea was solely to get Wyntoon going again, but the program began to look like a too grand and time consuming fiasco and the monastery was abandoned. Before it was entirely given up, it was agreed to have Bernard Maybeck have a hand in the project. Maybeck was a celebrated S. F. Architect who had been Phoebe Hearst's Architect for the original Wyntoon building. He was also the mentor for the young Julia Morgan who was a friend of Mrs. Hearst and did considerable work at Pleasanton. In any case I well recall the Sunday in '30 when Miss Morgan brought Mr. Maybeck to S. S. who produced a role of chalk drawings on brown wrapping paper of a fairy tale castle to be built on the old castle site. Years later some of these brown paper sketches were found by your mother in the Angel House. . . .

Anyhow we know that the big castle schemes were abandoned in favor of a Bavarian Village on the Waterhouse property which could be built rather quickly (and relatively economically) and so it was. Then The Bend came into view and efforts to convert the building there to usable condition—summer of 1933 as I recall [Hearst bought The Bend in 1934].

After The Gables burned [1944] there was a new source of insurance money and The Bend project became bigger. The present Bend looks rather grand scale compared to the Bavarian Village which are "frame" wooden buildings.

I regret that Mr. Hearst never saw the completed Bend. Neither did Miss Morgan to my knowledge. . . .

San Simeon is truly Miss Morgan's monument—Mr. Hearst's also. People comment on the religious indications by the architecture and decorations. The dining room and the [Gothic] study on 3rd floor indicate this particularly.

It was a handicap to be tied down by "hard times" lack of funds. Mr. Hearst never seemed to be able to accept the fact that 16 men could not produce what 60 did in the good old days.

George Loorz had been dead a few years when Mac wrote those letters. Had he still been alive, we can easily imagine his having concurred—can easily imagine his having written, "That's just how it was Mac and you told it better than anybody could." We can just as easily imagine his having signed off as he so often had in writing to his many, many friends over the years—with that warmhearted "Cheerio" they all knew was uniquely his.

INDEX

C

H

I

J

K

L

M

N

O

P

R

S

T

V

W

Y

Z